Warrior

Also by Robert Matzen

Dutch Girl: Audrey Hepburn and World War II

Mission: Jimmy Stewart and the Fight for Europe

Fireball: Carole Lombard and the Mystery of Flight 3

Errol & Olivia

Errol Flynn Slept Here
(with Michael Mazzone)

Warrior

Audrey Hepburn

Robert Matzen

GoodKnight Books

Pittsburgh, Pennsylvania

GoodKnight Books

© 2021 by Robert Matzen

Foreword © 2021 by Luca Dotti

Published by GoodKnight Books, an imprint of Paladin Communications, Pittsburgh, Pennsylvania.

Printed in the United States of America.

ISBN 978-1-7352738-3-9

Library of Congress Control Number: 2021936208

To Audrey, for a life that continues to inspire

Contents

Contents

Foreword

In Italy the term *seminterrato abitabile* technically describes a damp and poorly lit basement that is somehow still fit for residential use. This description perfectly matched my first flat in Rome. Nevertheless, on a morning some thirty years ago, its usual moldy scent had to briefly make way in order to pass one final test: my mother's inspection.

My flat passed with flying colors, and my mother and I hopped in a cab to the nearby studios of Rai 1 where she was to sit for an interview, the first of a tightly packed UNICEF Italy schedule, one that would jump-start the project to entrust 7,000 mayors of the world's largest cities with the protection of children's rights. By the end of the day I, having only chaperoned Audrey Hepburn from one meeting to another, was frankly exhausted while she was as crisp as her garden's roses in Switzerland.

"How do you manage?" I asked her.

She said, "Luchino, this is my work and it's so important. But let's talk about you. You must know that I was really moved to see you in your first ever flat. It's so important; it's the beginning of your life, of your independence. It may be small and smelly (damn, she got me!), but it's a place and time you will never forget."

Most people define my mother by her physique, her acting skills, her sense of fashion, all neatly tied up by grace and kindness.

Quite obviously she was all that, but what kept her going that day in Rome and every single day that she chose to dedicate to the less fortunate ones, was something older and bolder than her looks, or even her age, would suggest.

At the end of his first book on my mother, *Dutch Girl*, Robert Matzen poignantly describes her as being chased by a bullet, one of the many she was able to dodge in Holland during World War II and one that would finally get her in less than a year from that busy day in Rome.

That image sent shivers up my back and made tears well in my eyes but didn't totally match reality. I still didn't know what exactly was Audrey Hepburn's secret. What was the drive that got her out of that rose garden and into the dry hell of East Africa? How did she survive war, her own parents' and husbands' delusions, and a one-of-a-kind Hollywood career only to realize that all personal and professional accomplishments she achieved just weren't enough?

That image of a bullet chasing my mother certainly explains a lot of things. It explains the melancholy and the nightmares, as those are the badges of survivors. But in order to transform horror into beauty and live by it, she needed to turn around, catch that bullet, and put that evil where it could no longer hurt her, within the love in her heart.

My mother chose to become a soldier wrapped up in a uniform of grace and kindness, a soldier that makes time to visit her "troops" in the *seminterrato* and praise it like Versailles before jumping on to the next mission.

She chose to not turn her back on the bullet. In facing it, in confronting it, she became a warrior.

Luca Dotti
Rome
December 2020

Preface

This book resulted from my phone conversation with Audrey Hepburn's younger son, Luca Dotti, not long after our joint launch of the book *Het Nederlandse meisje* in the Netherlands—the Dutch edition of *Dutch Girl*—which proved to be a successful and satisfying series of events. We had stood together in the village of Velp on the former site of Villa Beukenhof, home of Audrey's family the van Heemstras, to unveil a small statue of Audrey as a teenage ballerina. I think we both had felt the weight of her wartime experiences while there and how the times shaped the remainder of her life, particularly her humanitarian work as a Goodwill Ambassador for UNICEF.

A book about those UNICEF years should have been on my mind then, in Velp, but it took another couple of months for the idea to germinate after the all-important phone call when Luca said to me, "UNICEF expected that Audrey Hepburn would be a pretty princess for them at galas. But what they really got was a badass soldier." That statement gave me chills and still does. I thought, if ever there was a theme for a book, this was it.

Once I started down the path, a story began to emerge that I didn't see coming. Hepburn biographers had skimmed over Audrey's war years because at age ten when the war began and fifteen at its end, she was simply too young (they thought) to experience anything significant. But I saw the story, tracked it down, and told it. In a similar vein, Hepburn biographers have glossed over the UNICEF years because she was *just* a Goodwill Ambassador engaging in a series of PR events. To which I say, thank you again, Hepburn biographers, for your oversight.

Imagine for a moment that you reach age fifty-eight having accomplished all your goals in life. You are enjoying retirement surrounded by everything you ever wanted—love, family, nature, and comfort. Then, suddenly, you move all that to second place and put a social cause first. You face bullets and bombs along with criticism and cynicism. Circumstances force you to leave your comfort zone and become political for the first time. You take on dictators and policy makers and deliver speech after speech, staring down stage fright each time.

But no, that's not a story because you were *just* a Goodwill Ambassador engaging in a series of PR events. "Mother Teresa in designer jeans," critics said, "crying crocodile tears."

The story told in this book resulted from hours of conversations with the people from around the world who are best qualified to tell it: Audrey's closest surviving friends first of all, and of course her son Luca—and UNICEF staff who worked with Audrey all over the world, photographers and journalists who covered her and military men who marveled at her guts in the line of fire. When I told the combat veterans about her experiences in World War II—surviving strafing by British fighters, artillery fire from both sides, and missions for the Dutch Resistance—ah, then her nonchalance at bursts of machine gun fire in Mogadishu made sense.

After spending two years walking in young Audrey's footsteps in the Netherlands while researching and writing *Dutch Girl*, I thought I knew her. I was wrong. Working with Luca revealed new, deeper layers to this woman's soul. He patiently helped me understand each of these layers, and then he would lead me on to new discoveries.

I believe Audrey would not be happy with the state of the world these days because so little has changed. Civil wars still rage. Dictators still terrorize populations. People are still judged by the color of their skin and not by the content of their souls. Refugees are still shunned at best and demonized at worst. And the planet is still dying, just as she predicted it would, from the greed and carelessness of humans.

But she stood her ground on all these issues and fought a good fight, for social justice for children and mothers in desperate circumstances. And she campaigned for the environment back when rain forests and glaciers still abounded and things seemed fine, even though they weren't. To her last breath, she battled.

In 1995, two years after the passing of Audrey Hepburn, Sophia Loren wrote that "Audrey was meek, gentle and ethereal." I now take umbrage at the very idea that this lion-hearted woman, this warrior, was in any way meek. She could be, at any given moment, wise, funny, engaged, determined, reflective, sad, evasive, playful, childlike, doting, fussy, or committed. But meek? Audrey Hepburn took a night flight in a single-engine plane into the war zone of southern Sudan sitting on a flak vest in case stray bullets came up through the fuselage. This is the story of that woman, the warrior Audrey Hepburn, engaged in the fight of her life.

Robert Matzen
December 2020

Comebacks

Kurt Frings pronounced to Audrey Hepburn in 1974 that the time for a comeback was now and he had found the right script. Coming back after years away from the screen would represent a headline decision to a world always thirsting for news about the legendary movie star who had dropped from sight in 1967 after a whirlwind career of fourteen successful years.

All that time she had been the unlikeliest of motion picture titans, an actress who had not come up through the ranks from drama school to the stage, but it hadn't mattered. She won a Best Actress Oscar for her first Hollywood picture anyway. Unlikelier still, she became a 1950s competitor for Marilyn Monroe despite a lack of big breasts or rounded hips or any curves really, except for a couple of shapely legs, and a personality that made headlines without the genetic makeup to grab a single one. She self-effaced her way to international acclaim, apologizing at every opportunity for not being good enough or pretty enough or—God forbid—sexy enough, and then she had walked away to begin almost a decade of silence while she raised sons born in 1960 and 1970.

The press had never understood her. Reporters found her too polite and too humble, and so they smelled a rat because behind the graciousness stood a brick wall they knew protected secrets. Time and again they would advise colleagues, "She never lets you get too close; when you try, she turns to ice." The less she revealed, the more people wanted to know, even five years, six years, seven years past her last picture, *Wait Until Dark*. She walked around as if in the eye of a hurricane, and about her swirled fans and paparazzi desperate for the latest news of a woman with no interest in being "news."

Since she had left the screen, Kurt Frings of the Frings Agency in Beverly Hills had acceded to her wishes for privacy because he knew better than to mess with Audrey Hepburn, a hard-headed woman with a keen nose for the business. Frings knew any plan to lure her back to the screen had better be iron-clad and so he bided his time until finally the right script dropped into his lap.

Frings was a short, tough ex-boxer who had represented, among many others, Olivia de Havilland during a comeback run of post-war successes that included Oscars for *To Each His Own* and *The Heiress* after a bloody battle with Jack Warner of Warner Bros. In 1954 Frings had become Audrey's agent at the urging of another of his clients, star-on-the-rise Elizabeth Taylor. By the end of the decade both Taylor and Hepburn commanded a fortune per picture thanks to Frings, with Audrey peaking first.

"Kurt became a devoted and fanatical defender of her interests," said Audrey's first husband, actor Mel Ferrer.

Into the 1960s Frings remained a Hollywood battle cruiser. His wife, Ketti, had written the novel *Hold Back the Dawn* and a number of Hollywood screenplays; she and Kurt comprised a power couple during their twenty-five-year marriage that ended in 1963. Kurt went on to deliver to Audrey mostly outstanding projects that included *Breakfast at Tiffany's*, *Charade*, *How to Steal a Million*, *Two for the Road*, and *Wait Until Dark*.

Audrey trusted Kurt's instincts, so when he called with what he regarded as a dynamite project, the recluse who considered herself a nobody listened as Frings blurted out a series of givens: Former 007 Sean Connery would star. Alexander and Ilya Salkind would produce; they had recently done *The Three Musketeers* and then *The Four Musketeers*. Richard Lester would direct; his hits went all the way back to *A Hard Day's Night* and *Help!* with the Beatles. James Goldman wrote the screenplay; his work included *The Lion in Winter* with the other Hepburn, Katharine, and the lush, tragic *Nicholas and Alexandra*.

Through the kind of serendipity that marked her career, Audrey already knew about the script that had excited Frings; she had read this screenplay a year earlier when James Goldman left it like an abandoned baby at the threshold of her Plaza Hotel room in New York City.

According to Goldman, "It always seemed incredible to me, but apparently Miss Hepburn had been waiting patiently and quietly in Rome for someone to call and offer her the role." Finally, Columbia Pictures called Frings and Frings called Audrey, and then she waited even longer for the production to come together.

Called *Robin and Marian*, it told the story of an aging, paunchy Robin Hood who returns to England from the Crusades for one last battle with the Sheriff of Nottingham and there reunites with his lost love, Maid Marian, now a nun. Audrey saw in the Marian part what she thought to be akin to a four-leaf clover: the chance at age forty-six for a starring role in a love story. "There's a great need in films today for mature women to be seen playing mature women," she told a reporter.

But even then, with a script she loved in hand, Audrey the mother of two wouldn't say yes to a return to the screen until Richard Lester agreed to shoot his picture over a summer, the summer of 1975, while her younger son, five-year-old Luca Dotti, would be on holiday and free to frolic with the Merry Men in Pamplona, Spain, where lush stands of trees would represent the Sherwood Forest of the twelfth century.

Audrey should have been more mindful of four-leaf clovers. The actress who had been nurtured to success in Hollywood's time-honored system, who had been made up to perfection and lit and photographed with great care to capture her good side, met Hurricane Richard in Pamplona, Spain. Self-professed as "impatient," director Lester embraced the filmmaking philosophy of "run and gun." Use available light, deploy multiple cameras, print the first or second take, and keep going.

When syndicated columnist Liz Smith visited Audrey for an interview on location in hot and sweaty Spain, the lady playing Marian said: "Things have changed since I made my last movie, *Wait Until Dark*. Today, there seem to be technical advances that make things easier and more fun. Dick Lester, our director, is so fast and unencumbered by ego or dramatics. He is a whiz-bang with his many cameras and single takes."

It was pure Hepburn spin.

Every fact she rattled off had, in Audrey's off-the-record view, made the shoot a nightmare. Multiple cameras rolling here, there, and everywhere put her good side, her bad side, every side on display. Lester's satisfaction with take one or take two reduced the concept of performance to a joke. To Lester, all that mattered was getting the words right. Worst of all, the script she had so loved, the baby left on her doorstep, had been rewritten into a leaner, meaner tale of self-pitying, endlessly philosophizing geriatric men reunited in a rotting Sherwood Forest. At the end she poisons Robin and then herself. Murder–suicide; lovely. Sure, Luca got to play with bows and arrows on the set, but Audrey knew now that her days as a leading lady had ended.

Publicity around the release of *Robin and Marian* focused on the Hepburn comeback. A curious public trooped to theaters to see Holly Golightly at forty-six years of age, but not in the legions expected. *Robin and Marian* did okay business, which prompted Kurt Frings to spend another two years attempting to understand the changing Hollywood motion picture landscape, especially as it applied to a client nearing fifty years of age.

During that time Audrey said no to an African picture called *Silence Will Speak*, which both she and Frings disapproved of. It was her friend Anna Cataldi's pet project. She had written the script treatment, which she hand-carried to Audrey's Swiss home in 1978, and then had pleaded with her friend to bring the story of Karen Blixen to the screen. Anna knew packaging Audrey's name with the script would boost its chances of moving forward, but Frings had reinforced Audrey's own feeling that the story was slow and uninteresting and so she passed on what would become, after the character of Denys Finch Hatton was written in as Karen's love interest, *Out of Africa*.

Even if she had known in 1978 what lay ahead for Anna's project, Audrey would have declined because six months in Africa couldn't be managed with an eight-year-old son. And the boys came first, period; Luca and his older half-brother, Sean Ferrer. But Audrey did say yes to another script Frings sent her way—*Bloodline*, an international melodrama with clunky elements of thriller thrown in, which died on arrival at theaters in 1979. When she followed that with a Peter Bogdanovich comedy called *They All Laughed* in 1981 (no critics laughed), Audrey finally conceded—this time she would stay retired.

Since divorcing Mel Ferrer in 1967, she had made Frings' job a difficult one by dictating her own terms and walking away from Hollywood when instinct told her she should.

"She was no pushover," said Sean. She manifested that independent streak by living not in Los Angeles but at La Paisible, the eighteenth-century farmhouse she had bought in the 1960s and renovated on Lake Léman—known to the outside world as Lake Geneva—in Switzerland. The farm, named with the French word for peaceful, and its fertile grounds sat in the Swiss village of Tolochenaz and became the place Audrey could find seclusion that proved essential to her soul. For contemplation she had but to look due south past lower Swiss mountains to see looming far in the distance the pristine, glistening peaks of Mont Blanc. So many things about this woman made people curious. Into the mid-1980s they wanted to know what exactly it was that made enigmatic Audrey Hepburn tick.

Literary agent Swifty Lazar sent a three-page letter seeking to represent her, and publishers made offers through Frings for "My Story, by Audrey Hepburn." As she told a reporter, "You know, the definitive book." But would Audrey really consider opening up about a lifetime of wounds inflicted upon her? When she was five both her parents embraced Germany's savior Adolf Hitler, tucked their daughter in the Netherlands with family, and traveled to Munich to meet the Führer. Soon Audrey's father separated from Dutch Baroness Ella van Heemstra, Audrey's mother, to work for the growing German empire. Her mother retained pro-Nazi ties for another eight years, all of which became a set of secrets locked in Audrey's soul for a lifetime. Would she now share these horrors with the world in a memoir?

Could she really discuss the way she felt about her early love interests—William Holden, John F. Kennedy, and others who had fallen under her spell over the years? How could she talk about her marriage to Ferrer, their battles and his betrayals? Or the second marriage to Italian Andrea Dotti and its heartbreaks and failure? Could she talk about the anguish of the miscarriages she had suffered? No, of course she would never set pen to paper. For some, the exercise might allow catharsis; for Audrey, it could only reopen wounds, with agony the outcome. She had gained a reputation as fiercely private for sound reasons.

Frings continued to send along screenplays for consideration. She leafed through the scripts as they arrived, read any that aroused curiosity, and found them "dull, more than anything. None of it's fun. Not that it has to be laughs, but something you can get your teeth into, something you can have fun doing, something you can make something of. I don't care how small a scene it is."

On another occasion she said, "People are inclined to send scripts to me for which the parts are too young. I'd love to do a picture with Michael Caine or Michael Douglas—actors who have style but aren't pompous about it."

The introvert loved her life in Tolochenaz, the village edging Lake Léman. She loved the house, the massive gardens with their fruits and vegetables and flowers. She loved her four Jack Russell "children"—Picciri, a long-legged rescue by Audrey's father-in-law, Vero Roberti; Jacky, renowned cat chaser; Penny, Audrey's personal bodyguard; and Tuppy, a present from Audrey to her love interest, retired Dutch actor Robert Wolders—the first dog ever in his care. Audrey loved visiting the twice-a-week village open market. She relied on best friend of twenty-five years Doris Brynner, who lived just up the hill.

Audrey would say of the 1980s: "It's going to sound like a thumping bore, but let's see: My idea of heaven is Robert, the boys—I hate separations—the dogs, a good movie, a wonderful meal, and great television all coming together. I'm really blissful when that happens."

But.

Ever practical, she wanted enough money to care for her sons—Sean and Luca. She had bought Sean and his bride, Marina, a house in the Hollywood Hills as a wedding present in December 1985 since Sean was out on his own and successful in the movie business. Audrey wanted an education for Luca, her bookworm-turned-monster teenager. And, God help her, despite the box-office failures of her comeback pictures, some little part inside missed the excitement of a Hollywood production, the travel to locations in Rome or Paris or the Congo, and the challenge. Yes, the challenge of a nice, juicy role, whether a troubled nun or a kooky call girl or a blind, would-be murder victim. She missed being doted on, draped in gorgeous clothes, and lit like the work of art that everyone thought her to be. She missed devouring the script and noting in the margins in her careful hand every nuance of scene and character. She missed having a place to be with so much excitement and so much investment of souls, the band of motion picture brothers and sisters. She missed the ultimate father figure, the director—whether Blake Edwards or Billy Wilder or Stanley Donen. "What my directors have had in common is that they've made me feel secure," she admitted, "made me feel loved." To Audrey Hepburn, love always mattered. When she spotted it anywhere, she gave chase.

And yet the reality grew ever harsher—if roles proved elusive while she was in her forties, what hope did she have in 1985 in the youth-obsessed film industry, where every wrinkle diminished the number of parts offered? Audrey lamented, "The older you get, the more you have to resign yourself to not working or taking inconsequential or frightening parts."

To a reporter she said, "As the years go by, you see changes in yourself, but you've got to face that—everyone goes through it. I can't be a leading lady all my life. That's why I'd be thrilled if people offered me character parts in the future."

Finally, a project with a character part did excite her—a novel by her friend Dominick Dunne, *The Two Mrs. Grenvilles*, was being made into a miniseries by Lorimar for NBC, and she found the role of New York society matron Alice Grenville right up her alley. Alice suffers the murder of her son by his wife, Ann, whom Alice hates. But Alice protects Ann for the sake of the family name. Juicy stuff! It was, Audrey thought, something she could get her teeth into. Something she could have fun doing.

Audrey called Kurt Frings in Beverly Hills and put him on the case. On Thursday, July 11, 1986, a headline in the States named Audrey Hepburn as "in the hunt" for the role of Alice Grenville. Unfortunately, Bette Davis and Claudette Colbert had also expressed interest. Audrey's heart sank. Compared to these two Hollywood heavyweights, real actresses of great accomplishment, she thought herself to be ninety-eight pounds of nothing.

"My mother didn't take herself seriously," said Sean. "She used to say, 'I take what I do seriously, but I don't take myself seriously.'"

In the end Colbert got the part, but the Lorimar connection would bear fruit. Producer Karen Mack, Lorimar alumna, approached Frings with the exact tonic Audrey needed: a romantic comedy caper picture with a working title of *Here a Thief, There a Thief*. In a sentence—and Hollywood bought and sold concepts based on a sentence—this picture was "*Charade* meets *Romancing the Stone*." Best of all, Audrey wouldn't play someone's mother. Audrey's part would be that of a glamorous baroness-slash-concert pianist turned high-class thief on a wild adventure spanning the American Southwest. And production would last only one month, which meant a return to Tolochenaz before the weather turned colder. The only catch: *Here a Thief* would be a 100-minute, made-for-television enterprise and not a theatrical release, a fact offset by a salary of $750,000 and knowledge that her contemporary Liz Taylor had made the jump to television and extended her career; maybe Audrey could do the same.

"If I was going to do something, I wanted to do something cheerful," she told the press. "There's so much tension in the world and in our lives, and stress and misery around us, and a great deal of it is also on the screen and on television. I'm not condemning that. I think serious things have to be done, too, but selfishly I wanted to have fun if I worked again."

The question became, who would co-star with Audrey in her television comeback? Enter Audrey Hepburn's recent obsession with American television, something she had once despised and now found captivating despite the handicap of only six broadcast stations in the Geneva area. "We don't have the ninety-nine stations you have here," she told a reporter while visiting the States. Her favorite show until its cancellation two years earlier had been *Hart to Hart* featuring Stephanie Powers and Robert Wagner.

"Mum never missed an episode, whether she was in Rome or Switzerland," said Luca.

"I have seen all of *Hart to Hart*," she said. "I think they bought it very quickly for Europe. I saw it in Italian. I saw it in French. I saw it in Spanish. I loved that show."

Robert Wagner, known as RJ, had been a member of Gstaad's rat pack, dubbed "Hollywood in the mountains," along with David Niven, Roger Moore, and Julie Andrews and husband Blake Edwards, and others in a revolving all-star lineup that featured Doris Brynner as mistress of ceremonies. They'd gather at Gstaad's exclusive Hotel Olden to ring in the New Year and ski, which meant Audrey and RJ knew each other from way back. Now Wagner's most recent U.S. television series, *Lime Street*, had gone on hiatus after Samantha Smith, the thirteen-year-old actress who played his daughter on the show, had perished with her father in a plane crash. Tragedy seemed to follow RJ—he was less than five years past Natalie Wood's death by drowning, and that brought out Audrey's mile-wide maternal instincts.

Hepburn asked *Here a Thief, There a Thief* producer Karen Mack if Wagner might be available to star with her—after all, he had just worked with Liz Taylor on that recent TV movie and word on the street was the production had gone well.

"I was flattered—very flattered," said Wagner when he heard Hepburn had requested him. "I said, 'Show me where to go for makeup and let's get started.'"

The production revved up just that fast and spanned August 1986. With Luca in Sardinia on summer holiday with the Dotti family, Audrey and Robert Wolders, her "Robbie," embarked on the adventure together for production locations in Hollywood, San Francisco, the mountains of Dulce Agua southwest of Palmdale, California, and the Old Tucson film studio in the desert to the west of Tucson. Summer blazed for the mobile production every day as only summer can in the southwestern desert.

"Do you know how much it was every day we worked?" Audrey said to David Hartman in an interview for *Good Morning America* shot the following February in Gstaad. "105 in the shade. And that means working. I mean, a half hour for lunch, in which time you barely have time to eat, get your makeup on, and go right back under that sun again."

As thirty-five-year pros, Hepburn and Wagner endured it, in part because, claimed RJ, "It's a wonderful script." He would issue this proclamation more than once when interviewed during and after production, as if willing it to be true. At fifty-six he was half a year younger than Audrey and had come up through the old studio system at 20th Century Fox while Hepburn toiled at Paramount. Both had been schooled from their earliest days on what to say to the press about a picture and how to say it. But the script for *Here a Thief, There a Thief* gave every appearance of being thrown together in quite a hurry, to the extent that much of the final product seemed ad-libbed.

Audrey took the glass-half-full approach and called the screenplay "a lark, a romp." Less optimistically, critic Judy Flander would tell her United Feature Syndicate audience upon the picture's broadcast six months later under the title *Love Among Thieves* that the material came off as "a pathetic attempt to duplicate those sophisticated movies of the '30s and '40s that lit sparks between leads."

Audrey had been weaned on the intimate relationship between an actress and the film's director, a wise artist capable of drawing the performance out of her mind and body through all means of communication, whether laughter or gentle guidance or cajoling or outright anger and frustration. It had all come from a place of love with earlier father-figure directors. The director this time, forty-four-year-old Roger Young, had begun his career in television as an editor and graduated to directing shows like *Magnum P.I.* and *Lou Grant* before working with his pal Tom Selleck on the feature *Lassiter* in 1984.

Audrey showed up on time, knew her lines, and hit every mark, but the slapdash nature of the production—set up here, shoot, strike the set—reminded her what she had learned making *Robin and Marian* for Richard Lester: The dream factory of yesterday had gone. La Paisible, Luca, and her Swiss life felt an ocean away—because they were. Luckily, she lived in the present and could wring a drop of enjoyment from the experience and play Hollywood star one more time, living a month of lights, excitement, and all the bustle of working movie sets and the people who made them go, from assistant directors to grips, makeup artists, gaffers, and second assistants. They all worked so inhumanly hard to make an impression and be remembered for the next job, wherever that job might take them.

Shooting progressed through the month at various desert locations, all equal parts dust and sweat, doubling for the mythical country of Yaruba. It was a physical picture with lots of setups and running around, dodging bad guys and bullets, and the exertion and stress melted pounds off Audrey by the day, to the detriment of her health and the final product.

Wraparounds for the front and back of the picture were shot last in San Francisco, where City Hall doubled as a Yaruban concert venue. Production in the heart of city government required shooting off-hours, in this case at 1:00 a.m. Then and there, Audrey experienced an uncomfortable moment on-set, when in her role as pianist she wore a black Givenchy evening gown and stepped up to a grand piano before more than 100 extras to give a simulated piano recital.

Wagner said, "When she came out to do her concert pianist thing, they all stood and applauded her for three minutes. At that hour! She treated everybody so beautifully and created such a positive atmosphere around her."

But after weeks of breakneck production, she knew how she

looked—wilted, undernourished, older than her fifty-seven years, and in no way up to a Givenchy design that exposed one bony shoulder. Somehow, just being away from the screen raising her kids, she had morphed into some sort of legend who merited a standing ovation from extras and crew members, and it was ridiculous. More than ridiculous, it was embarrassing. She stood on display, like the fake Cellini in her 1966 picture *How to Steal a Million*. That's always how she felt, sometimes a little and sometimes a lot, like a rather pretty forgery.

Then, after a quick costume change to another Givenchy gown, this one strapless, she shot scenes for the finale, looking emaciated and exhausted after the death march through the desert.

"I'm terribly critical of myself," she told David Hartman while discussing that awkward moment of the standing ovation in San Francisco. "I don't like what I see, and that's why it's always such a miracle to me because obviously, if I've been successful, the audience, the people see something I don't see."

In another blink it was over, and back she and Robbie were at La Paisible, taking the dogs for walks. It was September in Switzerland and, as she described, "There's fruit to be picked, jams to be made, and vegetables to take care of…. The day goes by very quickly." Luca returned from holiday in Sardinia and then headed off for the new term at school.

The restlessness of earlier in the year had been replaced by disillusionment and exhaustion at the film production just completed. She imagined the November of her years ahead with nothing but long walks and shopping at the market. One way or another, Audrey Hepburn was being turned out to pasture, a reality with only one accompanying problem: Audrey Hepburn still felt young and vital and craved something to go after, something to inspire her, in or out of the movies. She had already seen and done it all—fought the Nazis, won the awards, worn the clothes, traveled everywhere, and lived the dream of raising children. She hadn't climbed Mont

Comebacks

Blanc, but in a sense she had earned the mountain as her own; she had lassoed it for her own use as a pretty thing in the peaceful distance. Now she'd even achieved romantic love with Robbie. But nearing age fifty-eight, Audrey felt there must be one more dragon to slay, and feeling that way, she grew ever restless. Audrey Hepburn needed a quest.

Wings, Prayers, and Fate

July 6, 1949. The Pan American Stratocruiser, son of the B-29 Superfortress that had dropped atom bombs on Japan, lumbered through the air like a four-engine pterodactyl. In service from London to New York for just six weeks, the Stratocruiser was a Boeing 377 that boasted two decks and a pressurized cabin for the warmth of passengers. Pressurization also meant freedom from the full and deafening roar of those beastly engines just out the window—quite a step up from the DC-3.

Ninety minutes out of London, as the plane headed west over the Atlantic Ocean at 19,000 feet, one of the Pratt & Whitney R-4360 Wasp radial engines flamed out in a spectacular fireball. The aircraft lurched and coffee and snacks went flying. The crew of ten hurried into emergency procedures for fifty-three startled passengers, handing out life jackets to each. With the fire burning hot, thirty-nine-year-old pilot Haakon G. Gulbransen, a veteran of Pan Am's transcontinental routes, followed standard procedure: Cut petrol to the engine and begin a power dive to 6,000 in an effort to extinguish the flames. Down the pterodactyl shot, dials spinning in the cockpit until they reached 6,000 feet.

Gulbransen wiped sweat off his forehead. The maneuver didn't work, and the pilot reached for the interphone to speak with the main cabin.

"We were told we might come down in the ocean," said a passenger. "While I can swim, 600 miles is out of my range." That passenger, a redhead, age thirty-eight and dutifully wearing a life jacket, walked the length of the plane's two decks during crucial minutes as the engine flamed. He climbed forward and then aft grabbing seat by seat while the deck under him shuddered. In a voice familiar to some of his shipmates, curly red hair bouncing above his eyes, he cracked wise to keep passengers calm a mile up in the night sky. His secret: He took comfort in the fact the crew hadn't bothered to don life jackets themselves. In another moment, he sobered: "Then the crew did, too, and I thought, 'This is it.'"

Among those the redhead entertained in their "*Titanic*" moments were tennis stars Louise Brough and Margaret DuPont and former U.S. Ambassador to the Philippines Paul McNutt.

In a few more minutes the fire winked out and the passenger who had cracked wise, movie comic Danny Kaye, returned to his seat. The plane banked sharply north and then east and began an agonizing passage toward Shannon, Ireland, on three engines.

Danny Kaye's antics weren't false bravado; he had already proved his bravery entertaining troops in dangerous zones during World War II. Then came the 1947 Goldwyn picture, *The Secret Life of Walter Mitty*, which shot him to the top, and he had just inked a contract to make *The Inspector General* at Warner Bros. Would this be the end, right after the beginning, he had to wonder as he sat sweating the miles as the Stratocruiser skimmed over what might soon become a watery grave? Before long, the fire-damaged propeller gave up the ghost and fell into the ocean.

The plane landed safely in Shannon and Danny Kaye tried the trip to America again. "Sitting next to me on that second plane was a man named Maurice Pate," said Kaye. "Maurice was tall and stately, an imposing figure with silver hair and a quiet yet warm manner." Kaye and Pate struck up a conversation about the latter's organization, the United Nations Children's Fund, or UNICEF, then just three years in existence. They had set up shop in the world's poorest countries, Pate explained, and provided food and medicine to the youngest and most vulnerable among populations.

Pate looked into Danny Kaye's face and said, "If you would stop at some of our installations and then come back and go on the radio or write a magazine article, it would help us a great deal."

Kaye thought a moment and responded, "Well, I'll do a little better than that. I'll try to make a documentary." And he did, releasing *Assignment: Children* in 1955.

In another five years, Danny Kaye would begin crusading for UNICEF. During that time he made—among other pictures—the Goldwyn Studios feature *Hans Christian Andersen*, which cemented his connection with children around the world. Fate had brought Kaye to the UN children's organization through a flaming engine over the North Atlantic, and fate had brought his career in alignment with the UNICEF mission by leading him to portray the world's most famous writer of children's stories.

A lifelong appointment as UNICEF Children's Ambassador followed, as did trips around the world, including the Third World, to champion children in all corners. The Renaissance man would combine his love of symphony orchestra and fondness for children in engaging concert hall performances where he served as a passionate orchestra conductor—who in fact couldn't read music. He hosted television specials and made "Trick or Treat for UNICEF" a catchphrase in the United States during the 1960s.

"While UNICEF gives them food and medicines, I make them laugh," he said of his personal mission with children.

For thirty-three years Kaye rated his career second to his work as the children's champion. He logged hundreds of thousands of air miles on behalf of UNICEF while also serving as half of a power couple with songwriter-wife Sylvia Fine. Together they had a daughter, Dena, in 1946, and the three became a centerpiece of Hollywood. When Danny Kaye took up Chinese cooking, it required adding on a room to their Beverly Hills home in addition to the purchase of a commercial-grade, stainless steel Chinese stove. According to many, including Dena Kaye, some of her father's greatest performances took place in the Chinese kitchen where, reported Dena, "Audrey Hepburn said it was like watching a great ballet dancer" to see Danny preparing a nine-course meal.

But fate had another course change in store for the great children's advocate and chef. In February 1983 Danny Kaye underwent heart bypass surgery to correct clogged arteries and during that process contracted hepatitis C from contaminated blood. Still, he soldiered on until March 1987 when he lay dying at Cedars-Sinai Medical Center of complications of hepatitis C. Only something ghastly could have kept the ageless Danny Kaye from helping his charges, the world's children.

With Sylvia and Dena at his side, at seventy-four Danny Kaye breathed his last at 3:58 a.m., March 3, 1987. "He was truly a champion for children in every continent," said UN Secretary-General Javier Pérez de Cuéllar.

Kaye had been UNICEF's first Ambassador-at-Large and that title had been made permanent. Now the king was dead and who could possibly take his place? Yes, there were other entertainers also serving UNICEF, famous names like Harry Belafonte, Liv Ullman, and Peter Ustinov. But Kaye had made it his mission to serve children in every corner of the world at the expense of his own career, and these others were in mid-career. Yes, they wanted to serve, but within limits. It had taken the intervention of a flaming engine over the Atlantic to bring Danny Kaye to UNICEF; would more such divine intervention be needed to connect a new king with this vital mission?

As it turned out, the divine intervention had already taken place in April 1945, and all fate needed now was the right word from the right person, and Audrey Hepburn would become the new Danny Kaye. The king is dead—long live the queen!

Cinderella

The UNICEF experience began for Audrey Hepburn not as an all-consuming personal battle to the death, but as a lark. On Friday, October 30, 1987, she and Robbie flew into Hong Kong and ferried across the Zhujiang River Estuary as a brilliant orange sunset seemed to set the waters ablaze. Ahead sprawled Macau like Oz, like a thousand Ozes, like an other-worldly New York City, skyscraper upon endless skyscraper, lights blinking to life as the sunset receded to dusk. A limo awaited at the dock to take the couple to the Mandarin Oriental Hotel in time for a dinner appointment with the governor. A strange set of circumstances had brought them here. Leopold Quarles van Ufford, Audrey's kin because of Ella's first marriage to a Quarles van Ufford, represented UNICEF in Portugal, which had claimed Macau. Leopold invited Audrey to serve as hostess for closing night of the First International Music Festival of Macau, with proceeds benefiting UNICEF.

Macau was a place she had never visited, and when "cousin" Leopold invited her, she asked Robbie what they should do. So much was converging here, not just a Quarles van Ufford issuing the invitation and Macau as the destination, but years of chats with a Swiss neighbor, Prince Sadruddin Aga Khan. Sadri, as he was known, had been the United Nations High Commissioner for Refugees, facing issues involving displaced populations, including and especially children. He had discussed such issues often with Audrey and encouraged her to become involved.

She had yet another connection to Macau and this event. Her father-in-law, Vero Roberti, had written a book about the pirates of the South China Sea after making his way into the pirates' den and interviewing their leaders. As seen through Vero's eyes—and Audrey loved, absolutely loved, Vero and his stories—he had painted Macau as a place of sheer romance.

Robbie already knew how he should answer Audrey's "what should I do?" question when he saw the light in her eyes. He was always up for a trip, he said, and she accepted UNICEF's invitation for an October 31, 1987, appearance in Macau.

The kidney-shaped region on the southern Chinese coast near the South China Sea had been a part of China since the Qin Dynasty around 200 B.C.—that is, until the 1550s when Portuguese ships sailed in, and the next in a long line of European powers laid claim to the next in a long line of Far East territories. Portugal's reign over the area of less than thirteen square miles, which would eventually contain the densest population in the world, continued unbroken into March 1987, when the Joint Declaration on the Question of Macau established a process and timeline to transfer control to the People's Republic of China by 1999.

Macau had been fostering a cultural scene and trying desperately to infuse classical music into the mix. The local arts committee planned an international music festival for Macau that would invite top performers from around the world, and some of the proceeds would benefit UNICEF. Portions of the program would be televised across Asia and for an event of this magnitude the committee needed a name—someone with drawing power to serve as master of ceremonies for either the opening or closing night of the week-long festival. Peter Ustinov was the first and only choice, but a query found him shooting a Hercule Poirot picture, *Appointment with Death*, and unavailable. Needing a replacement, cousin Leopold thought of another obvious choice.

Rushing out of their suite that evening for the dinner appointment with the governor, Audrey bumped into a man at the bottom of the grand staircase who would change her life. Jack Glattbach, UNICEF's regional information officer stationed in Bangkok, stood with mouth agape watching Audrey descend the stairs like Cinderella on her way to the ball.

"She looked quite stunning and regal in a haute couture evening gown," said Glattbach. "I'd just crawled off the ferry from Hong Kong and felt quite serf-like, scruffy and subdued." He cut in to introduce himself. "She was very keen to talk about what she could say for UNICEF and asked if we could meet after dinner." They arranged an 11 p.m. meeting in the Hepburn-Wolders suite.

At the appointed hour he knocked on their door. "By this time Audrey was wearing T-shirt and jeans," said Glattbach, "still stunning but absolutely down-to-earth and charming. She wanted to know all about UNICEF and we went over the message I'd drafted for her to give at the next night's gala concert, which was also being recorded for television."

They sat around drinking scotch as Audrey studied her speech and smoked the suite into a hazy, L.A.-like cloud. Jack asked her why she had agreed to appear for UNICEF, and she told him about her longtime interest in the UN sparked by relief efforts at the end of the war that had brought food along with clothing, blankets, and other goods to the Dutch people, including her teenage self. She gushed about her love of children. She said her sons were grown and she was, she stated, "living quietly and contentedly in Switzerland and don't really want to travel very much, but I would be happy to help UNICEF wherever I could, if they ask me."

A plan formulated in Glattbach's brain this night that would play out in coming weeks and over the next five years. "I tried to make sure in my reports and in drafting various official 'thank you' letters that she was asked. Fortunately, she was."

The next evening's Opera Gala Night proved to be a first-class affair. Headliners included the Radio Symphony Orchestra from Beijing, the Goldberg Chamber Group from the UK, and several top European musicians.

"You can always tell when there is quality and I noticed it at once," said Italian coloratura mezzo-soprano Lucia Valentini Terrani, who performed along with Romanian soprano Ileana Cotrubas. "Everything went very well: the chamber ensemble from England, the Beijing orchestra, the performers, [and] the presentation of the Gala Night by the great actress Audrey Hepburn."

"Audrey delivered the sixty-second message for UNICEF just perfectly," said Glattbach. Of course, his brief compliment failed to capture the iceberg of fear inside Audrey's body as the moment onstage approached. The shy, introverted girl had learned forty-five years earlier that public performance of ballet released her from torment. Dance allowed her to communicate before twenty or two hundred or two thousand people. The size of the audience didn't matter—she was free to be herself. But place her before any audience and ask her to speak into a microphone, and Audrey Hepburn turned to hot wax. She threatened to melt at any moment.

She told one reporter, "I never was the ideal performer because I suffer so terribly from fear … my stomach goes to pieces, and my head starts to ache."

Robbie had grown used to the torture Audrey put herself through, and speaking on behalf of UNICEF in particular for taping and broadcast brought new terror. She wouldn't be representing just any cause—funds raised this night would be channeled to desperate children. That October evening "she knew little about what was expected of her and was pacing outside in her evening dress beforehand because it meant the world to her," said Wolders.

Robbie himself was an odd duck and filled the role of Audrey's shadow—quiet, stoic, happy to stand by, and with zero need to occupy any portion of the spotlight. Already, in this first UNICEF exercise, he was proving to be a catalyst who could make such charity work possible.

After her speech she returned to her seat beside him. "Did I do all right?" she asked. He could assure her with confidence: She was perfect. The evening at the Government Palace in Macau went very well indeed. With Audrey as headliner the Opera Gala Night enjoyed the best attendance numbers of the week of performances.

At their hotel afterward, they met up again with Jack Glattbach and "we repeated the nightcaps and I heard how terrified she had been by the whole occasion. Performing had never been easy for her, apparently. But you don't expect stars like Audrey to be scared of public appearances."

So ended Audrey's brush with UNICEF, and Glattbach went off and set his plan in motion; the retired actress appeared as a blip on UNICEF's radar. But this celebrity, Glattbach said to UNICEF branches around the world, was different than others who had committed to doing this and that for the organization. All the other names fixated on their careers, which made booking them catch-as-catch-can, as with Ustinov for Macau. Only the late Danny Kaye had been prepared to put all career aspirations second and the world's starving children first. But Audrey—Jack had heard with his own ears that Audrey was "living quietly and contentedly in Switzerland." Retired. At liberty.

UNICEF decided to test the waters. Would Audrey be interested in appearing at another music festival, this one in Tokyo, before Christmas? The role would be identical to the one she had undertaken in Macau—serve as mistress of ceremonies, present a short speech, and make introductions for the musical acts. Macau had gone well; Audrey and Robbie weighed the offer. The trap was snapping shut and she didn't realize it. Yes, UNICEF was a nice idea, she mused, and maybe she would go to Tokyo. But for now there were more important issues to think about—autumn at La Paisible meant it was time to make jam from the apple harvest.

The Square

Sunday, June 4, 1961. A Hollywood party celebrating the tenth wedding anniversary of Tony Curtis and Janet Leigh drew Audrey and husband Mel Ferrer during production of *Breakfast at Tiffany's*. At the party the always-shy Audrey struck up a conversation with Yul Brynner's young bride, Doris—the pair had married the previous March. Doris was a striking blond some years younger than Audrey and a fashion model from Chile, her accent European thanks to Yugoslavian parents, her eyes a dazzling blue, and her manner coolly confident in a way Audrey could only envy.

"We just bonded upon meeting," said Doris of that first encounter with Audrey. "We got to talking about children, and we were chatting, and I didn't know anybody. Audrey said she liked my dress and the way I look."

"With me, it's all fake," Audrey asserted.

Doris gaped at the woman already renowned for beauty. "What do you mean, it's all fake?" she asked.

With a sigh, Audrey began the usual litany: "My eyes are too small. My face is too square. And the rest—the rest is makeup."

Doris couldn't decide if Audrey was kidding. "Don't be ridiculous," she told the stranger.

At a little after six the next morning, a knock sounded on the door of Bungalow 12 at the Beverly Hills Hotel. Doris opened the door and it was Audrey, dressed for comfort and in a scarf and sunglasses. She removed both to show how she looked without makeup, a voilà moment to prove the honesty of her self-assessment.

"See? I told you," said Audrey. "I have small eyes and a square face."

What Doris beheld, of course, was a magnificence all the world saw. All the world but Audrey.

"Since that day, I only and always called her Square," said Doris, "and she only signed notes and letters to me SQUARE."

A great friendship had been formed and, said Doris, "I carried her secrets, and she carried mine." They would spend the next thirty-one years like sisters, with Doris close to the action with Mel and many times seeing his mistreatment of a dutiful wife. Doris would never consider herself a fan of Mel Ferrer.

Said Yul Brynner of the Ferrer-Hepburn relationship, "Mel was jealous of her success and could not reconcile himself to [the fact that] she was much better than he in every way, so he took it out on her. Finally, she couldn't take it any longer."

Ironic that these words issued forth from Brynner, who would divorce Doris months later. Best friends Audrey and Doris commiserated about their bleak lives, each of them responsible for a young child. "We cried a lot and we were miserable a lot," remembered Doris.

For Mel, marriage had been all about making it in Hollywood, socializing, playing the game. And he had browbeat and criticized Audrey for fifteen years to the extent that it would take that many more years for her to come to an understanding with herself: "I've decided I'm not so bad after all."

Mel and Hollywood had been so entwined that she rebelled against the town and its lifestyle and, by no coincidence, settled a couple of continents and an ocean away from it.

Soon after the separation, in the summer of 1968, Audrey received an invitation for a yachting trip on the Aegean Sea that had been wangled for Square by Doris; her jet-set pals owned the boat and were now busy charting the adventure.

Doris persuaded Square that setting sail on the Aegean would allow them both an escape from the gloom of messy divorces that lay ahead for each. They boarded in Istanbul and docked for a day in Izmir, during which time Audrey accepted a dinner invitation made by a young Italian man also on the cruise. Andrea Dotti was a student of psychiatry, not yet in practice and not yet thirty, which made him a whopping decade younger than Square—astonishing given that Ferrer had been a dozen years her senior. Aboard the yacht *Calisto*, the new couple fell in love "between Ephesus and Athens," as Andrea phrased it. Audrey possessed a playful, child-like sense of humor and the good-natured Dotti could make her laugh. Such a joy that was after years with serious Mel Ferrer.

The following January in Morges, near La Paisible, Hepburn married Dotti in a civil ceremony that was followed by lunch and a celebration at Doris's house. In short order the couple produced a son they called Luca. Audrey had always adored children, and now had two from polar-opposite fathers.

Mrs. Andrea Dotti gladly left her name and actress reputation as Audrey Hepburn behind and settled into a housewife's role in Rome, raising ten-year-old Sean part time and newborn Luca full time. Audrey had lived in Belgium as an infant, in England as an elementary school student, in the Netherlands through the war, and in Amsterdam and London afterward. With Mel she had played Hollywood socialite before finding her dream home in To-lochenaz. As a citizen of the world, Square expected to fit like a square peg into a square hole in the culture of Rome. After all, her first big picture, *Roman Holiday*, had been shot there over a six-month period.

What a shock awaited. Luca said, "I believe that, for certain Roman social circles, the fact that she was too much a housewife, too 'square,' took its toll more than her celebrity." He described the city as a sea of clannish neighborhoods with no appetite for outsiders.

Audrey's friend, writer Anna Cataldi of Milan, put it more bluntly: "People in Rome, they were not nice to Audrey. They were absolutely not nice. She needed desperately to have friends and warmth. People were absolutely awful."

Two other sets of villains would surface during her years in Rome: paparazzi and kidnappers.

"The cities are not a place for you if you're famous," said Audrey. "With the paparazzi in Rome, there is no privacy."

Much worse, the startling July 1973 kidnapping of sixteen-year-old heir to the Getty oil fortune J. Paul Getty III—Luca was only three at the time—sent a wave of terror through every affluent Roman household. The boy was recovered that December minus an ear that had been cut off by his captors, and security ratcheted up for every parent thereafter.

The horrors seemed unending for Audrey in Rome as day by day she learned the price of marrying a charming and fun-loving man with wild oats yet to sow. Mrs. Dotti began to read reports in the press of Andrea's dalliances—this was how her marriage to Mel Ferrer had gone; she had learned of his romances in gossip columns. As during that first marriage, she clung to the institution for the sake of a son, so that on paper the Dottis remained married for fifteen years but spent only a portion of that time as a couple.

By the 1980s Audrey only ever felt safe and secure tucked inside a Switzerland that cared not who was who. Tolochenaz represented Fort Knox to Audrey: a place where she could lock herself away. But following her success in Macau, UNICEF had called and offered Japan, and Audrey knew what that meant. For Japanese women, the love affair with Audrey Hepburn began with a haircut—the one she received as a princess on the run in *Roman Holiday*. That picture began playing at Tokyo's Hibaya Movie Theatre in April 1954, and there Princess Ann's act of defiance struck a chord with Japanese women then burdened by traditional long hairstyles that were costly and time-consuming to care for. More than that, Japanese women bore the weight of second-class citizenship in their post-war world. Well, Audrey showed them a different way of life, this young woman who rebelled against custom. *Roman Holiday* sent an unexpected shock wave through the country. By August a fad had swept the islands—Audrey's short hairstyle was seen everywhere as a symbol of a new woman emerging in Japan.

It wasn't just the hair that captivated a nation. The way she looked, the way she moved, and her demeanor all felt vaguely Asian to the Japanese and therefore familiar—they simply fell in love with Audrey Hepburn. She would first set foot on Japanese soil in March 1983 with Sean and Luca to celebrate the thirtieth anniversary of the Givenchy brand. It might as well have been the arrival of the Beatles, she was still that adored by the Japanese people. She stayed more than a week and charmed the pants off a country already under her spell.

Now four years later she was coming back, this time on behalf of UNICEF, to serve as hostess for the Japan Air Lines-World Philharmonic Orchestra annual concert. By coincidence or not, another shock wave would course through the islands. Audrey's arrival should have made headlines in every newspaper—Audrey and Robbie were due in on the 18th, but at 11:08 a.m. on Thursday, December 17, 1987, an earthquake struck Japan, epicentered 350 miles south of Tokyo. Two were killed and ten injured in the quake, which dragged on from seconds into minutes as buildings swayed and office workers screamed for their lives. Preliminary estimates rated it 6.6 on the Richter scale.

"We were working and organizing the big event," said Christa Roth, forty-six-year-old UNICEF Goodwill Ambassadors and Special Events Assistant. "That was the first time I experienced an earthquake. It was quite something and, thank God, it happened the day before and not when they were there."

The next day UNICEF Executive Director James Grant arrived and checked into the elegant Tokyo Prince Hotel, as did Audrey and Robbie. Then Roth received a call that she should report for an audience in the suite of her girlhood idol, Audrey Hepburn.

"I was extremely nervous meeting someone I had admired my whole life," said Roth with a laugh. But like so many, the German national who had been transplanted to Geneva fell under the Hepburn spell. "I must say, it was like we had known each other forever," said Roth. "It was very easygoing and very friendly. We started to work on the program; she was very professional. It was a wonderful first meeting."

There Hepburn and Grant ("Please, call me Jim") sat down together for the first time, forging a bond that would endure for the remainder of her life. Grant at age sixty-five was in the midst of a world-changing career. Bill Gates would say of him twenty-five years later, "The person who's done the most amazing things and is the least known for it might be Jim Grant. It's important to remember the 1980s were a very troubled decade in the global economy and so he had a lot of headwinds. In fact, that's why his work is particularly inspirational to us right now, because he did that by getting people to focus on the right priorities. By making things more effective, by bringing the countries in and making sure the measurements were there so everybody felt good about this work."

Grant had come into his directorship with a mission to make UNICEF more relevant. He scrapped the model of holding splashy galas, saying the organization needed to be more "down-to-earth."

Careworn, charismatic, and still quite handsome, Jim Grant had Audrey Hepburn at "hello." He pressed every button without pressing any—a Berkeley undergrad and Harvard law graduate, world traveler, relaxed and funny, suit always rumpled, he had a bit of William Holden's looks about him. Audrey had always been a sucker for father figures, and Grant's gravitational force pulled her further in UNICEF's direction. Grant and Roth gave Audrey the basics of the message she should deliver at the concert and, that evening, deliver she did.

The World Philharmonic Orchestra, directed by thirty-two-year-old Venetian conductor and composer Giuseppe Stripoli leading musicians from fifty-eight countries, performed in Tokyo's most prestigious venue: the Ryogoku Kokugikan Sumo Hall, a cavernous amphitheater with a capacity of more than 11,000. Audrey's reputation in Japan preceded her, and "the sumo hall was full, full, full. I've never seen so many people in one place," said Roth.

With passions stirred by Stripoli and his orchestra, Audrey's job was easy—to give an impassioned plea for the world's children and introduce Jim Grant, who brought a lifetime of experience to bear in driving the point home. The result was a tremendous success of a fund-raiser for UNICEF. By nature a recruiter on behalf of the world's children, Grant could see an opportunity when it presented itself—getting Audrey into the UNICEF family might elevate his organization like never before.

Baiting traps was the UNICEF way, as Peter Ustinov could attest. A Yugoslav UNICEF representative had, according to Ustinov, "first contaminated me with the happy virus of enthusiasm for this vital cause." Once infected by the UNICEF message, Ustinov could see "the selfless work of those often-maligned international civil servants who have a passionate interest in their work and who are content with the knowledge of its constructive nature as a moral recompense."

Now, Grant wondered to himself whether delicate-looking Audrey Hepburn could step into a preeminent fund-raising role. She had connections the world over, and a passion for children. Might she even be convinced to take a trip into the field?

If Grant harbored doubts as to the potential effectiveness of Audrey Hepburn as a UNICEF torchbearer, they were put to rest by the funds raised that evening and by the next day's press conference organized by Christa Roth for Hepburn at the Prince Hotel.

Roth had met with an event manager at the hotel and arranged for a room that could accommodate thirty to fifty journalists. Roth knew her business; she had been arranging press conferences for UNICEF Goodwill Ambassadors across Europe for years. She eyeballed the room, gave her okay, and settled in bed.

"The next morning I went downstairs and there was a line outside the hotel," said Roth. Well over 100 Japanese journalists had queued up and Roth panicked, approached the hotel again, and commandeered the Prince ballroom, luckily available. There Audrey held court to drive home the message of UNICEF—a message lost amid questions about the woman who had captured Japanese hearts thirty-three years earlier. Where do you live? How do you spend your days? Will you get married again? Will you make any more pictures? Which is your favorite?

Her responses didn't matter; they hung on every lyrical word that tumbled out her mouth. Where do you live: a little village in Switzerland. How do you spend your days: gardening and listening to music. Will you get married again: Why should I? Robert and I are happy the way it is. Will you make any more pictures: not unless a very attractive script comes along. Which is your favorite: It's like asking which is your favorite child, but if pressed, "The film that meant the most to me emotionally was *Roman Holiday*."

It was clear even the hardened Japanese press corps loved Audrey Hepburn with every corpuscle in their collective bodies.

James Grant knew he'd captured lightning in a bottle and sought at once to secure the cork. "He immediately realized the potential that Audrey presented in order to get UNICEF more into the public eye," said Christa Roth.

Grant made his move, asking Audrey if she might consider more work on behalf of UNICEF, perhaps with a title like Special Ambassador; Audrey didn't commit, but said she would help in any way she could. And that's how they left it in Tokyo.

The War Diet

Audrey had spent much of her first twenty years, up until 1949, struggling to find pockets of happiness under the thumb of a domineering mother, Ella, Baroness van Heemstra, with secrets tied to a Nazi past. Audrey's father had abandoned her as a small girl, causing a wound that never healed and influencing her choice for a husband. Mel Ferrer, a Hollywood actor. Ferrer's serious nature and quenchless ambition intrigued her at first, but time revealed a moody man who could be rigid and dominating. Audrey would spend the length of their marriage arguing with the press about whether her husband was a Svengali. She would admit privately, yes, often he was.

By the time their son Sean arrived in July 1960, six years and two miscarriages into the marriage, the relationship had already eroded. As an adult, Sean would describe his father as a "difficult and demanding man," but Mel also understood the emotional scars of the war and helped Audrey deal with them.

She said in 1966, "I still wake up in the middle of the night with a feeling of overwhelming horror, sometimes in an icy sweat. It's Mel who has eased me out of this, who has given me an understanding of safety, of warmth, of security. Mel has always woken me when I've been having a nightmare and forced me to talk about it. This does me good." The term post-traumatic stress disorder hadn't been invented back then, but that didn't mean millions who had survived the war weren't experiencing it. "It's never the same dream," she said, "but it's always about German soldiers. I had them all the time after the war."

Luca confirmed, "She had nightmares about the war all her life."

Audrey worked hard at overcoming the trauma and the dark memories generated by World War II. She stated that the war instilled "enough fear to have riddled my life with apprehension about life and people," which had, in turn, caused her to adopt a philosophy that made her "resilient and terribly appreciative for everything good that came afterward."

Rarely she would slip, as when Luca as a boy of eleven walked down to the corner store and bought an alarm clock so he could wake himself for school in the morning. For a boy used to spending money on toys, he considered the move quite grown up, practically a rite of passage. He had used his own money, made the purchase himself, and proudly showed Mummy his new possession.

The blindsiding that followed made a memory for a lifetime. "She completely flipped out," he said. "I couldn't understand—it was like she found a loaded gun under my pillow."

"How could you do such a thing?" Audrey demanded. He could see devastation, anger, and pain in those famous eyes. She pounded up the stairs and slammed the bedroom door behind her.

Luca stood there bewildered. Her response had been so extreme, so unlike her, that he remained downstairs and waited.

"She stayed in her room for quite some time," said Luca and when she finally emerged, Hyde was gone; Jekyll had returned. She pointed at the name on the clock, Krups—the same name she had seen on the sides of the tanks that parked for months in front of her home, Villa Beukenhof, in the Dutch village of Velp before and after the battle of Arnhem. These tanks clattered down the main street dealing all manner of death. The last sounds of combat she heard before liberation had been tanks in the distance.

The fact that the name on the tanks was Krupp and the name on the alarm clock was Krups didn't matter a bit. The resemblance had set off a trauma reaction.

Luca conveyed to her that he couldn't possibly have known this, "and from that day she started talking more about the war."

Those final months of war, from September 1944 through April 1945, generated most of the nightmares that plagued her. Artillery shells sailed over her village and sometimes strayed off course and pulverized homes. Neighbors simply ceased to exist. The Red Cross provided young people in the village, Audrey included, with pendants to wear around their necks. On the pendant was printed a name and address in case the child was blown to bits by a bomb or stray V-1 and couldn't be identified.

Allied fighter planes growled overhead incessantly, looking for armored columns to attack. Those British pilots who cruised above in Spitfires and Typhoons firing rockets would lock onto German tanks or trucks, not the faces of Dutch men, women, and children in homes that might be destroyed. It was a war waged by Hitler, Stalin, Roosevelt, and Churchill—they and their generals decided who would attack and who would defend. Who would live and who would die. Which city or town or village would erupt in flames. God help the poor Dutch caught in the middle. They had no say in it.

By the end of February 1945, thousands of Dutch civilians had died in the Hunger Winter after the Germans cut off all food flowing into the Netherlands. Old people passed any meager bit of food to the young who must live past this darkness. After all, these children would be the citizens of tomorrow's world. But then came a time when no food at all remained for the children—Audrey called it "the war diet." At that point edema set in, the inability of the kidneys to function due to malnutrition. Swelling started in the feet and worked upward to the ankles and then the knees. All the children in Velp experienced it, including Audrey. She would say decades later as a movie star, "I still have stretch marks on my ankles from where the skin was stretched by the edema." Anemia ravaged her as well—almost all the children endured it.

These memories, darkest of all, never left her—the inability to get warm no matter how many clothes or blankets. The aching joints. The short tempers that turned family members into strangers. Hunger made seconds pass as minutes and minutes as hours. The empty belly conjured a tunnel and then a cavern that stretched into blackness for tomorrow and the next day and the next.

Finally, toward the end of March the famine in Velp was broken by emergency food supplies arranged through Sweden. It wasn't much, but it kept the townspeople alive going into April and the last gasps of the Nazi empire. British and Canadian forces liberated Velp on April 16, 1945, bringing with them K-rations and chocolate bars shared with the desperate Dutch.

Clan Visser 't Hooft, daughter of the local Resistance leader, remembered that the first quantities of emergency food supplies arrived "out of the air! Great silk parachutes with huge tins filled with English biscuits. Dropping site was the empty terrain behind the burnt down Hotel Naeff.... The Red Cross distributed these tins among shops in the village. Everyone was allowed just one pound per person. People hurried to fetch those in pillowcases for want of paper bags."

After five long years of ever-worsening conditions under German occupation, freedom hit like a thunderclap. Cheering crowds waving Dutch flags greeted the Allied tanks and half-tracks that roared into town and whipped dust from destroyed homes and buildings into enormous clouds. Members of the Dutch Resistance movement, identified by armbands emblazoned with the word ORANJE, rounded up Nazi collaborators and pushed them through gauntlets of angry townspeople. Village officials shaved the heads of Nazi-loving women. Bottles of wine and champagne hidden away years earlier now appeared to toast the liberators and the free air they had brought with them.

The people had been hunkering down in their cellars dodging bombs and bullets for weeks. They hadn't even seen the sun. Now the friendly Canadian boys offered smiles and cigarettes and ever more chocolate bars. Next came a distribution center set up in the village to receive supplies that began to flow in from something called the United Nations Relief and Rehabilitation Administration, or UNRRA.

"There were UNRRA crates," said Audrey. "There were boxes of food that we were allowed to take home—blankets, medication, and clothes." But to the Dutch girl, first and foremost the food arriving in Velp made an impression. "I remember lots of flour and butter and oatmeal and all the things that really feed a child, and all the things we hadn't seen in ages! And I must say one of the first meals I had was oatmeal made with canned milk, and I put so much sugar on it and I ate a whole plateful and was deadly ill afterwards because I couldn't absorb it. I wasn't used to rich food anymore. I was hardly used to food anymore, let alone that kind of thing. But it was everything we dreamed of—it was a dream."

Among the items given freely by the liberators were packs of Players cigarettes. Audrey took up smoking on Liberation Day and never gave it up, with Kent her preferred brand. The love affair with cigarettes coupled with vestiges of starvation cast war's shadow on the remainder of her life. But what did she care at sixteen as relief crates poured into the Netherlands?

The Latin school, a brick building in the city of Arnhem, next door to Velp, became a clothing distribution center. Said Audrey, "After a few days I remember going to a huge classroom where we could pick out clothes, sweaters and skirts, and they were so pretty, and they had come from America. We thought, how could people be so rich that they could give away things that looked so new, because I literally was wearing things made of old curtains, and my brother's shoes."

She would always remember the clothes she picked: "I chose a white blouse with a Peter Pan collar and a navy blue pleated skirt. There was a Saks Fifth Avenue label in the blouse. Hence my love ever since of fine clothes."

The resourceful Dutch also retrieved parachutes from those food supplies dropped behind the Hotel Naeff. "The silk material from the parachutes immediately was transformed into skirts and blouses," said Clan Visser 't Hooft.

Another young teen from Velp, Rosemarie Kamphuisen, said of the UNRRA relief effort, "I remember a lot of American goods coming to us. At school we got extra food: Ovomaltine, porridge, and soup, half a liter per person in a special enamel cup that was white with a blue brim, also from the U.S.A. We were told to keep the cup and bring it for more food. No cup—no food! We also all were given identical reversible coats, one side wool, the other side for rain, three-quarters length. And for decades we used your army blankets—I only threw them away when I was fifty years old."

The United Nations Relief and Rehabilitation Administration, based in Washington, D.C., worked to "plan, co-ordinate, administer or arrange for the administration of measures for the relief of victims of war in any area under the control of any of the United Nations through the provision of food, fuel, clothing, shelter and other basic necessities, medical and other essential services." The United States provided most of the funding; hence U.S. supplies and food products flooded into newly liberated parts of Europe. A multinational team of nine (French, Belgian, and Dutch) set up each UNRRA site—a director, doctor, welfare officer, warehouse officer, supply officer, food officer, nurse, and two truck drivers.

Audrey often talked about the consequences of too much food flooding into Velp. "I went on an eating binge. I would eat anything in sight and in any quantity. I'd empty out a jam jar with a spoon. I was crazy about everything I could lay my hands on when food started appearing. I became quite tubby and put on twenty pounds."

She also said, "Fortunately, the feeling of being hungry, in that sense, has left me. But you never forget the experience. So it leaves you with an enormous respect for food and for everything. For life."

Decades later, after enjoying limos and gowns and piles of cracked crab and smoked salmon, she would come back again and again to the darkest moment of all, with four starving van Heemstras—Audrey, her grandfather the baron, Ella, and Ella's sister, Audrey's Aunt Miesje.

It was Miesje who said, "We have nothing to eat tomorrow. Let's just stay in bed."

Those days seemed almost quaint in comparison to what she knew of Ethiopia in 1985 and 1986 and 1987, with international aid organizations and worldwide media raising the alarm. About 20,000 Dutch died in the Hunger Winter; Africa's poor were dying by the millions of disease and hunger. Audrey would never dare to compare Holland's situation with Ethiopia's, yet Audrey understood what the Ethiopians were facing. She had met and become acquainted with hunger, which made her one of them. Now that she had been infected by the UNICEF bug like Danny Kaye and Peter Ustinov before her, the ambassadorship offered by Jim Grant demanded only one answer. And that was a problem.

The voice of Ella van Heemstra was always in Audrey's ear and that of her grandfather Baron Aarnoud van Heemstra—her family of Dutch nobility had generations ago embraced the concept of *noblesse oblige*, the obligation of nobility to help those less fortunate. They believed it and had lived it. Said Audrey, echoing what she had been taught in her youth, "There is just no question that there is a moral obligation that those who have should give to those who have nothing."

Her friend Anna Cataldi knew the direction UNICEF was taking and understood what such a commitment would represent for Audrey. She would be "witnessing the sufferings of child victims of poverty, disease, or armed conflict," said Cataldi. "Above all, it would mean undertaking long, tiring journeys under difficult conditions and exposing herself to the emotional stress of confronting children in dangerous and vulnerable situations."

Anna knew the score, as did a vocal member of Audrey's household. "Giovanna the housekeeper was very much against it," Cataldi said with a chuckle.

"La signora need to rest!" Giovanna would scold—rest not just occasionally, but as a lifestyle. In the early 1960s Audrey had employed two young Sardinian women, Giovanna and Tina Orunesu, as family cooks and housekeepers. Tina had married and left the farm, but Giovanna became a relied-upon member of Audrey's family.

Giovanna was, said Luca, "talkative, emotional, and dependent on my mother." More than that, Giovanna had become Audrey's barometer, able to interpret the needs of the lady of the house. And Giovanna's understanding of her lady's well-being was unerring.

A few years later, Audrey added to the staff by hiring another empathic character, Engracia de la Rocha, a native of Toledo, Spain, as a housekeeper—a woman as silent as Giovanna was talkative. "I could tease Giovanna," said Luca, "but when I annoyed Engracia, she would point a finger at my throat and say, 'Do it again and I'll bring in my brother from Toledo, who has knives as big as this.'"

But it was Giovanna who had la signora's ear on the issue of UNICEF, and Audrey valued and respected the concerns Giovanna raised about what she interpreted as a threat to the home. As far as Giovanna was concerned, UNICEF had no business asking her mistress for anything.

Luca felt the same way, and so did Doris; Square's distraction was palpable as she fell under the influence of this new man, Jim Grant. Yes, Giovanna, Luca, and Doris could admit to a certain jealousy, but they all also sensed danger. Working against the three of them was the fact that UNICEF's European office sat in Geneva, just a thirty-minute drive from La Paisible; had it been in, say, Stockholm, Audrey would have nixed the idea for practical reasons.

But so many factors pointed her in another direction. The fact that UNICEF offices in Geneva's Palais des Nations were so close to home amounted to a sign. Sean was well-established in Hollywood now, and Luca was off to college. Audrey had lived up to long-standing obligations; she had held Ella's hand as she passed in 1984 at age eighty-four and had done the same for eighty-eight-year-old Miesje in 1985. From hand to hand had gone the torch of family leadership and the obligation of family service, and Audrey had lived what she had lived and seen what she'd seen. However improbable, she was an international celebrity and always, always in the cross hairs of every nearby camera. Audrey Hepburn loved children almost to obsession. Audrey Hepburn knew war and famine so well that her nerves scrambled at any triggering sight or sound even forty-plus years later. No one alive was better positioned to spread the message of UNICEF.

Giovanna may have been correct, Audrey did need to rest, but there was a higher obligation born of UNRRA, precursor to UNICEF. As she would express it, "UNICEF saved me as a child.... To save a child is a blessing. To save one million is a God-given opportunity."

From afar she had watched Danny Kaye beat UNICEF's drum and entertain the world's children. Audrey and Danny had been friends and his death a year earlier so saddened her. But his situation and hers weren't the same. "He did it in a different way," she said. "He would make occasional trips with them, did some fund-raising concerts over thirty years, and I don't have that kind of time." In her mind the plan coalesced: She would "do as much as possible in the time that I'm still up to it." No one foot in, one foot out for Audrey Hepburn. Once in, she knew she would be all-in for the duration, doing whatever she could to raise funds and awareness. And "whatever she could" took in a lot of territory for a past and future workaholic.

"When they asked me to help, I was only too happy to accept, but I didn't know what I was getting into," she would tell her friend Dominick Dunne three years later. In a sense she was signing a blank contract, with the details to be filled in later, and as her own worst enemy—a bleeding heart unable to refuse any opportunity to help—accepting UNICEF's offer placed her directly into harm's way, which had set off alarm bells in those closest to her. "The whole thing terrified me, and still does," said Audrey. "I wasn't cut out for this job."

She wouldn't be able to take on this new UNICEF role without Robbie, so he would have to say yes to all that a UNICEF ambassadorship meant and required. About this time the Geneva office floated the idea to send Audrey to the obvious place, Ethiopia, to bring the crisis there more sharply into world focus. The invitation became another factor in the discussion—was Robbie up to being Audrey's wingman not just for an occasional Macau or Japan, but on field missions of several days and the multi-continent news conferences that would follow each?

"So now, an answer to the mystery of Audrey Hepburn," wrote an interviewer. "All her life, she has been searching for a man capable of returning her love. And I believe she has found that man in the gentle, decent, psychological father figure of Wolders." Father figure and also friend, social secretary, and conscience who insisted she get nine to ten hours of sleep a night. Joining UNICEF required a "yes" from Robbie.

They talked; Robbie remained 100 percent solid and predictable. Wherever she went, he'd be right there with her. By now Audrey's La Paisible family had grown; Giovanna's brother Giovanni Orunesu and his wife, Rucchita, had moved in and could now watch the house and tend the grounds while Audrey was away. The Orunesu children came along: Marilena, who became Luca's best friend, and her younger brother, Pierluigi.

Against the wishes of Doris, Giovanna, and Luca, Audrey reached agreement with UNICEF on Wednesday, March 9, 1988. The announcement came Thursday, March 10: Audrey Hepburn had been named a UNICEF Special Ambassador. Jim Grant said in the official press release, "We are indeed fortunate that people of renown, like Audrey Hepburn, with huge talents, are prepared to give so generously of their time and energies. During recent ad hoc missions for UNICEF, including appearances at benefit events in Tokyo and Macau, she has demonstrated her remarkable talents as an advocate for children."

Audrey broke the news to Luca in a much less formal way, presenting UNICEF to him as another lark. "Look," she said, pointing to the new United Nations sticker on Robbie's Volvo, "We can park anywhere we want! I have diplomatic immunity!"

The Visionary

When had the "Ethiopian situation" begun? Was it the 1960s, when civil war engulfed the Ethiopian regions of Eritrea and Tigray? Was it 1974, when Marxists overthrew Emperor Haile Selassie? Was it 1981, when a drought wiped out that year's harvest and famine resulted?

All were turning points and sent the country spiraling downward into 1984, when another drought killed one million Ethiopians as the Western world failed to take notice because, after all, Ethiopians were black and, even worse, ruled by Marxists. Then a BBC film crew led by British newsman Michael Buerk ventured into Ethiopia and the footage they captured shocked the world. Among those riveted to the television were Audrey and Robbie at La Paisible and, in London, an Irish rock 'n' roller from a fading band called the Boomtown Rats. Up to this point, Bob Geldof's worry had been the release of his next album, which threatened to become the third in a row to land with a thud. But the drama of that BBC film footage shown on the air November 15, 1984, rooted him where he stood. To Geldof, the issue wasn't skin color. He gaped at humans in crisis.

"The pictures were of people who were so shrunken by starvation that they looked like beings from another planet," said Geldof. "Their arms and legs were as thin as sticks, their bodies spindly.

Swollen veins and huge, blankly staring eyes protruded from their shriveled heads." And thousands upon thousands of these creatures filled the frame of the camera.

Geldof would say in retrospect he found himself perfectly positioned at this moment in time to do something. "I wasn't out on tour or trying to follow up a hit record. My band's fortunes had already failed to a large extent, and we were bringing out a single and an album, but there was no indication they would be any more successful than the last two."

The Boomtown Rats had been a galloping chariot leading the charge of something new in music with hits that included "Lookin' After No. 1" and "I Don't Like Mondays." One reporter would say of Geldof's run as head Rat, "The marketing phenomenon known as 'punk rock' was tailor made for such an incorrigible loudmouth and, to his delight, Geldof discovered that every pronouncement, no matter how witless or uninformed, was rewarded by acres of newsprint."

But now Geldof had a cause: the plight of Ethiopia. Within a day he had set to organizing a fund-raising record using his fading name and that of his band, the Rats. He envisioned throwing together an all-star single in time for Christmas 1984, less than six weeks away. Others had seen the BBC broadcast and responded thumbs-up to his invitation. Along with veteran musician Midge Ure of the band Ultravox, Geldof wrote a song inspired by the Ethiopian starving masses called "Do They Know It's Christmas?" On November 25, 1984, some of the biggest names in popular music turned out in unprecedented fashion to sing the new song, working together and at least trying to cast egos aside. Their super-duper supergroup—led by George Michael, Sting, and Boy George and including three dozen other names from popular music—was dubbed Band-Aid.

Through the force of Geldof's will, "Do They Know It's Christmas?" zoomed through post-production for release eight days later, on December 3, 1984, and changed the landscape of popular music. It became an instant number one in fourteen countries and sold millions of copies worldwide.

At the beginning of January, Geldof arranged to visit Ethiopia and see the disaster firsthand and up close. In Addis Ababa he met Mother Teresa, the "tiny giant" as he called her. He learned something by observing the nun's handling of reporters and politicians that Audrey would later discover and, in her way, master.

"She was outrageously brilliant," said Geldof of the tiny giant Mother Teresa. "There was no false modesty about her and there was a certainty of purpose which left her little patience. But she was totally selfless; every moment her aim seemed to be, how can I use this or that situation to help others." Geldof also realized the tiny giant was media savvy, and knew where the cameras would be, and used her saintly image to back politicians into corners for the good of the less fortunate. Geldof would always lug around his reputation as a loudmouth boor and never possess the polish of Mother Teresa, or of Audrey Hepburn. Geldof simply muscled his way forward, all bluster, Irish temper, and F-bombs in the name of the starving masses in Africa.

Geldof's Ethiopian visit galvanized his commitment to further action. The Band-Aid Christmas record raised £8 million, which proved to be a drop in the bucket of Ethiopian humanitarian needs. Geldof had to think bigger, much bigger. Luckily, the limits of his imagination matched those of his bluster—none. What if he could stage a one-day concert at Wembley Stadium in London and sync it with a venue in the States the same day? A big venue in the States. Never shy, he put out feelers to Wembley for a date in summer 1985. Initially, he received an indifferent response, but then a letter arrived in the post. If what he proposed was a concert for charity, like Band-Aid, he could probably get Wembley at no cost.

He didn't hesitate. The success of Band-Aid made this a fait accompli. Within days Elton John said yes to the still-theoretical concert, and Mark Knopfler of Dire Straits threw their hats in the ring. Roger Taylor and Brian May of Queen said they'd try to convince Freddie Mercury. Off to the races went Bob Geldof with his idea for a one-day concert on two continents that he would call Live Aid. "People are dying out there!" was his rallying cry, and for those who found him self-righteous, or self-serving, or trying to resurrect a failed career on the backs of famine-plagued Ethiopians, Bob Geldof had just two words: "Fuck off." If he said it once, he said it a thousand times.

By now the headwinds had grown fierce and cynics abounded. Critics said: The narcissist's band had tanked, so he needed a new stage. He was a rich musician asking others to fund rescue missions. He was in it for the glory and not the cause. Precious little of the Band-Aid money actually reached the people of Ethiopia. He had made compassion "hip" and, just wait, it will all go away.

To each of these assertions he said in response, "Yeah, but people are alive. This criticism irritates me, but then I think it makes people question even further: What price criticism when the end result of a bunch of people in the studio is without doubt millions of people being helped to stay alive?"

Audrey Hepburn could only admire the activists from the sidelines. She was, she said, "overwhelmed by a sense of helplessness when watching television or reading about the indescribable misery of the children and their mothers." She knew it all too well. She had lived it.

Geldof kept at it and suddenly it was summer. Saturday morning, July 13, 1985, focused on two issues: the weather and the Beatles. Would rain fall on Wembley Stadium where 70,000 were set to see the biggest rock 'n' roll show of all time? And the question of questions: Would the living Beatles reunite on that stage, wet or dry, to be joined by John Lennon's son Julian standing in for the slain fourth Beatle? After all, Paul McCartney was set to close the day's mega-sets with "Let It Be." George Harrison had been spotted at Heathrow. Julian was already performing. It was a natural, and the music world held collective breath that finally, after fifteen years, today it would happen.

An ocean away, a city had sprung up beside John F. Kennedy Stadium in Philadelphia that included thirty-seven broadcast trucks and mobile homes and a portable Hard Rock Café. About 82,000 were expected to fill the Philly venue, and weather there wasn't a concern.

In London, Bob Geldof, mastermind of what had grown into a seventeen-hour event he hoped would draw a billion sets of eyes worldwide to the issue of Ethiopian famine and raise $10 million U.S., prowled backstage like a panther at the zoo. The acts went on at a pace of twenty-two minutes each. Joan Baez, Ozzy Osbourne and Black Sabbath, Crosby, Stills, and Nash, the Beach Boys, U2—so many killer acts, and the money didn't pour in. Finally, with Dire Straits finishing "Sultans of Swing," Geldof headed along a rickety series of gantries high above ground level with his destination the BBC booth located in Wembley's roof, with his Irish temper ready to blow the mop top off his head. Halfway there, from the top catwalks, he heard Freddie Mercury singing "Radio Ga Ga." Freddie and Queen, the '70s glam group, had recently played South Africa and become pariahs for their trouble, at least among the rock elite. Apartheid was wrong, and Queen had played anyway. But today was about Ethiopia, not apartheid, and down below, something crazy had brewed up. Geldof staggered from the tremor of 70,000 in the audience clap-clapping in time to the music—he could feel it in the metal gantry.

Geldof stole a peek down below. "All we hear is radio ga ga," sang Mercury, "radio goo goo, radio ga ga." And the ocean of an audience clapped along as one! At any other moment in his life, Geldof would have cried. But not now. Now he pounded along the gantry and into a sweltering television studio where he found in progress a quiet talk show that infuriated him. Live Aid wasn't a telethon; it was "finely tuned politics!"

He squeezed in between TV host David Hepworth and, on the couch beside him, Pamela Stephenson, Billy Connolly, and Ian Astbury. Geldof said, "I was wound up by how great this was, having seen these guys [Queen] being magnificent. Suddenly, I'm there and it's cozy, celeb, DJ, poptastic stuff."

Geldof pleaded with viewers to stay home from the pub and send him their money instead—send your damn money to Ethiopia. "People are dying now," he snapped, pounding the table, "so give me the money!" And when David Hepworth tried to read an address for people to send donations via post, the punch-drunk Geldof snapped, "Fuck the address, let's give the [phone] numbers!" It was an F-bomb on live TV that catalyzed with Queen's performance to change Live Aid's fortunes. Geldof didn't realize what he had just done. In a day of firsts, and lasts, and onlys, when Led Zeppelin reunited for the first time in years and played horribly, and the Beatles failed to reunite at all, Geldof became a legend for his guts and his F-bomb, and Queen had dazzled the world. Between them, torrents of cash poured in.

About 500 miles due southeast of Wembley Stadium, Luca sat in his mother's bedroom at La Paisible. They had watched the day unfold on two continents, with additional performances satellite-beamed from Sydney, Vienna, The Hague, Moscow, and Belgrade. Luca, who had been an amateur DJ in Rome, sat enthralled by the '80s British pop groups who were performing while disdaining old-guard bands like Black Sabbath, The Who, and Judas Priest. Audrey's focus gradually intensified from casual interest—the closest thing that day to Henry Mancini in Audrey's mind was Sting—to captivation at what unfolded before her eyes.

"We were watching the ads where, for the very first time, you were informed live about the donations," said Luca. Audrey sat transfixed, watching roll-ins about the situation in Ethiopia, famine and millions of innocent people dying. Children dying. And there was Geldof, tirelessly, courageously present, driving the point home. Geldof wasn't a politician or some slick salesman. Geldof pounded the message with the relentless fury of a prizefighter.

"People were seeing it in that moment," said Luca. "You could see the money rolling in. That lit up a light in my mother's mind and eyes and heart and that's where she realized, as she clearly put it, 'This is a fantastic idea. You should be giving money because you want to give money.' She had never been a big fan of the Catholic Church—you know, give money so you can go to heaven. With Live Aid she realized those guys were doing their job, which was entertaining people. People were not there because they had to be—it kind of reversed the equation. Usually they say, 'Look at the dying children; give me the money.' This was, look at the best show on earth, and on top of it we're raising money for Africa."

Audrey watched with Luca, and by the time the Band Aid supergroup assembled on the Wembley stage to close that portion of the show with "Do They Know It's Christmas?" and USA for Africa gathered to close Philadelphia with "We Are the World," the existence of the retired Hollywood star had changed. She was no longer able to escape the fact that she, Audrey Hepburn, needed to do something, and she could do something. Geldof had discovered a powerful tool. Celebrity power. His doubters piled on every chance they got, berating this unkempt youngster, this has-been from a flash-in-the-pan band who claimed to care so much. He was self-serving. He was uncouth. They said horrible things about Bob Geldof, but Audrey could draw only one conclusion at the end of Live Aid when the world had been confronted with video of starving masses in Ethiopia, when the $10 million Geldof hoped to raise had become $70 million, and the dreamed-of audience of one billion had grown to three, or half the population on Earth: "Shit!" Audrey exclaimed. "He did it!"

You Just Decide

Late in 1939 Ella brought Audrey, age ten, back to Arnhem from boarding school in England. Audrey's introduction to much of her Dutch family took place at a city-wide event sponsored by the van Heemstras to benefit Polish victims of the Nazi invasion—just one of many charitable activities in which Audrey's family engaged.

Baron Aarnoud van Heemstra, Audrey's maternal grandfather, would profoundly influence the ten year old. The baron had been appointed governor of the Dutch possession Suriname in 1920, nine years before her birth, and proved to be a progressive in dealing with the melting pot of inhabitants he found there. Van Heemstra believed in governing all the people, including those with dark skin who had ended up on the northeast coast of South America against their will—many on slave plantations until the abolition of slavery sixty years earlier.

The baron's color blindness would later put him at odds with his firebrand daughter Ella when she became enamored of Hitler's Aryan beliefs. Ella's decision in favor of Hitler deepened Audrey's commitment even as a teenager to equality among races. Especially after what she had seen the Nazis do to the Jews, Audrey saw everyone as a person, not a white or a black or a red or a brown person. You are a person and if I can help you, I will.

From September 1944 to the spring of 1945, the van Heemstra household in Velp transitioned from helping the less fortunate to becoming the less fortunate, with no running water, no heat, and no food due to the attempted strangulation of Holland by the Nazi occupiers.

Audrey had during the war years been Arnhem's most accomplished ballerina. Soon after liberation, she would star in a benefit ballet recital in Velp to benefit the Netherlands Red Cross. Two years later she participated in a Red Cross fashion show in The Hague. From there she espoused many causes, and in February 1953 as a star on the rise passionately led the charge for aid to the Netherlands after the worst flooding in 500 years hit the southwestern coast and killed more than 1,000. The next month she canvassed New York City carrying a collection can for the American Red Cross and the next year engaged in a grueling five-day tour of the Netherlands for the Dutch Association of Military War Victims.

She described her charitable activities in a 1989 interview on French television: "Throughout my childhood, every member of my family was doing something to help others ... but we didn't talk about it. It was embarrassing to receive compliments because it was our ethic; it all went without saying. It was natural to help."

With her official Special Ambassador appointment made in the March 9 UN document, Audrey accepted about her shoulders a mantle of responsibility for as yet uncounted millions of defenseless souls. She entered the job with big brown eyes open and an understanding that the struggle ahead would be mortal. She didn't cipher it as a final countdown, and yet a final countdown had begun. She would live out another 1,777 days, all of them fighting under the UNICEF banner.

She embraced the breadth of the mission to save children, including a $22 million funding gap for operations in famine-plagued

Ethiopia, the place so in the news these past several years, the place
Geldof had aimed spotlights at. Ethiopia became the obvious first
destination for an Audrey Hepburn mission.

The Ethiopia budget reflected the scope of horror there and
not tens or hundreds of thousands but millions of souls in peril:
$8 million for emergency drugs, vaccines, medical supplies, and
equipment for clinics and food distribution centers; $5.1 million
for projects to bring clean water to villages and distribution centers; $5 million cash for food to families in exchange for work on
community development projects; and $3.9 million for supple-
mentary feeding and relief supplies, high-protein biscuits and falfa
(locally produced enriched food products) for malnourished children and lactating mothers.

The catch was that UNICEF didn't receive funds from the
general United Nations budget. UNICEF was its own operation,
responsible for its own fund-raising, and always ready to go under-
water. Nobody was kidding anybody—Audrey was ready and willing to use her name for the children, and UNICEF was happy to
use her name as its newest and perhaps biggest drawing card ever.

Logistical planning began at once to get Audrey into the field.
She and Robbie drove into Geneva for a meeting with UNICEF
PR liaison Christa Roth at UNICEF headquarters in the Palais
des Nations. Roth outlined a program that would put Audrey and
Robbie in drought- and famine-plagued northern Ethiopia for five
days, flying out of Geneva Sunday, March 13. They were game
to take this on, to give it a try, because, as Robbie said of Audrey,
"She was persuaded [by UNICEF] that she could do it." At the
same time, there was no way she could become grounded in all she
needed to know in a matter of a few days.

Robbie would later lament the lack of planning: "We had no
idea, in fact, what was expected of her." But she was determined to
go in prepared.

In New York Jim Grant set Audrey up with Fouad Kronfol,

chief of the Africa section, program division, at UNICEF head-quarters. "A few days later I was on the phone with Ms. Hepburn and we went through almost two hours of questions, answers, statistics, information, and other aspects related to Ethiopia," said Kronfol. "I was extremely pleased with her charming personality to start with, but also impressed with her knowledge and consideration of issues; she was very attentive, asked intelligent questions, absorbed a great deal of pointers on policy, program issues, and activities. Naturally I also pointed her in the direction of important documents to read and other UNICEF staff to talk to. The whole briefing went off remarkably well and it was a most gratifying and memorable bit of official business I had been involved with, especially with celebrities."

Another program officer in the Africa Section, George Kassis, became her go-to resource after Kronfol's initial briefing. Audrey "was given my phone number to call with any last-minute queries or updates," said Kassis. "Sure enough, especially in the beginning, she would call ... with pointed questions, and I took advantage of every call to put her on speaker phone. You can imagine how jealous and impressed my colleagues were overhearing our conversations on the phone. She was so concerned and keen to do a good job."

One of those colleagues was Shahida Azfar, who said: "One day George was generous enough to ask me if I wanted to hear his interaction with her. He immediately dialed her and her response was prompt, personal, and warm, almost affectionate. This further increased my admiration of her and envy of George Kassis!"

With the stakes for Audrey's first field mission so high, she would have overseers throughout her stay in-country. "The trip was half organized by the American committee for UNICEF and the president was also with her in Ethiopia," said Christa Roth, who now had to coordinate the itineraries of Audrey and Robbie and also President and CEO of the United States Committee for

UNICEF Lawrence E. Bruce, Jr., and John Williams, executive secretary of the UNICEF board.

Roth's PR role included prepping celebrity ambassadors for their missions and working with the country's UNICEF office to develop a program based on the needs within that country. Then, "I would discuss it with her and with Robert," said Roth of the agenda. "We would take things off because there was just too much on it sometimes. There was no time for her to rest in between visits to projects or to government people. Then we would send the revised program back—there was a lot of faxing back and forth."

Then all at once it sunk into Audrey's brain that a large part of her job would involve public speaking. Said Robbie, "When she realized that she would have to address a large group of people, she requested information. And when she found out the staggering facts, the statistics that 40,000 children a day [worldwide] die needlessly of totally preventable diseases, die of hunger, that made her realize there was a tremendous responsibility in conveying this to the public."

Roth arranged flights, visas, and forms for all the participants, a mountain of paperwork in short order, as Audrey sat at home studying everything UNICEF could provide in terms of background material on Ethiopia, applying the same laser focus to this new job as she had devoted to studying each line of each movie script in her career. The routine was quickly established: Cram at the dining room table for hours each morning. When Luca visited and came down for breakfast, he would know how long she had been studying by the number of cigarette butts in the ashtray.

Audrey learned that a UN photojournalist named John Isaac had made several trips to Ethiopia as part of an impressive resume that had taken him to Beirut to cover the Israel–Lebanon conflict, to Southeast Asia to document the Vietnamese boat people, and to Iran where American diplomats were held hostage. Christa Roth believed he could be an asset on Audrey's first field mission and she asked Jim Grant if Isaac could be included on short notice and meet the party in Ethiopia.

Packing for the trip proved to be the easy part. She would go Spartan, which had always been Robbie's custom anyway. "I am not here to be seen," she said, "but so that the rest of the world can see others." One carry-on and two suitcases would see her through five days in Ethiopia, even counting press conferences afterward.

Audrey Hepburn's UNICEF career began inauspiciously when their Sunday, March 13, Swissair flight from Geneva to Addis Ababa was canceled, prompting a mad scramble on both ends to reschedule the flight and rearrange the program as the would-be travelers killed a day back at La Paisible.

The next morning, Monday, March 14, 1988, the schedule proceeded in more orderly fashion and the Special Ambassador went wheels-up on her first official flight. Six hours later they landed at the facility formerly known as Haile Selassie I International Airport, its name changed after the emperor's 1974 removal from power—symbolic of a country that had been spiraling downward for decades.

Larry Bruce, John Williams, Audrey, and Robbie met with the local UNICEF team, including Mary Racelis, director of the Eastern and Southern Africa Regional Office. Racelis understood the gravity of the new Special Ambassador within minutes. "After resting at her hotel, she joined the UNICEF staff for an initial briefing on the Ethiopia situation and UNICEF's role there," she said. "We were awe-struck, not only because *the* Audrey Hepburn was among us but because of how quickly and ably she had grasped the key points of our briefing." Racelis hadn't seen the early morning dining table sessions or the many phone consultations with UNICEF staff.

The team then met with government officials; Audrey wanted to know about the new resettlement policy enacted by the ruling Derg four months earlier, which had displaced somewhere between

100,000 and 200,000 Ethiopians. Their goal, they said, was to remove people from the worst of the drought-plagued areas and resettle them in better lands. Or was it just an attempt to depopulate rebel areas in the north of the country, namely troubled Eritrea? When she pressed officials on this matter, they admitted to a "terrible mistake." As she said later, "They told me their soldiers had been overzealous and brutal." The rebel response to disrupt truck traffic into and out of the area, which kept food out, was "a tragedy within a tragedy," said the government. As a novice diplomat, she didn't know if she was being humored but had to suspect it.

This first meeting as part of a UNICEF team opened her eyes to problems that would only grow worse over time. Said UN photographer John Isaac, "Working with the UN is sometimes very frustrating because you're in the middle. You can't support this or that side. Initially she was frustrated by that. You want to sympathize. But she took a stand on a lot of things."

After an evening to unpack, Audrey and Robbie sat down with Larry Bruce, a tall American, age forty-two, with movie-star good looks and a wicked sense of humor. Three years earlier, Bruce had gained instant buy-in during his first staff meeting in UNICEF's New York office when this native of the backwoods—Huntington, West Virginia—promised the city people he'd wear shoes in the office. He had a soft side as well. When his secretary left her job and moved away, Bruce was absent from her going-away party and then found sitting in his office, crying because he would miss her.

Bruce spoke passionately to Audrey and Robbie about his UNICEF work, describing for them how he had come around to Jim Grant's four-pronged strategy for child survival that initially Bruce had resisted. He recited the acronym for them; GOBI—Growth monitoring, Oral rehydration, Breastfeeding, and Immunization. He said he didn't believe such a simple strategy could work until he visited Chad several hundred miles west of where they now sat. "I had my doubts," Larry told them, "but I saw GOBI work in Chad, and if it could work there, it can work anywhere."

Audrey realized her good fortune at having both Larry Bruce and John Williams at hand to show her the ropes.

"Since it was Audrey's first mission to a sensitive country, I wanted to give her and the Ethiopia country office support in managing this supremely important UNICEF mission," said Williams.

The next morning, the team met up with Isaac at the hotel. "I was a bit nervous since I had seen Audrey's films like *My Fair Lady*, *Roman Holiday*, and so on," said Isaac. That morning at the hotel he didn't meet a movie star; rather, this was a slight woman who looked more like a tourist, dressed in a blue sweater over a polo shirt and khaki pants. She wore her hair pulled straight back in a ponytail and had tucked her folded aviator sunglasses in the shirt's V neck.

Whatever Audrey was expecting visually in a "photojournalist John Isaac," the guy before her wasn't it. The dark-skinned Isaac, sporting a mop of black hair and whiskers, had been born in India, emigrated to the United States at age twenty-five, and "landed at JFK airport with a dollar in my pocket and a 12-string guitar in 1968 wanting to be a folk singer in New York City—but that's another story," said Isaac. While still chasing his dream, the aspiring hippie had appeared as a yodeler in a July 1970 nationally broadcast episode of the *Ted Mack and the Original Amateur Hour* television program, and a good yodeler at that. But the United Nations came calling and Isaac had spent the past year as the UN Department of Public Information photography chief after so many assignments in the world's hot spots that he couldn't keep track of them all.

Audrey confessed embarrassment because she assumed with a name like John Isaac he'd be British. But as she did with Christa Roth, Audrey put Isaac at ease right away and made it clear she would be relying on his expertise in what they were about to see and do.

The entire UNICEF team, including Mary Racelis and other field representatives and a film crew in addition to Audrey and Robbie, Larry Bruce, John Williams, and John Isaac, drove to the airport and boarded a C-130 Hercules cargo plane operated by the Belgian Air Force. Also aboard were eighteen tons of dried milk from Canada and grain from Germany being routed to an orphanage the group would visit. The flight toward the northern-most region of the country, which had become a danger zone, circuited high above harsh brown landscape—how could anyone live down there?

On final approach to the airport in the war-torn city of Asmara in the Ethiopian region of Eritrea, Audrey saw batteries of manned artillery in position along with Soviet MiG fighters parked off the runway. She would be asked later about why she would jeopardize her life traveling into Ethiopian war zones. Her answer to the question revealed a van Heemstra single-mindedness of purpose.

"You just decide," said Audrey. "Once you've decided, yes, I'll deal with it, then you don't think about it anymore."

As she stepped off the plane with Larry Bruce in Asmara, a shy little girl of perhaps eight wearing pigtails and traditional Ethiopian dress handed the Western lady a bouquet of flowers. Audrey had been just a little older than this girl when she presented flowers in just such a fashion to Sadler's Wells ballet director Ninette de Valois and principal dancer Margot Fonteyn in Arnhem in May 1940. Audrey reached down and hugged the girl for a long moment and thanked her for the gesture. Then she held the girl's face in her hands, and they posed together for pictures. Audrey carefully unwrapped the flowers and plucked a stem to give to the girl, who beamed as if holding treasure.

Local UNICEF representatives took Audrey on a quick tour of the rundown city, many buildings long ago wrecked by artillery fire and the hulks of cars and trucks appearing at random along the streets. She was shown the UN transportation and logistics operation, described to her as "the heart of any relief program."

She saw trucks distributing water desperately needed by city inhabitants and refugees who had fled fighting to the north and east. The regular water system was being repaired and upgraded with the help of UNICEF, she was told.

The party returned to the airport, where Audrey, Robbie, John Isaac, and some others piled into a Pilatus Porter PC-6 single-engine turboprop with UN painted in blue on the side. This powerful short-takeoff-and-landing, single-wing aircraft was used for unpaved rural runways, which should have indicated the going was about to get rough. The remainder of the UNICEF contingent crawled into another small prop plane and off they went, speeding south.

The small planes flew much lower than had the Hercules, and John Williams observed Audrey "gazing down at dried river networks, naked mountains shimmering under burning blue skies, and occasional patches of green, teeming with people. She was awed."

On the dusty runway of the Alula Aba Nega airstrip in the Tigray region, waiting UNICEF jeeps took the party on a short drive to Qwiha. There the Audrey Hepburn UNICEF experiment began in earnest, and John Williams harbored doubt that the former movie star would be up to it. "As we approached our first village and I saw her wiping her face and hands on a paper towelette, the kind airlines give you, I thought that this frail-looking, elegant lady was too far from her own environment." Then Williams had his eyes opened. "A minute later she had gathered a flock of dusty, scabby children to her, hugging and holding hands."

Looks could be deceiving, however. Audrey had developed a crusty shell in World War II. She had worked at Ziekenhuis Velp, the hospital in her village, tending wounded and injured townspeople and soldiers after the battle of Arnhem. She had stepped over body parts in the streets after V-1 explosions in the last months of the war. She had watched friends and family members shrivel to their bones in the Hunger Winter. And what she saw now in the desert shook her mightily.

"I went into rebel country and saw mothers and their children who had walked for ten days, even three weeks, looking for food, settling onto the desert floor into makeshift camps where they may die," she said. "That image is too much for me."

Here in Tigray, for the first time she stood before those victimized by the kind of evil she had experienced in the war. As an empath—which Robbie knew she was—such sights hurt her terribly, and each human interaction took something from her that could never be returned. She learned quickly to compartmentalize for her own survival, but mere rationalization couldn't dam the flooding emotions. She felt the suffering of these people too deeply for her own good and her own health. Drop by drop, she began to dole out her life force to those she met, a drop here and a drop there, all along her path through Ethiopia and on through the years and missions. Drop by drop, she would grow weaker from this point on as she tried to give strength to the thousands, the tens of thousands, that she met.

The touring party visited a single-story clinic with a white three-by-four-foot sign that read Qwiha Health Centre. Near the sign a white flag bearing a red crescent, symbol of a humanitarian site, flew stiff in hot morning winds that nearly knocked Audrey over as she exited the car. Overhead the sky was relentlessly, punishingly blue, a blue tinged with tan as those gusts whipped the dusty earth skyward into clouds. Robbie, said Racelis, "regularly reminded us when it was time to stop and let her get some rest." He would already see the dangers of field work for someone as sensitive as Audrey. But with so much to see and do, rest was rare.

Audrey forced a smile as the group passed many mothers and children milling about on the sandy, rocky grounds. Inside the health center, the UNICEF team received a tour of the facility from a tall young doctor and said hello to many mothers and children sitting in the corridors. All were painfully thin, some quite frail looking.

Audrey moved about awkwardly, not speaking their language, not knowing what to do to help them—they all, every one of them, so desperately needed help. Back outside she became fascinated by mothers sitting on the ground with white garments draped over them. She quickly learned they were sheltering their small children from the sun in what looked like little tents. She began playing hide-and-seek with some of these children, who giggled in response. Finally, she had found a common language: laughter.

She watched as families dipped buckets into piles of grain on the ground. Wherever she turned, cameras pointed at her. Still cameras, motion picture cameras—this was why she had come, to show the world. For a decade and a half she had been annoyed by paparazzi, and now the camera operators were her allies.

Next, the UNICEF caravan piled back into their jeeps, leaving Racelis without a seat. Audrey inched over close to the driver and wound her long legs around the gear shift to make room for Mary. Audrey waved off her protests, "urged me to get in and off we went," said Racelis.

The vehicles drove a short distance to the west, to the southern edge of the town of Mek'ele where the Ethiopians were constructing an earthen dam that would catch water in the rainy season—if there was a rainy season this year. The locals, Audrey was told, were building the structure by hand. The effort to construct this dam, one of several being thrown up in the area, was incredible and involved thousands of civilian builders participating in a UNICEF work-for-food program—one of the projects in the $22 million plan for Ethiopia.

Audrey and the others exited their cars and she beheld something that required descriptions that couldn't be conjured, something Cecil B. DeMille would have directed for *The Ten Commandments*. But for Hollywood to recreate the scene she witnessed this moment would have cost maybe a half-million dollars.

At least a thousand men, women, and children were scattered over a vast depression in barren landscape that may as well have been the surface of the moon. Overhead the sun beat down in a sky that remained dusty blue as relentless wind gusts swept the plain. The workers dressed in all manner of clothing, the men often in Western shirts and jeans and the women mostly Muslim, their heads wrapped in rags to protect from the sun and their bodies covered to the ankles in various wraps and robes. All went about their tasks in what Audrey described as "complete silence." She would say a week later, "This almost Biblical scene ... showed the importance of water to their people and their yearning to help themselves. Some of the rock dug by women and children was carried away in wheelbarrows, but there were not enough of them. There were no trucks. Children were carrying earth in a rag between them, or children carried rocks on their backs."

All the workers were in motion. People of all ages lugged rocks and earth in a never-ending procession and deposited it over the top of a steep sloping earthen wall—their new dam—that might one day soon save their lives.

She had traveled much of the world in her lifetime. She had seen the war. She had worked in the Belgian Congo making *The Nun's Story* in 1958, and that area had been remote, the people quiet, respectful, and dignified. But she had never witnessed anything like this. It was a stunning scene, breathtaking and inspiring in its way, so much movement and energy almost as far as the eye could see as these people sought to make a difference for themselves, their families, and their village. A local UNICEF representative explained that all who arrived and worked from seven in the morning until four in the afternoon building this ten-meter-high earthen wall received three kilograms of grain to feed their families, about seven pounds of food, in exchange for their labor.

The film crew asked Audrey to walk among the workers and she complied as John Isaac covered a broad area shooting images.

He worked quietly and efficiently, calling no attention to himself and wasting no movement. Take one's eyes off him for just a moment and he'd be gone, only to reappear in ten minutes far over yonder. As he worked, Audrey continued to wander through the scene, a wisp of a Western white lady in a sweater and khakis amid a sea of black faces and bundled figures. When their curiosity got the best of them, the workers would stop her and take her hand or simply stare—they had no idea who or what she was. But they liked the lady. Something about her made many of them smile.

A little farther on she watched young men with pick axes breaking up the rocky earth, which was then loaded into wheelbarrows and taken to the dam wall. Then she noticed it wasn't just young men—women were also hacking at the earth with axes; lines of workers waited their turn to break the hard-as-cement earth into dirt for their dam.

She learned here a message she would pass along in the press conference later: "This whole tragedy is because there's no water. We can't make it rain, but when it does rain—when the good Lord will let it rain—at least we can help provide the country with ways to contain it."

From the dam project the group moved on to an old stone building nearby that served as an orphanage run by the Italian Catholic Church for children whose mothers had died of disease in local camps. Audrey shook the hands of each aid worker in the cavernous and immaculately clean building, which featured long rows of bunk beds lining the walls. She listened to an explanation of how the facility had come to house 500 children whose mothers had died. She learned the church had decided to plant acres of young trees around the building to memorialize the mothers. Audrey thought to herself how beautiful this idea was, as she would say later, the idea of trees "not only for reforestation, which this country desperately needs to attract the rain, but in memory of all the people who died there."

Outside, a dinner bell rang and children aged perhaps five to twelve walked in orderly fashion into the building. All were practiced in the art of shooing flies off themselves so as not to bring them inside.

The children were served soup with injera—sourdough flatbread and a staple in Ethiopia. She watched perhaps 200 children sit and eat in ordered silence. Some were clean, some dirty, but she adored each one, patted heads, took hands in hers, and kissed the backs of the hands of some of the most irresistible of the children.

The exhausted visitors piled back into their turboprops and flew north; they would spend the night at the Nyala Hotel in once-glamorous Asmara. Awaiting their arrival was the city mayor, Afework Berhane, who had never heard of someone called Audrey Hepburn. Journalists explained she worked for UNICEF but had once been a Hollywood movie star. They rattled off the names of her pictures until the mayor waved his hand to cut them off.

"I would like to see tapes of those films," he declared. "Do you think she will have some with her?" When Audrey and her party finally arrived, she received Mayor Berhane with great dignity and apologized that, no, she didn't bring any tapes with her. For his part, the city official barely concealed his disappointment that this was not Marilyn Monroe but a shabbily dressed older lady bathed in perspiration.

Said John Williams, "She never complained [when] the hotel had no water." Asmara, an old Italian protectorate, had forty years earlier been considered by many to be the most beautiful city in Africa. Then came civil war and years of fighting in the surrounding area. Government troops guarded the roads in and out of the city, and landmines kept rebels at bay in the terrain between checkpoints. Civil war had dragged on among the ruling Marxist Derg and rebel forces, also Marxist, for more than a decade. This was the source of the troubles of all those people Audrey had been seeing and kissing and heartening. Each side blamed the other for weaponizing famine as machine guns rattled and rockets whizzed through the air—Audrey knew it all oh, so well from being caught in the middle of the war for Europe.

From the vantage point of Asmara, the *Washington Post* observed, "Over the years, the rebels and the government have pounded away at each other in the north, and the reach of their conquests has expanded and ebbed like a bloody tide."

The hotel did indeed lack running water, and yet had been deemed safe enough, as guarded by soldiers with machine guns in the lobby, to become the haven of UN people from diplomats to pilots. Safety, or lack thereof, came in many forms: Audrey and the others were warned that spies were listening carefully to every conversation in case sentiments against the Derg were expressed in the open.

Audrey wasn't interested in politics as they sat in the hotel lobby—she wanted to hear everything John Isaac had to say. Isaac had left the group to explore the region and document with his camera what he found. At dinner he told Audrey, Robbie, Larry, and John Williams about an encounter moments earlier with a half-blind old woman who lived with a chicken in a slum called Gaza Tanika.

"She was a gentle old soul, and she was worried about me because she had nothing to offer to me," said Isaac in his elegant Indian accent. "She kept apologizing for that and kept saying to my interpreter to tell me not to leave yet. I was worried because my ride was waiting for me since it was past curfew. Suddenly she came rushing out of her shack and said, 'You can leave now!'"

The group hung on Isaac's every word. "Why did she make you wait?" they wanted to know. Such a day it had been, and now their fate hung on the next decision by an old woman with a chicken.

The Good Egg

Inside the Nyala Hotel, John Isaac set an egg on the table. Those at the table stared at the egg. "She gave me *this*," he told them. "She had just one chicken and she was waiting for the chicken to lay an egg that she wanted to share with me." It would have been her dinner, he told the group, but she wanted him to have it instead because he was out there in the war, and she worried.

Audrey swiped at tears. "Oh, John," she said, "may I use that story? This is what giving is all about."

John Isaac would prove to be an early and profound influence on the neophyte road warriors. "I try not to take anybody's dignity away," Isaac said, vowing never to snap a photo that would compromise a vulnerable soul within range of his camera. "I'm a human being first. I don't care about the Pulitzer Prize."

Said Wolders of Isaac and Audrey, "He really inspired her. He spoiled us. We were looking for more people like that, and they don't exist."

Isaac said, "This makes me feel happy and humble to learn they felt that way." But then, Audrey also spoiled him. "Her humility, her transparent behavior impressed me the most, her love for animals; whenever we saw cats or dogs she would straight away go and pet them even if they were on the street. When I was growing up, I always trusted people who loved animals."

After an uncomfortable night in the Nyala Hotel, the UNICEF people took to their small planes the next morning and flew south to the remote town of Mehal Meda in the Shewa province. The pilot nimbly brought the turboprops in, but such an exercise on a short runway had the feel of an amusement park ride that left some of the passengers a bit shaken.

The industrious film crew hopped out first and caught a doting John Isaac asking Audrey repeatedly if she had unbuckled her seatbelt before she attempted to leave the aircraft. Finally, she snapped, "Yes, I'm not taking the plane with me!" Those within earshot giggled, but they were now indoctrinated to Audrey's sense of humor.

"The elf was always in her," Williams observed, as when she plopped down on his hat in the Nyala Hotel lobby and then, "carefully pushed out the crumples and, with a grin, a little bow, and a kiss, returned the hat to my head."

Earlier, when Isaac sat in front of Audrey in the airborne PC-6 he had dropped the battery pack still attached to his camera. As it dangled, Audrey leaned forward and said in his ear in her best Holly Golightly, "Is it all right for me to help you with your … apparatus?" The way she said it drew snickers. Isaac responded that he would appreciate her help with his apparatus, and she retrieved his dangling battery. Hours later, on first sight of him at the Nyala after his adventure with egg woman, she said loudly and with great sincerity, "How is your apparatus, John. In working order?"

"After that, there were no secrets between us," said Isaac.

Now, after the steep and short landing, Audrey stepped out of the plane undaunted as the others paused to collect themselves. In fact, she complimented the pilot for a "super landing!" The group then stepped into jeeps for a ride into Mehal Meda. Upon arrival, more bouquets appeared in small black hands. More hugs and kisses from Audrey in return. Audrey and the group walked through a long gauntlet of locals clapping in unison for their guests. Some of the women issued forth with the Arab custom of trilling in joy as a special honor for Audrey. She was hamstrung by not being able to speak with any of them. She could only smile and shake their hands. Some of the women kissed hers.

At the local farm the visitors watched oxen pull plows through rough earth as had been done here for thousands of years, and Audrey and Larry Bruce asked questions about how the village was managed. They saw precious water supplies doled out for drinking and for washing clothes by hand in community sinks.

Audrey's curious mind needed to connect all the cramming she had done with the practices she now witnessed in villages like these. It was explained to her: Victims of drought are given cash to buy food at the nearest market. In return the village commits to undertaking a project—in this case a water project supervised by an engineer, with all the hands-on work done by villagers. The result was water flowing through a communal system complete with wash sinks.

By the middle of this second day working together, John Isaac got a sense of the dynamo UNICEF had landed: "She didn't demand special attention. She was one of us. Starving people were on the streets and sidewalks with their children. She would walk up to them and carry babies with flies on their faces and runny noses and kiss them and hug them. That to me was noble and I knew right then and there that this was where she came from. She was respectful to everyone. Most of the time she would address people as 'Sir' or 'Madam.'"

John Williams said, "I was very impressed by her empathy to the victims of the disaster and by her political sense in how she handled tricky media questions."

Larry Bruce must have been equally impressed by the depth of Audrey's knowledge of Ethiopia, her intellectual curiosity, and the way she had charged headlong into each situation that day. He was used to working with celebrity ambassadors, but this one was different. Bruce saw in Audrey Hepburn what he himself felt—a genuine love for all these children placed through no decisions they had made into perilous situations. He remembered a moment when she had knelt in front of a little boy sitting under an umbrella for shade eating a nutritional wafer. He took a bite and Audrey said to him encouragingly, "That's right! That's the whole idea!" And really, that captured all of it in a nutshell. He had also witnessed Audrey inside an immunization tent with mothers and babies as she gave her first immunization to an infant girl. Holding an oral syringe Audrey was all thumbs as if fearing she might break the child, but she managed to land four drops of liquid in the little mouth and enthused, "Oh, that's a good baby!" and swabbed a mixture of drool and medicine on her finger and scraped it into the baby's mouth to make sure she had received all she needed. Little things like that told Larry Bruce this isn't your usual celebrity in the field. Soon Audrey grew slick with the syringe and immunized child after child.

Inside the village she observed blanket making done by women sitting in a line on the bare ground who would first spin cotton into strands, then hand over their materials to a man working a wooden loom that must have been ancient. A woman proudly bowed and handed Audrey a newly made blanket. Audrey beamed at the gift and thanked all the workers.

The UNICEF people then made their way back to the planes and flew on to Addis Ababa, the field work at an end, but the day far from over. The moment Audrey dreaded was at hand: an evening press conference at the hotel that would bring all her fears and insecurities bubbling to the surface. She and media expert John Williams went over questions and answers as Larry Bruce and Robbie listened. She wrote out her speech in pen as she smoked up a storm, her hands shaking because what she said this evening might be life and death, and her effectiveness would be captured in funding—or lack of funding.

Audrey cleaned herself up, applied some blush and lipstick,

and stepped out before the firing squad. Her first official words for the press, spoken slowly and carefully, packed a wallop: "I'm very impressed by the people of Ethiopia," she said. "By their beauty, by their dignity, by their patience, and by their enormous desire, their enormous will to help themselves. Not to simply sit there waiting. Their patience is a patience which comes, I think, partly from their religion, partly from their character, of dealing with their luck the best they can, facing facts the best they can."

Larry Bruce's mouth hung open. After hours in the field under that hot sun, after too long without food and water because she didn't want to be the one to take a bite or a drink, after long and loud plane rides, here she was, holding onto the pages of her speech but speaking extemporaneously based on what she had written out. How could she form coherent thoughts after a day like today? But on she went, the most magnificent ad-lib performance he had ever seen.

"Everywhere I've been, every center, or hospital, or dam that's being built, it is they who are doing it," Audrey said of the Ethiopians. "And it's also the marvelous part of UNICEF. There aren't any banners anywhere saying, 'This is a UNICEF project!' UNICEF has a wonderful long arm which is trying to reach wherever it's most needed. The important thing is that given a spade, which UNICEF can give them, they will dig a well. What we have to attain is that they don't use it to dig graves for their children."

Tears welled in her eyes as she said it; tears welled in Larry Bruce's eyes hearing it. Photographers sensed what was happening and clicked away; these were the only sounds in the room.

"She was magnificent," said John Williams, "combining passion and logic in an alliance of eloquence for children. Only she thought she could have done better."

She concluded her speech with, "Mahatma Gandhi once said, 'Wars cannot be won by bullets, but only with bleeding hearts.' And surely caring is better than killing. We care for our own children when they go through a crisis—when they have an accident or are stricken by disease. Not only during that moment, but also through what may be a fairly long convalescence. If we can do that for our own children, I certainly think we can do it for all those silent children that I saw yesterday and today. And I firmly believe that those children are our sacred charge."

She then took questions and answered them like what she was—a woman who had been handling the press for thirty-five years. Audrey had to wonder; maybe she *was* a warrior after all.

After Addis Ababa, she and Robbie flew to New York City with Larry Bruce and John Williams. Early on the morning of March 23 she taped *Good Morning America* and then proceeded to UNICEF House at the New York headquarters to describe the Ethiopian situation again for two dozen reporters. Afterward she sat for three individual interviews.

"The country suffers from two grave injustices," she said at UNICEF House. "One is man-made—they get too little aid. And the other from God—they get too little water. But I plan to talk to Him."

The next day she appeared on the *Today Show* for NBC, *CBS This Morning*, CNN Live *Showbiz Today*, *CNN International Hour*, and *Entertainment Tonight*. She also participated in tapings of four television appeals for the U.S. UNICEF Committee and attended an advocacy luncheon and reception for major supporters.

The next morning, Friday, March 25, she was in Washington, D.C., and walked into a U.S. Congress working breakfast like a gunslinger in spurs. U.S. Representative Dante Fascell of Florida hosted, with attendance by twenty-five senior staff from the Foreign Affairs Committee and five members of Congress. The woman of the world who had held heads of studios in her spell now appealed for additional funding for Ethiopia. Her wish would be granted; aid wasn't cut as the administration of U.S. President Ronald Reagan had advised; it was plussed-up. Who, after all, could say no to Audrey Hepburn?

"They were chaaarming," she would say later of her Congressional hosts and their breakfast. "And it wasn't easy to field some very difficult, unexpected questions about Ethiopia dealing with the political situation over coffee and grapefruit. But I was very gratified to hear that after this meeting, the United States had augmented funds for Ethiopia."

She met with U.S. Senator Daniel Inouye of Hawaii and traveled to the Kennedy Center for a lunch with the Washington Advisory Council hosted by D.C. businessman and philanthropist Abe Pollin. Among the guests were Katherine Graham, publisher of the *Washington Post*, Mrs. Anwar Sadat, Mrs. Averell Harriman, and Hodding Carter, late of the Jimmy Carter administration.

Larry Bruce watched in astonishment as the UNICEF press release inviting media to request interviews with Audrey Hepburn returned unprecedented interest. That afternoon she sat for interviews with the *Diane Rehm Show* on National Public Radio, the *Washington Post*, *Washington Times*, *WRC TV News*, *WLJA TV News at 5*, and *USA Today*. With each she appeared fresh and interested no matter how many times she answered the same questions.

Saturday, March 26, it was on to Toronto and a lunch with senior management of the Canadian UNICEF Committee followed by another press conference to share Audrey's now well-crafted message. When she, a war veteran herself, said Ethiopians deserved support because of their dignity, willingness to work, and faith, the world decided it should listen.

The *Toronto Star* and the *Toronto Globe and Mail* interviewed her, and she completed TV news features for the CBC, CTV, and Global and City TV, as well as radio features for the CBC and Standard Broadcast.

She and Robbie flew to London for several more media appearances. At the press conference there, Stuart Wavell, a reporter for *The Guardian*, entered the appointed room with *Roman Holiday* in mind; he had watched the old classic recently on television. As a journalist who had seen it all in real life, he found the climax of the picture to be embarrassing in its lack of realism. He said, "Rome's hardened hacks" fawned over teenage Princess Ann as she held a press conference after her twenty-four-hour "illness." But on a Monday in March 1988, London's hardened hacks got some schooling in royalty and, admitted Wavell, "We were struck dumb." He described Hepburn as "a slight figure, demurely clad, chestnut hair swept back, those huge eyes suddenly misting or flashing with impishness." It wasn't the first time that her sincerity would melt a cold journalist's heart. He said, "Others have given the same accounts of horror and hope. To hear them from Miss Hepburn, who at fifty-nine still evokes the quick hurts of a deer, was moving. But even more eloquent was the fact that she was speaking as a wartime victim of famine." That message resonated with a London audience—a parachute drop by their own British Airborne on Audrey's city of Arnhem in 1944 had set a catastrophic series of events in motion, with the Hunger Winter and nearly 20,000 dead Dutch as a result.

Once again, the fact that she had survived that period of the war in the Netherlands gave her credibility on the subject of hunger and famine. The press needed an angle into an otherwise unpleasant story for readerships—Third World people, black people, who were otherwise put so easily out of both sight and mind. And really what could Givenchy's clotheshorse Audrey Hepburn, who lived in Switzerland and had famously ordered a bidet shipped to the Congo when she made *The Nun's Story*, possibly be able to say about starving wretches in Africa? Well, she had a lot to say, and the press couldn't help but eat it up.

Criticism bubbled below the surface about Audrey's "naïve" fund-raising work that could only benefit the Marxist regime in Ethiopia. Who knew how money funneled through UNICEF into the country would be used? As she recounted it, she was asked,

"Why are we sending money to Ethiopia? It's a Marxist government run by a terrible man." She answered with the subtlety of a cobra poked by a stick.

"It was just like a child that had just had a road accident being asked about its father's political stand. We shouldn't be thinking along those lines! Our job is to help the children survive, no matter what the religious or political background of their situation may be." She blazed on, "And in any case, we aren't helping the regime, the government; we're bringing relief to the children directly. Not even money gets there. It's medication, technical assistance, well-piercing equipment, anything you can imagine for those circumstances. And for me, it is totally unacceptable not to help them; it's illogical, inhuman, and I think in theory is totally without love. That person who would have made such a judgment, would he or she have said the same after Armenia—not to help the victims—or after the Second World War, when the whole of Europe was ruined and there were twenty million people who had no homes?"

After two weeks on the road she had developed a certain subtle ferocity at the ongoing intercontinental barrage of questions about her motives for the UNICEF work and her future plans in the motion picture industry. She had begun to channel just enough Bob Geldof to do her some good.

In London she looked a reporter dead in the eye and said, "If people are still interested in my film career; if my name makes them listen to what I want to say, then that's wonderful. But I am not interested in promoting Audrey Hepburn these days. I am interested in telling the world about how they can help in Ethiopia, and why I came away feeling optimistic."

In the afternoon she was still talking in her suite at a five-star hotel in Mayfair, where Lynn Barber of the *Sydney Morning Herald* managed to land an interview. The latest in a long line of cynical reporters sat down with the "former film star, dressed in Givenchy and staying at Claridge's, talking about starving children." Barber was first impressed by the size of the tumbler of scotch that Hepburn waded into at mid-afternoon.

"I am *not* a lush," Audrey smirked, wagging a finger at Barber, "but I've been up since four and I need a pick-me-up." Then Barber noted the chain-smoking, another unlikely point of realism in the star's favor.

Robbie was conspicuous by his presence and when Audrey caught Barber giving Wolders the snarly eye and willing him out of the room, Audrey made it clear this wasn't going to happen by saying, "We've done all this together," which prompted a reporter's question about living in sin and when would they make it legal?

"We're living in love," said Audrey with a swallow of scotch.

"I'm a romantic woman," she had told another reporter on the tour. "What is there without it?"

The sit-down with Barber was her last of however many interviews in a week, dozens, maybe a hundred, and she sat there without really being there. Barber asked about compensation from UNICEF, and Audrey said unless the customary dollar a year counts, she isn't compensated. She confessed, in fact, that her contract with UNICEF had been drawn up but nobody had actually signed it yet, which meant she had been somewhat at risk through the entire Ethiopian enterprise. Barber had attended the press conference, so she already had recorded the Hepburn spiel about UNRRA in 1945 and conditions on the ground in Ethiopia in 1988.

Audrey mustered her strength to answer the reporter's question about lasting memories of Ethiopia. She spoke of a food distribution camp. "That terrible silence, the beauty of the people, their stillness in this vast, empty, moon-like landscape—that image stays with me."

Lynn Barber walked out of the suite another convert. She saw that Audrey was "clearly ragged with exhaustion," but "her commitment is passionate and sincere."

After fourteen punishing days on the road, Audrey and Robbie finally were allowed to drag themselves back to La Paisible. The din of all those days in-country and then all the cities, reporters, and events rang in their ears amid the utter quiet of home. Here the lake rippled peacefully, the snow-tinged mountains rose up in the distance as they always had. There were berries and grapes and flowers in the garden. And only now did it hit them both: We flew into an armed city and ventured into rebel country and might have died. We met government officials there and in Washington. We made it through hundreds of reporters and a half-dozen press conferences. What we experienced had been a thrill and an honor and so very important.

When Doris Brynner saw the condition of her best friend after just two weeks of field work and press conferences, she became alarmed. Audrey was obviously giving no thought to her well-being, kicking Doris into gear to worry for the both of them. "She came back absolutely exhausted, telling me all about it," said Doris, "and I didn't want to hear all these horrid stories. She was full of emotions and very happy she had done it, but it was absolutely exhausting and so depressing. She was really completely done in."

A sixth sense in Doris flashed danger in response to this new phase of life Audrey had begun; in only two weeks so much energy had drained out of her friend of nearly thirty years! What would become of her if she repeated the experience?

Now not one but two people who loved Audrey—Doris and Giovanna—expressed concern that UNICEF and Audrey Hepburn were a bad match. "Anytime Audrey returned from a mission, Giovanna was worried," said Anna Cataldi.

"La signora need to rest!"

So okay, Audrey rested, but only for a few days, and then she appeared at the Palais des Nations in Geneva for another post-Ethiopia press conference on Wednesday, April 6, 1988. Downtime at home had only sharpened her senses to relive moments, hours, and days with the desperate people she had encountered, all those lovely souls who had welcomed her into their land. They were so humble they never even asked for food; they just sat quietly and smiled when they were able, and offered their own meager crumbs, or flowers, or a blanket, or an egg. In Geneva forty journalists from several countries heard her appeal. She also gave individual interviews to Swiss TV and Antenne 2 of France.

Larry Bruce and John Williams were amazed at the stamina and popularity of their high-profile Special Ambassador and the results she had achieved in just one trip into the field. Back on their first day together in northern Ethiopia, they had noticed the same thing as had John Isaac. This wasn't just another celebrity ambassador lending a big name to a funding appeal: "I didn't see the same kind of reactions from the other ambassadors," said Isaac. "Many were concerned about their own safety and health and I never saw anyone hugging or kissing a child with flies on its face. Audrey kissed them without even wiping away the flies. I have dealt with many celebrities during my career as a photojournalist, but Audrey was unique. She was bigger than life in every way."

Hepburn had managed to rivet the world's attention on Ethiopia for the first time since Live Aid, landing photos and captions and often feature articles in just about every newspaper in the Western world. The number of calls into UNICEF offices from would-be volunteers skyrocketed as did the donations.

Audrey had done everything UNICEF asked of her, no matter how many press conferences, interviews, and events, and no matter where they were. Larry Bruce and John Williams had Jim Grant's ear after Ethiopia to report that their preconceptions were all wrong about "frail-looking, elegant lady" Audrey Hepburn—as Williams had initially described her—and what they had imagined might be a need to revive the concept of galas to capitalize on that elegance. They now had the experience of working with her in the field. They had flown in a C-130 with her and landed in the middle of a civil war. They had shared a hotel with her—a hotel with no running water and guards with machine guns in the lobby. They had ridden in a single-engine turboprop and felt their stomachs drop out when the plane came in on a short runway—her reaction had been to compliment the pilot on a great landing. They had watched her power through such fear they wondered if she might throw up before the Addis Ababa press conference. But she had completed it flawlessly. No, Audrey Hepburn was anything but frail; Audrey Hepburn was a badass soldier waging her own kind of war, her own crusade for the children. Hell, she probably would have parachuted into Ethiopia if they had asked her to.

After the debriefs and results of Audrey's press tour, Jim Grant decided two things must happen immediately: First, Audrey Hepburn must be elevated from Special Ambassador to Goodwill Ambassador. And second, UNICEF needed to get this badass soldier back into the field, and fast.

Two Worlds

February 1980. Eight years before the Ethiopia trip, Audrey had secluded herself at 615 North Beverly Drive in Beverly Hills during what she called "the worst period of my life." Divorce proceedings with Dotti were dragging on and when final, she would find herself a signed and sealed two-time loser. So much for chasing love. Her most recent attempt at following her heart had been a crush on actor Ben Gazzara, with whom she worked on the features *Bloodline* and *They All Laughed*. But the infatuation went nowhere and she ended *They All Laughed* feeling lonelier than ever.

Constance Polan Wald, widow of successful movie producer Jerry Wald, owned 615 North Beverly. Still striking at age sixty-five, with a mane of silver hair long before the look became Hollywood-chic, Connie Wald possessed a big heart and an outgoing, chatterbox personality delivered with a West Virginia twang—almost the drawl of a Southern belle, but not quite.

Luca said, "She called me, 'Keydeechee, Keydeechee' from Italian 'Che dice, Che dice?' or 'What is she saying?' At age five I couldn't speak a word of English and was constantly asking Mum for a translation of Connie's speed-talk."

The style of her home, which had been designed by architect Gerard R. Colcord in 1939, was Pennsylvania Dutch Colonial Revival, which meant sprawling rooms, rough-hewn floors, wide doors, shuttered windows, and lots of woodwork, including beamed ceilings. Because of Jerry Wald's generally unerring sense of what made a good picture and reputation as a genuinely good guy, and their location central to everything in the movie capital, 615 North Beverly became the beating heart of Hollywood. Here Connie Wald hosted low-key get-togethers with the Henry Fondas, the Jimmy Stewarts, Billy and Audrey Wilder (who lived up the street), and on and on. Everyone who was anyone wanted to be invited to the Wald's for dinner. In turn, said Connie, "my highest compliment" was when someone who had been invited said yes.

The connection to Billy Wilder, Audrey's director for *Sabrina*, had brought Mel and Audrey Ferrer into the mix in the 1950s while Jerry was still alive and could introduce Audrey to people who would remain friends for her lifetime—especially Connie Wald, who became like a sister to Audrey and second only to Doris in Audrey's heart.

The house sat just far enough back from the street, and Jerry Wald's name didn't rate inclusion on maps of movie star homes; therefore, "the Starline tour vehicles filled with happy, credulous tourists cruise right by," said the *New York Times* of 615. Audrey might have been at La Paisible; she was that well insulated from the paparazzi and public at Connie's home in "the Flats" of Beverly Hills that became her hideaway.

Luca said, "At Connie's house Mum reconnected with friends and spent hours in the kitchen, making small talk and exchanging recipes."

"We would regularly gather there for wonderful family dinners, after which they would usually wrestle over who would do the dishes," said Sean. "Mother would plead that a good houseguest should at least have the right to do the dishes. They cooked together, laughed a lot, and loved each other to death."

Aside from the kitchen, Audrey gravitated to Jerry Wald's library. "She'd sit by the fireplace day and night," said Connie. "She liked the warmth of the library."

Connie claimed that during Audrey's February 1980 visit, there was no plot to connect her with Robert Wolders; the two of them just happened to end up at a Wald dinner party, a let's-cheer-Audrey-up party that included Sean and Marina, Billy and Audrey Wilder, and Kurt Frings. In fact, Connie had almost forced Rob Wolders to attend; he used to visit 615 often with his wife, Merle Oberon, but Merle had died the previous November and Rob was quite alone and hurting. Connie believed this group in particular, low-key and welcoming as it was, would be a safe one for Rob. After all, Audrey and Merle had enjoyed a kinship as international personalities with their share of secrets.

Wolders said, "When Audrey and I met, the first thing she did was to talk to me about my wife. Neither one of us was exactly looking for a love relationship."

"It was very curious," said Audrey. "I never met him with Merle. I knew Merle, adored her. I met her several times during my life. But when I was living in Rome, I didn't go to Hollywood much, and Robbie and I never met."

Audrey and Rob shared more than Merle in common; both spent the war in the Netherlands and both were actors. Wolders had been three years old when the Germans stormed through the Netherlands, and his earliest memories of childhood featured Nazis. Like Audrey, his pretty face had gotten him into the movies; his debut had been playing a corpse in Federico Fellini's 1965 feature *Juliet of the Spirits*. A year later he moved up to sixth billing in the Universal Pictures remake of the French Foreign Legion picture *Beau Geste* starring Guy Stockwell and Telly Savalas, and then Universal kept him around to star in season two of the western series *Laredo* with Neville Brand and Peter Brown.

But the quiet Dutchman never possessed the killer instinct to keep a career thriving. Maybe he was just too … Dutch. When Godefridus Wolders died at age fifty-one leaving wife Cemelia, a son, and four daughters behind, Rob, the middle child, became the man of the family, displaying maturity and responsibility beyond his years. He was a pleaser who loved his mother and sisters; he became their knight in shining armor.

"I was charmed with him that night," said Audrey of the meeting at Connie's party, "but he didn't register that much. We were both very unhappy."

Still, Audrey went away from that evening both intrigued and attracted. "We drifted together because of, I don't know," said Robbie. "There was an affinity for one another."

On Monday April 11, 1988, Audrey said of her man, "He is solid in every way. I can trust him. I trust his love; I never fear I'm losing it. He reassures me. He's very loving, an affectionate man, and we like the same life—being in the country, the dogs, making trips together—and we're both avid readers, and go shopping together. Everything we do together is fun."

Ethiopia had not been fun. Their first UNICEF adventure had revealed sights neither expected to see, like a thousand Ethiopians building a dam by hand. But, oh, the suffering of these people. Audrey and Robbie had claimed a few days at La Paisible to rest and check on the staff and the dogs, then flew west for an evening in what a reporter called her "other world," the one in Hollywood— although she blanched at the idea.

"I don't think in terms of that world and this world," she said. "It's all my life. It's all me. I don't think of this and that world as different jobs. There's a time for everything, but it's all you. I find no delineation. Nor am I cut off when I go back to California."

And it was indeed Hollywood calling—she was asked to present an Oscar at the sixtieth Academy Award ceremony at the Shrine Auditorium in Los Angeles. She agreed to participate only because her co-presenter of the award for Best Original Screenplay would be Gregory Peck, one of her favorite humans on the planet going all the way back to their Roman holiday together. She felt she owed her whole life to Greg and to their director, William Wyler. Imagine if she had had mere mortals as director and co-star for her first picture; there may never have been a second.

Once again Connie Wald and 615 stood ready in Beverly Hills, a port in new storms for Audrey and Robbie, as she wound herself up for yet another UNICEF press conference, this one in Los Angeles on Wednesday, April 13, for local reporters and also TV crews from West Germany and Luxembourg. By now she had established a routine and her speech had become theater. The tears were real—it had been difficult not to cry since Ethiopia. But she had refined and sharpened the message to a fine point. By now the questions had become predictable, including the inevitable, "When do you plan to make another movie?" and "When are you and Mr. Wolders planning to marry?"

L.A. reporters heard Audrey tell her matter-of-fact story of flying into the battleground of Asmara. Those reporters then cornered Robbie and asked if he thought she was brave to take on her new role. "She doesn't consider herself a brave person," he said with a wave and a smile, "so you're not going to get me to say it." He did allow, however, "We were amazed when we got back that we had not dwelled on the element of danger."

UNICEF was already proving to be a hungry beast with requests for her help from a number of countries, including Turkey, and, said Robbie, "In our enthusiasm, we accepted them all." UNICEF Turkey inquired about Audrey joining Prime Minister Turgut Özal to host the 10th International World Children's Day, a gathering of 786 child delegates from 33 countries. The offer held special interest because UNICEF was working with Turkey on an immunization drive against the six main child-killing diseases: measles, tuberculosis, tetanus, whooping cough, diphtheria, and polio. Audrey well recalled her talks with Larry Bruce about the importance of GOBI—growth monitoring, oral rehydration, breastfeeding, and immunization.

The idea of a trip like this one appealed to her—the gathering of children was the kind of event her friend Danny Kaye would have loved to attend, and the immunization drive offered a chance at life to potentially tens or hundreds of thousands of children. Yes, Doris and Giovanna would wag fingers and tell her it was too much too soon, but Audrey rationalized that Turkey was weeks away and until then she could rest. How could she possibly say no?

Audrey had the Ethiopia mission under her belt and understood what would be expected of her in the field. She knew she must prepare much better for Turkey and asked for Christa Roth's help to get ready.

"We always worked at her house," said Roth. "I went with all the papers and everything to their house because we didn't have an office for her in Geneva, and I didn't want her to have to come back and forth. I would usually just take everything and go and spend time with her and Robert together with the program and all the papers on top of the dining table. We would go through all that, and I would stay for dinner and go home."

Then Audrey would take over, repeating her habits dating back to *Roman Holiday* when she would rise early and study the day's schedule and shooting script, usually three or five or ten pages, getting to know it until the words became part of her skin. She would make notes in the margins, little reminders to herself, questions to the director, or impressions how she should play a scene.

Audrey remained Audrey, whether in 1952 or 1988. She slipped on her large-lens reading glasses before dawn, lit her first cigarette of the day, and sat at the table learning about Turkey. All the facts, all the figures, all the needs of the people and challenges of the government. She learned the history, the political landscape—of course there was a civil war. Wasn't there always a civil war? This time it was the Kurdistan Workers' Party, or PKK, versus the democratic government, and once again children, mainly Kurdish children, were caught in the middle. It proved to be another crash course, this time with a more positive message—a UNICEF campaign to vaccinate Turkish children had been ongoing for years and was mostly successful. Promoting it could raise awareness among other countries.

On Thursday, April 21, Christa drove Audrey and Robbie to the Geneva airport for a flight to Ankara. On arrival reporters mobbed the pair as they stepped off the plane. A young boy and girl placed bouquets in Audrey's hand as the UNICEF children's song blared so loudly from speakers, she couldn't hear anything said by dignitaries greeting her. Inside the airport she was asked to sit for photographers and provide a quick, impromptu message to the children of Turkey. All she could manage was, "Well, for the moment, I've just arrived and it's difficult to provide the few perfect words right now. The best thing to say is that I love them all. That's my message to them."

The next morning she and Robbie began touring health care facilities for mothers and children. At one, she displayed skills learned in Ethiopia and administered oral polio vaccine to several infants as photographers snapped away. A UPI photo capturing this event would make many American newspapers. She also met with the Children's Day delegates—children and parents from thirty-three countries.

On their third day in Turkey, she and Robbie attended the International World Children's Day ceremony, and she faced the stomach-churning exercise of a speech in an amphitheater before more than 2,000 assembled, many in the traditional garb of their countries. She considered the message she would deliver before such an impressionable group to be critical. She hailed the delegates, "all here to manifest their love for all those children around the world who are the innocent victims of hunger, thirst, sickness, and war. Recently visiting Ethiopia, I saw these children. I saw their faces, faces of pain, suffering, and despair." She contrasted those children with the happy and high-energy group before her now and hoped one day all the world's children could be raised up with the help of UNICEF. She praised Turkish radio and television and the Turkish government for the success of the immunization campaign and announced that the government had declared that this day be proclaimed National Independence and Children's Day.

Through eight grueling minutes, she read her speech, hands shaking. She delivered it in English, a language many in attendance didn't speak, which made her pauses awkward as she awaited translations and then applause that was sluggish at best. But she plowed ahead in the too-hot venue and then posed for photos with the delegates.

In the evening at the hotel Audrey and Robbie learned that *My Fair Lady* was showing on broadcast television in her honor. The lingering memory of this production for Audrey was a stinging one—the dubbing of her voice by Marni Nixon—but Robbie had never seen *My Fair Lady*, so Audrey said yes when he switched it on. But the broadcast was dubbed in Turkish—except for Marni's singing. "I had to turn it off," said Robbie.

Audrey concluded the Turkey trip with the obligatory press conference, this one as well attended as all the others. Her message was a far happier one than anything delivered regarding Ethiopia. "I would first like to express my gratitude and immense admiration to you the media," she stated. "Turkish radio and television cooperation, and your newspapers, have made an unprecedented success of information in rallying your vast country, even in its most far-flung areas, around your monumental immunization campaign for children. It's clear from your achievements up to this day that you will succeed. Please know that you will continue to have the full support of UNICEF in any way that we can help to nurture, love, and protect your children."

On Sunday, April 24, they flew back to Geneva. Another mission accomplished.

By now Audrey recognized some trends emerging with the press. First, reporters had begun to burn out on the topic of starving children in Africa. Yeah, yeah, we already covered Audrey Hepburn talking about famine. It's old news. And the cynics among the reporters, the ones who hadn't been there to see her in person, didn't believe the tears.

Besides, other news cycles had begun. The Middle East was heating up, with bombings in Lebanon and saber rattling by the Reagan White House against the Iranians. Reagan was finishing out his second term as a suddenly doddering president, and the campaign to replace him was on, with Massachusetts Governor Michael Dukakis, Senator Al Gore, and civil rights leader Jesse Jackson on one side and incumbent Vice President George H.W. Bush and U.S. Senator Bob Dole on the other.

Beyond the fickle nature of news cycles, another trend emerged that infuriated Audrey. If she devoted her time for an interview to speak about the plight of children in Ethiopia, the resulting article might take a very different turn.

"Many times, people would ask for an interview about UNICEF when they really just wanted to talk about movies," said Christa Roth. "She would talk an hour about, say, Ethiopia and five minutes about films, but the story would be ten percent UNICEF and ninety percent movies. It bothered her a lot. So we started to restrict the interviews to publications that gave her solid footage. It worked out quite well. She got a lot of coverage."

Audrey's relationship with the press had always been courteous on the surface and icy underneath because Audrey had secrets she remained determined to protect for the length of her life. Of course she kept hidden her mother's pro-Nazi stance in the 1930s. But Audrey had performed in ballet recitals as a young teen at Arnhem's Wehrmachtheim—rest-and-recreation headquarters for the German army—in 1941. Then through the beginning of 1944 she had danced in public and yes, some in the audience had been German soldiers. She had always been anti-German, but if one wanted to perform as a ballerina, there was only one place to do it—with the Arnhem Dance School, which performed at the Arnhem city theater. The idea became moot when she turned fifteen and was required to join the Nazi union of artists, the Kultuurkamer; she refused and that ended her public career. But she never could admit that she had danced for Germans; keeping reporters away from this information meant in many cases a certain polite ruthlessness.

As far back as 1954 a reporter asked her about "pryers and probers" and how she dealt with them. Audrey said then, "It's hard work, really, harder than preparing for a play. You keep giving performances all the time." A year later another journalist described Audrey's "aloofness toward people she didn't know," and a third would say at the end of the 1950s that "when the questions get personal, she changes the subject." Her private life was her own. Period.

Now it was 1988 and, if anything, her recent deep dive into press relations for UNICEF only strengthened her beliefs. She would talk about what she wanted to talk about, and the first two rounds of press, about Ethiopia and Turkey, had been an education. From here on, she and Christa refined the message and kept reporters toeing a mark. Getting Audrey's time on behalf of UNICEF was possible, yes. But anyone not playing by the rules never got a second chance—Audrey would make sure of that.

Camels with Solar Panels

The forty-first International Film Festival at Cannes opened on May 11, 1988. The beautiful gathered on the Riviera whether their films showed or not, just to be there, to be seen and to view other beautiful people. Clint Eastwood was there as director of *Bird* and Robert Redford as director of *The Milagro Beanfield War*. Over here, Willem Dafoe; over there, Forest Whitaker, Sonia Braga, Gérard Depardieu, Jean-Paul Belmondo, Nastassja Kinski, Richard Gere, Sophie Marceau.

The same day that Cannes opened, May 11, Audrey and Robbie prepared for their third UNICEF trip in three months, part of that "we accepted them all" run of invitations, this time to Helsinki, Finland. The first trip as Special Ambassador had been gut-wrenching, and she still saw the faces of Ethiopian mothers and children in her dreams. The second had been a lark by comparison, visiting Turkey to promote an already successful immunization campaign and visit with hundreds of well-fed children from many nations.

Helsinki would be something else again; as the film festival at Cannes held the attention of the international film community, its former queen Audrey Hepburn would slip into Finland to auction off a piece of her artwork on live television.

Not many people knew Audrey Hepburn as an artist who

could draw and paint. Born in Belgium, she had fallen under the influence of the French comic strip character Bécassine from the weekly girl's magazine *La Semaine de Suzette*. Bécassine became so popular that entire volumes were devoted to her adventures as the young housekeeper of a bourgeois family in Brittany. Much more than just a menial, Bécassine had been hailed as the first heroine for young girls in the time of Audrey's childhood. The artwork was simple and modern, with rounded lines that would influence 1930s Walt Disney and Richard Fleischer among American animators and young artist Audrey Hepburn among those in Belgium and, ultimately, the Netherlands.

Since childhood Audrey's brain had worked in such a way that she could make a quick sketch or watercolor that conveyed deeper meaning—Audrey's art became a pathway into her mind, her portfolio revealing a delicate world of simple, pretty things. Vaguely Dutch, a touch Far East, Audrey's art resembled Audrey—international, unique, and difficult to describe.

When the Finnish UNICEF committee asked her to donate an item for a televised charity auction to benefit immunization in Africa, she created a small piece of original art based on her favorite photo taken by John Isaac in Ethiopia. Isaac's photo showed Audrey smiling, with a beautiful, small black boy, also smiling, wrapped in a blanket on her back. It became an instant, definitive UNICEF moment captured for posterity.

Audrey's simple illustration based on the Isaac photo showed a woman with a child on her back. But in place of Audrey's smiling face was a blank Ethiopian mother's face, with a tear descending her cheek. Instead of the little boy's impish smile, the child in the artwork was stoic. The mother's neck was swanlike, as was Audrey's, and the mother appeared to be wearing false eyelashes. The look was as much Egyptian as Ethiopian, but very much in keeping with Audrey's mind's eye.

In evoking sadness through art, Audrey achieved something

she couldn't allow herself in the field. Her natural inclination among suffering children was to bring them joy, to smile, to lift them up even if only for a moment, which worked against her mission to serve as an eyewitness to human suffering. Photo after photo taken in Ethiopia shows a beaming Audrey with beaming children that reflected her million-dollar impact, her natural pizzazz even among humans in dire circumstances, wracked with pain from hunger and malnutrition as most were. But after her return from Ethiopia, through a simple painting, she could show the moment before and after the smiles, the anguish of the mother, the bravery of the child.

Christa Roth didn't know of Audrey's artistic talent until she saw the illustration: "No, no, I was very surprised when I saw it, and I learned that as a girl she had done a lot of artwork for special occasions and used to design her own Christmas cards that she would send off."

Audrey's illustration of the Ethiopian mother and child raised the equivalent of $16,500 US when she appeared at the auction in Helsinki.

"It was a fund-raiser for camels," said Robbie. "For the vaccination campaign in Chad, they used camels with solar-energy panels in order to keep the vaccine refrigerated. They could buy a lot of camels with that $16,500," he estimated—four camels equipped with solar panels, to be exact.

The success of the auction inspired Roth to go one step further using Audrey's design. "I immediately suggested that we do a greeting card with that drawing. Our director was very much in favor of that. We asked the owner for permission; that was very important. Then we approached our greeting card department, and they made a special edition on special paper and it was a big hit."

When asked in the second half of 1988 if she knew how massive the job of UNICEF Special Ambassador would be, Audrey thought about the question and said, "Probably not. It's also snow-balled, you know." And thanks to the knee-jerk reaction to accept every invitation thrown her way before and after Ethiopia, due in part to Jack Glattbach's secret entreaties to representatives in UNICEF countries, demand for Audrey Hepburn really had snowballed. In June she appeared in Switzerland, West Germany, and the UK. Then finally she yielded to Doris and Giovanna and took July and August off to enjoy the fruits of the estate.

"She loved the quiet life," said Rucchita Orunesu. "She ate healthily and much of what we cooked came from the garden that my husband, Giovanni, tended. We ate in a very seasonal manner; whatever we grew in the garden and what [Audrey] would buy from the farmers market in Morges: cheese, bread, and special items sold by local farmers."

Not until Friday, September 23, did she climb back in the saddle for UNICEF when she served as host—along with Harry Belafonte—of the first International Danny Kaye Awards, held at the MECC building in Maastricht, the Netherlands, with Dutch Princess Margriet in attendance. In a sense Audrey was home, back in the place where she had hunkered down with her family and endured the war, although in a city much farther south than her village of Velp. Audrey could mention a royal connection to the princess in that her aunt Marianne, Baroness van Heemstra—Ella's sister—had been a lady in waiting to Margriet's mother, Princess Juliana, during the war.

The first Danny Kaye Awards, a benefit for UNICEF and celebration of the life of the trailblazing Goodwill Ambassador, would be a grand event created by Dutch media personality Ivo Niehe and broadcast with Hollywood production values on Dutch television. A rested Audrey, luminous in a black strapless Givenchy evening gown paired with a cropped fuchsia jacket, radiated confidence and showed none of her usual stage fright to an audience of 3,000 in evening attire. She would present the first-ever Danny

Kaye Award, a small bust of the entertainer, to exuberant twelve-year-old Tara McDonald of the UK, who won over the world by belting out "Make Your Own Rainbow" as she clutched her award.

Audrey said at the conclusion of the evening, "Tonight's real winners will be the millions of children who depend on our compassion and support and who are the concern of this unique organization, UNICEF."

A week later Audrey and Robbie hit Dublin for a quick stop to launch a UNICEF fund-raising appeal, her first trip there since dark times when she had visited her recalcitrant old father, Joseph Ruston, in Dublin. She had found him living in a rented apartment that "was all a little bit beneath him," a neighbor opined.

This was the price Ruston the Nazi-in-exile paid after walking out on his family and playing German agent. He had spent the war imprisoned but he had never reformed; he would die a Nazi at heart, and this fact would cloud the fragile association that developed between father and daughter. It had begun at the insistence of Mel Ferrer in 1959. It was Mel who tracked down Ruston and took Audrey to Dublin to reconcile with him. From there a letter-writing exercise progressed between them. But the association was strained at best and tortured at worst; Ruston had never wanted the responsibility of a daughter and she had felt the lifelong sting of his abandonment. Sean said he recalled seeing Ruston in Switzerland; Luca remembered the letters. Then in September 1980 Audrey had visited her father in Dublin again as he lay dying, this time accompanied by Robbie. She could savor the fact that a physician from India tended this man so intolerant of so-called impure races. "She found it wonderfully ironic," said Robbie.

Audrey attempted to make amends with her father despite his betrayals to family and country. "What's important is that she had no bitterness toward him," said Robbie a bit optimistically. He paused to add, "She didn't hate him for his fascism, but she became what she was in reaction to it." That much was true—because of what both her parents had been before the war, supporters of Hitler, Audrey had become a soldier for love and peace. And for all her goodness, she could never forgive either for what they had once believed and espoused. She didn't forgive; nor did she hate.

"I have hatred for no one, I must say," she told the *New York Times*. "You can't if you have any common sense at all—common sense doesn't allow it. You can hate any individual for what he or she does, but then we have to hate ourselves as well."

So here Audrey and Robbie were, back in the city where she had, to a degree at least, gotten to know her father. This time, in September 1988, the fates smiled and Audrey was surprised by an unexpected visit by Greta Hanley, her nanny in Belgium until about age six. Sean said that Greta "had heard that my mother was coming to Dublin and showed up at the hotel. Upon hearing Greta was there, my mother rushed through the crowd and into her arms. They were both elated."

Dublin served as the last warm-up act before Audrey's next mission as her relationship with UNICEF deepened. She told an interviewer, "What I really am is a messenger for UNICEF," and the message was that the Children's Fund did a lot more than just provide food to areas experiencing famine. Immunization had been the focus in Turkey, and now UNICEF's involvement in education initiatives would be front and center on her next mission, this time to Venezuela and Ecuador in South America.

"There's so much involved apart from seeing [a country], and meeting the media, and talking to people," said Audrey. "In general, it's advocacy for the needs of a child. And there are so many children that there's lots to do."

By now she and Christa were refining the foundational work involved with each country visit. Preparation for a mission would begin at UNICEF world headquarters in New York City. "New York usually prepared a packet of information and also very often the names of people she would meet," said Roth. In the packet would be "statistics from the office in the country—UNICEF had offices in all these countries who worked together with the NGOs [non-governmental aid organizations] on specific programs and UNICEF financed some of the programs, which were then executed through the NGOs and the field office. So New York would have reports from the field office in which there would be all the details of the project and the programs that UNICEF had in those countries. This is what they would send us and what I gave her to look at."

Then came visits by Roth to La Paisible where Audrey and Robbie scrutinized the preliminary agenda and decided what they could and couldn't manage. Audrey wanted to do everything asked of her; Robbie pushed back and required rest periods each day.

Phone calls with UNICEF officials followed, with detailed questions asked and answered. Then came early morning cramming at the dining table—on more than one occasion, Giovannawould "find la signora asleep at the table surrounded by all these papers—maps, conditions, numbers, and histories of the countries she's going to visit," reported Anna Cataldi.

On the first two missions Audrey had applied a Hollywood script-reading formula to UNICEF study. Now she added the next piece of the Academy Award puzzle: instinct. She had come to trust her instincts during her film career to take her unexpected places with each character as the cameras rolled. An Oscar and several Best Actress nominations resulted. Every action now for UNICEF followed this same formula: prepare, question, react on instinct, and perform. She had once famously said, "There's a science of war—why couldn't there be a science for peace?" At La Paisible, she created one.

Eye-Opener

The information packets that arrived from New York always revealed depressing truths about the developing world. People in these countries must be given a chance; how easy it was for Europeans and their American offshoots to look down on poor brown or black people and never understand that the system had been rigged against them long ago. Centuries ago.

September's UNICEF packet concerned Venezuela, a once-poor country that had become oil-rich and enjoyed a boom during the oil crisis of 1973—and then suffered a catastrophic crash a decade later when oil prices plummeted. By then the government depended solely on money from oil exports, and the economy collapsed. Wages decreased by seventy percent. Attempted coups, government corruption, and failed policies had combined to drive many Venezuelan citizens deeper into poverty than ever before.

President Jaime Lusinchi had won election in 1984, but four years into his administration, the economic situation remained dire. Poverty was so extreme here. The people owned nothing; no land, no resources with which to help themselves. And, of course, the children suffered. About one in ten Venezuelan children died before age five. Malnutrition raised the possibility of pneumonia, diarrhea, and malaria, and lack of education, particularly in rural areas, assured the continued misery of the country's children.

By the time Audrey's plane went wheels-down and landed at the Maiquetia airport just outside Caracas on Saturday, October 15, 1988, she could speak with authority on any subject related to the UNICEF projects in focus in Venezuela. And this would be an unusual mission in another regard—the photographer this time would be Victoria Brynner, Doris's twenty-five-year-old daughter. Audrey and Victoria had been close all the girl's life. As an adult Victoria had become an accomplished photographer and would now serve a key role as part of the UNICEF team. Her photos would enlighten the world about the conditions of South American women and children in need.

"Audrey asked me if I wanted to come on this trip," said Victoria. "I was a photographer for the French agency Gamma and was particularly interested in shooting people in news contexts. It was a great opportunity for me."

The Cavendes Foundation had invited UNICEF's movie star to Venezuela where she would serve as a magnifying lens for their ongoing educational activities in a country hit by those oil economy boom-and-bust cycles. Most inhabitants of Venezuela lived in the north, around Caracas, but there were many rural areas that sat far from resources, particularly in the south. Vicious, insidious poverty ruled everywhere.

Audrey and Robbie first traveled to Barinas, a city of a quarter-million 350 miles southwest of Caracas. There they viewed ongoing mother- and child-care projects by the Cavendes Foundation and a center that had been established for preschool activities, adult training courses, meetings, and social occasions.

Then, in one of the poorest areas of Caracas, Audrey and Robbie were taken to an early childhood education project supported by UNICEF.

Victoria Brynner said, "We were in the slums when we saw families—mothers and children. Audrey made it seem like wherever she was, she was at ease and put smiles on people's faces. She wanted to know everything; she asked a lot of questions and got involved in conversations."

A neighborhood house had been converted to a child and family center capable of caring for fifteen to twenty children under six years of age supervised daily by a mother who had been trained in preschool care by a teacher-specialist. Audrey was conversant in Spanish and she could communicate with the locals, giving her an advantage here she hadn't enjoyed in Ethiopia or Turkey. Later in the day Audrey and Robbie and other UNICEF officials met with fifty-nine-year-old President Lusinchi for a two-hour session on children's issues, including the problems of poverty and its effect on children and possible solutions for the most critical situations.

Audrey and Robbie also served as guests of honor at a ceremony commemorating the golden anniversary of the Cavendes Foundation, which included music by the Venezuelan Orchestra Juvenil. In her remarks before the group, Audrey hit hard on behalf of UNICEF—celebration or not: "Permit me for a moment to ask you to listen to the silence in this world," she told the audience. "The silence of children who ask for nothing. The silence of children who are the tiny victims of war—wars no longer confined to the battlefield. The silence of mothers and fathers who cannot feed their children because of abject poverty."

Victoria Brynner relished what she considered this "great opportunity for me to be with her in the context of her work, and to watch her deal not only with the suffering people in the field but with all the UNICEF officials, the governments, the media, constantly bouncing from one to the other. It was so impressive to see how giving and patient she always was."

Neither woman could know about another kind of silence that had doomed the South America mission. Consumers of news didn't much care about education for the poor in Venezuela. This wasn't life and death and because reporters smelled no story worth covering, even with Audrey Hepburn involved, they had passed.

If she had understood the coverage void, she would have been angered by it. Instead Audrey realized joy in making the rounds for education instead of wading into wars and famine. She would later realize: Her personal pain index served as a barometer for the news cycle.

On Tuesday, October 18, the UNICEF team flew 1,100 air miles south-southwest from Caracas to Ecuador's capital of Quito. This land had once been part of the Incan Empire before conquest by the Spanish under Francisco Pizarro in 1532. In recent times Ecuador, like Venezuela, had been ruled by a military junta until democracy and a new constitution gave Ecuador a fresh start in 1979. The new president, Rodrigo Borja Cevallos, was a descendant of the Borgias and had been in office a matter of weeks. UNICEF's packet included hopeful information about Borja, a representative of the Democratic Left who had run on a platform of improving human rights, including those for children. But severe poverty still plagued the people, which activated a UNICEF response. Here the focus would be on programs for street children—a new issue for Audrey and a dire problem in South America.

After the usual airport greetings in Quito, the team proceeded to Lucha de los Pobresere, what UNICEF called an "urban-marginal community" located near Parque Metropolitano Del Sur, a vast hilly park in the center of Quito. The landscape was spectacular—the peaks of the Pichincha volcano loomed high above no matter where in the city they moved.

In Lucha de los Pobresere the Ministry of Social Welfare maintained a preschool program with the assistance of UNICEF. As in Venezuela, private homes were used for preschool education, health care, nutrition, and early stimulation activities for children up to six years old. In the same neighborhood the visitors toured another center for preschool education where, in addition to childcare services, training took place for volunteer workers.

That evening they visited Acción Guambras, an open service

to young people living on the street. This program offered several initiatives for children who worked in various ways to support themselves since they maintained little or no relationship with their families.

The issue of street children came to vivid life for Audrey that evening. Some of these children had been abandoned by their parents or become orphaned when a single parent died. Others had been sent into Quito to earn money by families in extreme poverty. Many children had fled their homes because of violence or sexual abuse. Audrey was told they lived all over the city. They might be peddling chewing gum or newspapers to tourists or shining shoes. Aid agencies hadn't reached most of them, so for the sex industry, they became easy prey. Almost all had been initiated into sex by age eight or nine and in their teenage years were exchanging sex for money. Many would turn to alcohol or drugs to dull the pain of sex work, anonymity, and being forgotten. They slept wherever. Some on the sidewalk, others in back alleys.

She had heard that one of the children was asked, "What do you want to be when you grow up?"

"Alive" was the response.

Audrey could see a nightmare in the making not just for Ecuador but for the world, and it rattled her. They were growing up wild, these children of the streets, with no education, no moral compass, and total susceptibility to all the evils of the world. By adulthood, those who survived would be monsters without conscience. That realization crystallized UNICEF's street-children mission in her mind.

The *abandonados* wandered into Acción Guambras from all directions, in all sizes, and wore all manner of clothes, some shabby and torn but others seemingly fresh. Audrey was overwhelmed by how many had been drawn here—hundreds and hundreds—and by the care with which they were received and the breadth of services offered by her agency. It resembled a street fair, and here the small lost souls received moments of love.

She would later speak to the U.S. Congress about what she witnessed this evening: "UNICEF-assisted open houses for street children, who instead of being institutionalized, can come and go freely, be fed, sleep, wash, receive lessons—and are protected and respected."

Said Robbie, "Eventually, what affected her even more than those children who were suffering of hunger or disease were the thousands upon thousands of children that we saw who had lost their parents, who had nothing to relate to, who had no affection. That was something she could relate to even more."

Her eyes had been opened to the issue of street children. She would soon stand at a podium at UNICEF House in New York City and say, "Do you know how many street children there are in South America? All over the world? Even in this country? But especially in South America and India? It's something like 100 million who live and die in the streets."

Audrey and Victoria ended their first day in Quito by visiting the Jesuit Church of la Compañía de Jésus. The cut-stone exterior hid a Baroque nave gilded completely in gold leaf—many considered it the most magnificent church in all of Ecuador. "After what we'd just seen [with the street children], it was very moving," said Victoria. "We stood there next to each other and held hands and each said our own little prayer. It was almost like God was shining upon us."

The next day Audrey assisted President Borja in the kickoff of the PROANDES Project, a five-nation partnership to increase the fight against the deteriorating quality of life and provide basic services in the Andean region of Bolivia, Colombia, Ecuador, Peru, and Venezuela. This sub-region, made up of eighty-two million indigenous people, included twenty-four million living in absolute poverty with an inability to meet basic needs. PROANDES proposed intervening with additional resources in specific areas where critical poverty hit women and children hardest, complementing and extending regular UNICEF programs of cooperation.

In notes prepared at the hotel, Audrey told the gathered officials that she had witnessed the effects of the economic crisis on the welfare of women and children in both Venezuela and Ecuador and expressed her appreciation for the goals of the PROANDES Project. "One cannot wait until the crisis is resolved to take care of the problems of children," said Audrey. "They cannot wait."

In a lunch at the Government Palace, President and Mrs. Borja discussed with Audrey and her team the cooperation that UNICEF was giving to various institutions in Ecuador, and the efforts of the new government to bring basic services to all preschool children. Such meetings with heads of state, Lusinchi in Venezuela and Borja here, accommodated both sides. The leaders wanted to rub shoulders with a Hollywood royal and enjoy the photo op, while Audrey used the access to presidential ears to make sure they heard her every word on the subject of children. She would smile and defer and charm and, in a cunning way, influence.

She would say later, "I was received by the president of Ecuador, who I think is very committed to children. In fact, in his inauguration address, he said that 'the only privileged people under my government will be children.' And a very lovely thing has happened, and I was there for the launching of the PROANDES Project. These are five Andean countries who have united for common good—for education, for children, against poverty. And this is a big and very interesting project. And UNICEF is organizing and giving the know-how and raising funds for child care and immunization. There's very, very little immunization."

She had powered through another mission, seen thousands more desperate people, women and children living in property, and participated in her first meetings with heads of state. But she came back unbowed: "I usually go with a rather heavy heart," she told an interviewer soon after her return from South America, "because

I know what I'm going to see. I don't have to go to see it because I know what I'm going to see. Yet I must. But I somehow always come away much more light-hearted than when I go because one really can be optimistic when you see what's being done."

As bad as she found conditions in these countries receiving UNICEF aid, much worse were the attitudes of some members of the press. As a unit they had stayed away from this mission; some had also become her critics; armchair generals who perceived that she was shoveling sand against the tide.

"Somebody said to me the other day, 'You know, it's really senseless what you're doing,'" Audrey related around this time. "'There's always been suffering, there will always be suffering, and you're just prolonging the suffering of these children.'" Her own mother-in-law, Paola Bandini, had said these words to her, not a reporter, but she would use the quote now as a weapon.

"My answer is, 'OK then, let's start with your grandchild. Don't buy antibiotics if it gets pneumonia. Don't take it to the hospital if it has an accident.' It's against life—against humanity—to think that way."

Even in her own family the attitude seemed to be: Stick to your own kind, Audrey Hepburn. Indeed, her own kind had been beckoning. The Princess Grace Foundation had wanted Audrey to appear at a Cary Grant tribute gala to be held on Wednesday, October 19, at the Beverly Hilton. She felt bound to attend since her *Charade* co-star Grant had died in November 1986. His widow, Barbara, and Prince Rainier and Princess Stephanie of Monaco would attend the event in addition to R.J. Wagner and Jill St. John, R.J.'s *Hart to Hart* co-star Stephanie Powers, Liza Minnelli, Frank Sinatra, and a trio of Audrey's best guy-pals: Greg Peck, Roger Moore, and Henry Mancini. But as much as she felt obligated to laud Grant and support the Princess Grace Foundation, she felt a higher calling with street children in Quito—the place she needed to be.

Obliged

Spring 1944. The war in Europe had settled into routine—ground fighting had raged in southern Italy for seven months, and an invasion in France was expected at any time. Daily the Yanks flew bombing missions against strategic targets in Germany. Audrey saw formations of hundreds of big American planes fly over each morning of clear weather. The rumble of all those engines couldn't be missed. Many times German fighters intercepted, setting off life-or-death struggles high up over her head. At night she could hear the drone of RAF planes continuing the effort, bombing so indiscriminately and with such great loss of civilian life that the Germans labeled the Brits as terrorists.

The town of Velp carried a unique importance to the Nazi empire for its location only forty miles west of the German border and its resources immediately at hand—banks, hotels, shops, a railroad station, a hospital, and trees. The simple beauty of Velp's tree-lined streets could shield entire German columns of tanks and other armored vehicles. So far, the war had spared Velp and the city it adjoined, Arnhem.

As the Germans came to expect an Allied invasion, the Nazi occupation command moved its headquarters to Velp. Arthur Seyss-Inquart, ruler of all Holland on behalf of Hitler, became a neighbor of the van Heemstras. Hans Albin Rauter, head of the

SS, moved into a villa down the boulevard. Increased German activity in the area set off a like response by the Velp Resistance movement, which recruited Audrey to perform small but important tasks. In May 1944 she turned fifteen, still young enough and boyish enough with her tall, thin frame to seem nonthreatening to any Germans she encountered. But the Resistance coveted her abilities—she could speak English fluently, which was key to communicating with Allied airmen shot down by German fighters day and night, and Ella had raised her daughter to keep a level head in all situations.

One morning Audrey received word from Resistance boss Henrik Visser 't Hooft that a wireless operator had parachuted onto the lands of Castle Rozendaal after bailing out of a British Lancaster bomber set ablaze by German night fighters. Audrey responded at once since Castle Rozendaal, home of the van Pallandts, sat just a mile away at the end of her street, Rozendaalselaan. She walked up the long sidewalk and received direction to the flyer's location by her own kin; the baronial van Pallandts and baronial van Heemstras had been joined in marriage 107 years earlier.

Moments counted, Audrey knew, because the British flier would be a hunted man. Shyness made it difficult for her to speak with these heaven-sent heroes, but she had learned to force out key information. She informed him that he had come down just northeast of Arnhem on the grounds of Castle Rozendaal. Its master, Baron van Pallandt, respected an agreement with German authorities to turn over any Allied personnel he encountered. She asked if the airman held any valuables. He showed his hand, revealing a gold signet ring.

Audrey thought a moment. "Give me the ring," she instructed. "The Germans will only take it away from you. I promise to give it back to you after the war."

The flier hesitated, then handed over his ring and scribbled on a piece of paper: Max Court 5 Lyons-crescent Tonbridge. With that the girl wished him luck, repeated the promise, and walked home at a leisurely pace to avoid notice by the Germans.

Eighteen months later the world had changed. Arnhem and parts of Velp had been destroyed and the Nazis defeated. Ella had taken Audrey to Amsterdam to pursue a career in ballet. And with liberation, Audrey had written to Wireless Operator Max Court in hopes he had survived German captivity. Her letter reported that his ring was safe, and when he responded, Ella arranged for her daughter to meet up with Court at the holidays of 1946. At that time Audrey returned the ring to Max in an event covered by the *Kent and Sussex Courier*.

Since she had been old enough to take on such obligations, Audrey Hepburn felt their weight and fulfilled every one. And in October 1988 feel them she did, as two glittering Hollywood galas collided on her calendar. She missed the first, when the Princess Grace Foundation honored the memory of Cary Grant, but a greater obligation in South America had overruled.

But Hubert de Givenchy? Hubert was family, and Audrey insisted on drop-shipping herself from Quito to Los Angeles to serve as honorary chairperson for the Hubert de Givenchy Retrospective Black Tie Gala, a fashion show of his finest work staged at the Beverly Hilton to benefit the Los Angeles County High School for the Arts, which hoped to create a *"Fame"* high school in Los Angeles. Audrey and Robbie claimed some downtime at Connie's place to prepare, and her Givenchy gown for the occasion—a feather-detail evening sheath dress in red satin crepe with a sequin-embroidered bodice—arrived by taxi Wednesday, October 26, with two days to spare. She also waived her ban on Hollywood-related press that week to give interviews honoring the man and his work.

"I like unadorned simplicity," she told *Los Angeles Times* staff writer Rose-Marie Turk. "Somehow his clothes have always been right for me, for my body. It's never elegant and pompous. There's always that little bow or something that gives it a lightness." When pressed for a favorite of his designs, she said, "Something I loved was the short black dress and wonderful lace mask-veil I wore in *How to Steal a Million* with Peter O'Toole. I was trying to be mysterious and the mask was such a pretty way to be incognito. Hubert always had a wonderful understanding of the scenes."

For Audrey, Hubert had been a soulmate ever since the moment she walked into his Paris studio in 1953, just a year after its opening. She was about to begin her second starring picture, *Sabrina*, and had been sent to Givenchy—then a sensational young designer of twenty-six operating on a shoestring budget—at the insistence of director Billy Wilder because the press said Givenchy's signature use of white shirting fabric would perfectly represent the character of Sabrina Fairchild. The white fabric created looks, said Givenchy, that "were lovely and very young."

She remembered that first meeting with the designer: "The last thing he needed was this unknown actress walking in, asking, 'Could I see your clothes for a movie?' But in his usual simple, unpretentious way, he said, 'Why not?'"

Tall, elegant, broad-shouldered and two years her senior, Count Hubert de Givenchy—of an ennobled family with roots in Venice—could barely contain his excitement to be receiving "Miss Hepburn" that day. "I only knew of Katharine Hepburn," he said. "Of course, I was very happy to receive *Katharine* Hepburn." When he saw this other Hepburn, a young waif of a girl, he tried to dismiss her, but finally "for the sake of peace and quietude," as he put it, she was allowed to pick items off the rack from his current collection. Far from being offended that he wouldn't design wardrobe for her picture, she dug into the racks with the enthusiasm of a girl receiving an American blouse from UNRRA, made her selections and, she said, he "fixed them for me right then and there. We became great friends from that day."

Thirty-five years later she proclaimed, "He's my great love. I consider him one of my best and most important friends." And he really was. They met up anywhere and everywhere and enjoyed each other's company all those decades. He turned her into a glamour girl for the ages; she put his house on the map and he luxuriated in the stardust of Audrey Hepburn and considered her his muse.

Audrey said Hubert "is like his clothes: simple with a sense of humor."

Sean called Givenchy "the archetype of what a man should be. 'To be a gentleman means, as the word says, that you must first be a gentle man,' she taught us. And that he was."

Luca spent his youth finding his mother's friend Hubert to be aloof. Only as an adult would Luca understand the essence of Givenchy and the heart behind the reserved exterior: "When my mother needed to be a warrior, she was a warrior," said Luca. "Hubert was the same way. When things that matter happened, Hubert was there."

So, of course Audrey mailed herself from Ecuador to Hollywood to be there for Hubert, no matter the culture shock of taking off from an impoverished country overrun by street children and arriving in the overbuilt, sprawling dream capital of the world.

Of the Givenchy retrospective that Audrey walked into, Rose-Marie Turk of the *L.A. Times* said, "In the beginning, Hubert de Givenchy thought he would stage 'a simple retrospective' in Los Angeles. Thirteen months later, struggling with last-minute details and literally knee-deep in dresses from his past, the man who memorably dressed Audrey Hepburn for movie escapades and the Duchess of Windsor for her graveside farewell to her husband conceded the event had grown beyond his expectations."

Hubert had shipped twenty-seven trunks of dresses, shoes, and accessories from Paris; grateful clients from around the world flew in more dresses for his use. That evening, after a hectic morning and midday tearing his suite apart looking for keys to his trunks so he could "liberate the dresses," he sent top fashion models down a runway representing his finest looks from each era in a career of four decades.

Audrey looked on with pride on Friday, October 28, 1988, as her friend received the first State of California Lifetime Achievement Award for his significant contributions to the film community—primarily Audrey's costumes from *Sabrina, Funny Face, Love in the Afternoon, Breakfast at Tiffany's,* and *How to Steal a Million.* Ironically, Paramount Pictures and Warner Bros. refused to lend costumes that had been screen-worn by Audrey Hepburn to the event; copies were used in some instances.

Celebrities attending included Loretta Young, Roddy Mc-Dowell, Gene Kelly, Joan Collins, Jane Seymour, Donna Mills, designer Oscar de la Renta, and Apollo astronaut Buzz Aldrin.

Audrey and Robbie finally returned to Tolochenaz after the event, where she faced the inevitable "la signora need to rest!" But there was something Audrey needed to do first in celebration of Victoria Brynner's birthday on November 1.

"She came to our house carrying a little basket in which was a bird's nest she had found in her garden," said Victoria. In the nest was a small paper bird Audrey had painted. "And under the bird was a small cross on a chain and a note wishing me a happy birthday in memory of our special moment in that church in Quito."

Only then could la signora permit herself to rest, for a period of two weeks, at which time the UNICEF merry-go-round spun again.

Return of the Dutch Girl

Audrey Hepburn loved the Dutch people and all their foibles. She had grown up Dutch and seen their frugality, pragmatism, and industriousness up close. When the occupation came, the Dutch lived their lives hoping for the best but kept a wary eye on their Aryan "cousins." When things went to hell in the Netherlands, when Audrey's Uncle Otto was among the first to be gunned down by the oppressors, when all manner of privations hit her country, the Dutch didn't get mad; they got even. A Dutch Resistance movement became so sophisticated, so embedded, so formidable in her town of Velp that by 1944, the German occupiers were the ones living their lives hoping for the best. By then they had learned the Dutch would never be controlled.

Only as an adult would Audrey understand a stark truth about her country's oppression of foreign lands, when Dutch businessmen had, before the war, gone off to the "Dutch East Indies" or Suriname to make their fortunes. Their travels and success had seemed so romantic; it was anything but, and the truth emerged when, after the Japanese occupation of what became Indonesia, at the end of World War II, the indigenous people rose up against their former Dutch masters and expelled them.

But she loved the Netherlands warts and all, and whenever her country called, she would answer.

Tall, blond, and youthful Leendert de Jong had become film curator of the Filmhuis Den Haag in 1987. The Filmhuis promoted not only new world cinema but also film history, and so the energetic de Jong became involved in developing a major thematic festival every year. In 1987 it was Film & Architecture, and the success of this program led to 1988's theme, Film & Fashion.

The next idea was as simple as two plus two: The pages of Givenchy's film portfolio revealed Audrey Hepburn wearing this and Audrey Hepburn wearing that, so let's invite Audrey Hepburn.

Tracking down the mysterious Miss Hepburn at the beginning of the year, a month before she joined UNICEF and long before something called the Internet became ubiquitous, proved daunting for Leendert. She was after all a retired jet-setter and "only one book about her career existed as far as I knew," he said. "I had seen most of her films but was totally ignorant about her personal life."

De Jong finally secured her Tolochenaz address from the Givenchy studio in Paris and sent the invitation February 24, 1988.

Two weeks later—days after her appointment as Special Ambassador—de Jong's phone rang. The man on the other end of the line addressed him in fluent Dutch, which took Leendert aback.

"We received your letter," said the voice, "and Audrey appreciates the invitation to open your festival. She's interested in the idea, but she has some apprehension. Will the focus be on her, or on the designers you mention in your letter?"

Leendert responded that thirty films were selected for the festival that featured costumes designed by couturiers including Chanel, Dior, and Saint Laurent and by costume designers like Jean Louis, Adrian, and of course Edith Head. But the cherry on the cake? *Roman Holiday* by Head and six Audrey films dressed in Givenchy couture.

The man on the phone listened patiently to de Jong and had one more question. "Is there any way that the opening of the festival could benefit the United Nation Children's Fund?" he asked.

"Audrey has just been appointed a Special Ambassador and she's interested in anything that promotes this cause."

De Jong could see the positive direction the conversation was taking. He promised Audrey Hepburn's representative that he would find a way to fulfill this request.

"Then we would be delighted to come to The Hague for this event in November," said the man on the line.

About the call, Leendert said, "We were euphoric—Audrey Hepburn will open our festival! But immediately a feeling of shame came over me. I had forgotten to ask about the speaker's relationship with Hepburn. All sorts of questions popped into my mind: Is this Audrey's agent? A Dutch agent? How embarrassing!"

With Audrey's verbal okay in hand, the Filmhuis approached the Municipal Museum in The Hague to ask: Might an exhibit of film fashions be arranged, one that might include those of Dutch designers Frans Molenaar and Frank Govers as well as America's film design titan Edith Head and Hubert de Givenchy of Paris?

"The answer was a happy yes," said de Jong, who had been speaking with Robbie, he later learned. The trio would rendezvous at the Givenchy studio in Paris in mid-June 1988 to discuss details of the event. At the time Audrey was traveling across Europe giving interviews about UNICEF.

"We met at Givenchy's on Avenue George V," said de Jong. "It turned out to be a private fashion show for Audrey, two or three Egyptian princesses, and Marie-Hélène de Rothschild. After a first and brief acquaintance with Audrey, Robert, and de Givenchy, I was placed between Hepburn and Mme. de Rothschild—a somewhat overwhelming setting. After the show I was dropped at my hotel by Mme. de Rothschild and her chauffeur in a Rolls Royce."

The next day Audrey and Robbie met Leendert again, this time in the Hotel George V. In an elevator two attractive women began "chatting somewhat flirtatiously" with Robbie, said Leendert. When the elevator doors opened and Leendert, Robbie, and Audrey stepped out, she turned back with a sweet smile and said to the women, "Hands off. He's mine."

November arrived, with Audrey refreshed after her exhausting mission to Venezuela and Ecuador. She and Robbie arrived at Schiphol Airport the day before the gala and de Jong shepherded them to the Hotel des Indes in The Hague. Givenchy and his partner, Philippe Venet, arrived the day of the gala for an afternoon television interview during which, true to his word, de Jong made sure Audrey was asked questions about UNICEF.

Leendert arranged to present a series of films for the run of the Film & Fashion festival: "Amongst others we screened *Stage Fright* with Marlene Dietrich dressed in Dior, Catherine Deneuve dressed in Yves St. Laurent in *Belle de Jour*, and Vivien Leigh dressed in Pierre Balmain for *The Roman Spring of Mrs. Stone*."

But the opening evening of the festival on Friday, November 18, 1988, would be devoted to Audrey. Leendert secured a 35mm print of *Funny Face*—the film in which Audrey plays a fashion model—and arranged to have it flown in from the UK for viewing at the Metropole Theater, with the gate going to UNICEF. Hepburn hadn't seen *Funny Face* since the premiere and hoped "the colors were still bright and sparkling." They were.

De Jong had also tailored other portions of the evening to the cause—the fashion show featuring designs by Frank Govers and Frans Molenaar concluded with a Sotheby auction of three dresses, one each by the Dutch designers and a third by Hubert, who also donated a large Givenchy bottle of perfume. Total take from the auction was 40,000 guilders—roughly $50,000 US—which the press labeled "typical Dutch thrift" considering the fashions at auction. The number proved no surprise to Audrey, who could only smile at the frugality of the people. She quickly pointed out that the total represented 40,000 guilders *more* than they had before.

After the event the UNICEF representative mentioned that vitamins could save an African child from blindness at the cost of only four cents a year. "It would have been nice if she had mentioned that before the auction," sniffed a Dutch reporter.

Leendert would credit Audrey with hard work this "hectic night." She opened the gala with a speech—part in English, part in Dutch—to thank the directors, co-stars, and fashion designers of her films, including and especially Hubert de Givenchy. Despite discomfort at watching her own performances, she sat through *Funny Face* for the cause and then took an active role in the fashion show and auction.

The next day Audrey and Hubert jointly opened the exhibit "Haute Couture: Givenchy worn by Audrey Hepburn" at the Municipal Museum to a large, invitation-only crowd. In her speech Audrey expressed pride at her Dutch heritage, then turned her attention to her friend: "When I look back at my thirty-five-year relationship with Hubert de Givenchy, I look back at thirty-five years of my life. Yet no nostalgia prevails. Nostalgia has something sad about it. For me it was mainly the pleasure that surfaced and the realization how privileged I have been."

Later she became distracted by the presentation of one of Hubert's dresses on display. Consternation and a fury of activity commenced when Miss Hepburn tried to adjust the lighting on one of her friend's costumes. Givenchy understood both her intention to protect him and her penchant for over-managing any situation. He knew even better something she was blind to at this moment—the perception of her interference with the work of the lighting experts in attendance. He stepped in close and said, "Leave it, Audrey. They know what they're doing."

A young film curator's go-for-broke idea had nine months later become a win for UNICEF and a national event in the Netherlands. Audrey would leave this special place, the homeland of her youth, the always immaculate Netherlands, to prepare for her next mission to a blood-spattered and desperate corner of the world.

Dangerous Road

During a March 24, 1980, evening funeral mass in a San Salvador chapel, four gunmen from the government approached Archbishop Oscar A. Romero as he stood at the altar holding a communion wafer and shot him through the heart.

Months later in the same country, a government death squad cornered three Catholic nuns and a female lay attendant working as missionaries and raped and machine-gunned them.

The Jimmy Carter administration in the States looked past the atrocities and supported El Salvador's government because it was anti-Communist. The Reagan administration that next came to power in Washington rubber-stamped the policy of the outgoing Carter administration. Through the 1980s the United States funneled arms to the Salvadoran government of the murderous right to fend off the murderous left, which was receiving arms from the Soviets and Cubans. Washington's tried-and-true "domino theory" was now applied to Central America, and conflict would rage in El Salvador and neighboring Nicaragua. There, by mid-decade an American Marine Corps officer, Oliver North, busily funneled millions to anti-Sandinista forces for the purpose of buying arms to fight Communists. All the while civilian body counts mounted and the countries hemorrhaged refugees, thousands of which ended up in Honduras where their camps jostled for space with secret

U.S. military bases training Salvadoran troops.

The Central America of 1989 and recently promoted UNICEF Goodwill Ambassador Audrey Hepburn seemed to be anything but a match made in heaven. And that's where Audrey insisted on going in the first quarter of 1989. She would charge into the middle of these misnamed "civil" wars to pound home the devastating effects of poverty on mothers and children—effects compounded by warfare based, in theory at least, on the quest by one global superpower for individual liberty and the pursuit by the other of strength in a collective. In this struggle for the rights of man, women and children had no rights at all.

Horst Max Cerni, a UNICEF Public Affairs Officer traveling with Audrey, said, "This was a short trip—about two days in each country—with limited project visits and emphasis on public appearances. Naturally, in each country she attracted local media and gave several interviews." Scheduled meetings with heads of state and Audrey's charge to disseminate the recently published State of the World's Children Report reflected her growing clout as a working UNICEF representative willing to take risks and go where other celebrity reps never had.

She and Robbie, working again with photographer Victoria Brynner, began in Guatemala City on Monday, February 6, 1989, where Audrey received a relatively low-key welcome before heading two hours due west by jeep through the heart of Guatemala to the remote village of Panibaj on a mountain peak east of the volcanic remnant, Lago de Atitlán. Panibaj took the prize as the smallest and most isolated collection of dwellings she had yet encountered with UNICEF.

"We were accompanied by armed soldiers because of the ongoing civil war," said Cerni. With the aid of a translator who understood the unique dialect of the village, "Audrey interacted with the women and children and tried to find out their major concerns," said Cerni.

The subject of her visit to Panibaj was water. With help from UNICEF, Panibaj had just completed construction of a community drinking-water system, which Audrey inaugurated by twisting a tap after receiving a long explanation of construction of the system from the elderly project supervisor. Afterward she danced with children to a marimba band and took many small girls to the spigot, picking each up so they could turn it and feel the splash of mountain water.

The celebration at the water spigot became infectious, and Audrey beamed as she congratulated the people on their accomplishment: "It's wonderful to know that all these little girls won't have to walk those many kilometers as their mothers had to, because you now have water. Water is life and clean water means health."

East of Panibaj they stopped at the larger town of Patzún where she toured a health center and chatted with children and their mothers. Later, in Guatemala City, there was another chance to talk to mothers and children during a visit to the urban slum area of El Mezquital, as they walked down Calle de UNICEF, or UNICEF Street.

In the evening the UNICEF party met Guatemalan Vice President Roberto Carpio Nicolle, who formally introduced Audrey at a ceremony launching the 1989 State of the World's Children Report. In his remarks, Vice President Nicolle cited improvements in education and basic services for children as foundational steps leading to peace in Latin America. He indicated that Guatemala would support the call for a Presidential Summit on Children, and for the ratification of the Convention on the Rights of the Child. He closed his statement with, "There can be no peace without children's rights being protected." Audrey beamed a broad smile and applauded at hearing his words.

One country down, two others ahead.

The party flew on to the Honduran capital city of Tegucigalpa. There UNICEF Regional Director for the Americas and the Caribbean Dr. Teresa Albanez and Area Representative Agop Kayayan greeted the party and ushered all to the presidential palace for a meeting with President José Azcona.

During their meeting, Audrey invited Azcona to participate in the Presidential Summit on Children and to support the Convention on the Rights of the Child. The planned half-hour meeting extended to an hour as Audrey talked through the statistics in the State of the World's Children Report; the numbers on immunization drew the president's special interest. Azcona promised Audrey that the situation in his country would be improved. He was then presented with a copy of the report; he sheepishly requested that she autograph it to him.

Horst Max Cerni recognized that Audrey capitalized on each occasion of meeting a head of state, all of them starstruck to receive the great Audrey Hepburn. Cerni explained, "She used these opportunities to highlight the need of women and children whom she had just met and the possibility to improve their health through low-cost solutions, better training of medical personnel and provision of medications, especially oral rehydration salts to fight diarrhea, and which could be taught to be prepared by the mothers. Usually, our representative had already provided the details of what UNICEF could offer, and Audrey reinforced this and provided additional personal observation."

The next morning the team visited an urban marginal community that had just gone live with an economical drinking water system supported by UNICEF. Albanez told Audrey that the monthly cost of this new system for a family was twelve lempira—about six dollars; previously the people had to buy water from vendors at eighty-eight lempira per month—a third of the income of an average family. High atop an adjacent hill sat the system's water tank, and individual lines spidered out from the core to community spigots and even to some private homes. Albanez said a community water committee handled maintenance and administration. Most impressive was the fact that the system had become unexpectedly successful—in generating income for the community, the project had drawn international donors such as The World Bank, which also planned to duplicate this project in other communities.

Midday they reached another urban area, the Barrio Villa-franca, where construction of daycare centers had been assisted by UNICEF, which also provided furnishings and trained local women to operate the centers. Here Audrey met with female health volunteers who had trained for six months and then received a graduation diploma and a T-shirt emblazoned with the UNICEF logo—a source of great pride for the women.

That evening she joined President Azcona at a ceremony celebrating the 1989 State of the World's Children Report. There the president and the Goodwill Ambassador jointly presented the new annual National Media Awards, initiated by UNICEF to encourage journalists and media organizations to cover UNICEF activities—an effort to close the gap of apathy on missions like South America.

By this point in the trip, Audrey had become aware of a cancer of corruption that had woven itself into the fabric of government and society in this part of the world as a consequence of Cold War attempts by the United States and the Soviet Union to wield influence through weapons and cash. "The corruption is so widespread," Audrey lamented to Luca after the mission. She saw corruption as yet another burden for the oppressed and another obstacle to the efforts of UNICEF and other agencies. "She compared that burden to a devious war that taxed every aspect of the lives of the less fortunate inhabitants," said Luca.

The mission continued, and on the morning of Wednesday, February 8, the UNICEF team was off again, this time flying into El Salvador, "a very violent place," according to Victoria Brynner, where priests and nuns had been murdered—along with an estimated 70,000 men, women, and children culled from the population over a decade of horror and sorrow.

Audrey knew the statistics by heart and forged ahead, stepping off the plane to a children's chorus that greeted her in San Salvador. Then the UNICEF group was driven to the Government Palace for a meeting with Salvadoran President José Napoleón Duarte. Audrey knew the score with Duarte going in. He'd been in office four years, but his U.S.-backed government faced pressures well beyond his capabilities—leftist guerrillas attacked military targets at will; government death squads continued to operate beyond his reach; corruption ran rampant here as everywhere else; and perhaps due to the relentless pressure, Duarte had become ill. Stomach cancer now ate away at his sixty-three-year-old body, and a pale, gaunt, solemn man in a dark suit plodded in to meet Audrey.

As photographers snapped away, Audrey engaged Duarte in conversation, infusing what energy she could into a dismal, at times macabre, circumstance. Duarte had been a force behind the "days of tranquility" week-long cease-fire when government and rebel groups agreed to allow aid to reach families and children, with immunization the focus. There wasn't much positive they could speak about, but Audrey could single out this accomplishment as Duarte's alone.

"You're always here, but I'm in Europe," Audrey said to Duarte in an attempt to inflate him as if he were a shriveled balloon. "You can have no idea how respected and admired you are for that—for the days of tranquility. I think it's an inspiration to so many countries that because of children, there can be peace. What we hope now is that children can bring peace—lasting peace."

"Lasting peace, yes," Duarte rasped with a wan smile. "Not just a few days." Audrey could see he was ill, desperately ill, heavily medicated, and vacant.

He described his minister of public health as "a very devoted man working in this area; he has done a very good job. So we feel proud."

"You should be," she said eagerly.

She then pressed him on the idea of bringing up the issue of children at a summit meeting of five Central American presidents—Daniel Ortega of Nicaragua, Oscar Arias of Costa Rica, Vinicio Serezo of Guatemala, Ascona of Honduras, and Duarte of El Salvador—to be held the following week at a luxury resort on El Salvador's Pacific Coast. Specifically, Audrey wanted Duarte's commitment to bring up the idea of a separate summit meeting among the five on matters related to children who had suffered so terribly in the past decade because of unrest in all five countries.

Audrey didn't back off Duarte because of his frail health; she bored in on him until she received affirmation that he would try. Later he would tell the press with pride, roles fully reversed, "Miss Hepburn has asked me to be the spokesperson at the upcoming meeting with Central American Presidents, and to ask for a summit for children. I agree that this is a good idea because to speak of children is to speak of peace."

But in fact, Duarte was a lame duck to be replaced in the next month's elections. His main accomplishment after a full term as president of El Salvador would be a peaceful transfer of power to the new president—and then Duarte would die of stomach cancer a year after sitting down with Audrey Hepburn. She would meet with anyone, a president, a vice president, a Marxist—any leader at all if she spotted an opportunity to help the children.

Unseen Shield

In the most dangerous and bullet-riddled country in Central America, El Salvador, Audrey would spend two days looking in on self-help projects in health and education. In the urban community of Trujillo in San Salvador, she followed community health volunteers as they visited families in their homes, examining babies, weighing and measuring them. Trujillo housed many who had been displaced by a deadly 1986 earthquake. Audrey also participated in a public health session where mothers received vaccinations against tetanus—here she administered oral vaccines to children. Then she observed as mothers learned about the importance of breastfeeding, responsible parenting, and proper hygiene and health practices for the entire family.

The UNICEF party traveled to the rural community of La Libertad on the Pacific coast and witnessed the "Literacy by Radio" program in action. Through special radio broadcasts and accompanying workbooks, Literacy by Radio provided reading and writing skills to illiterate people in urban slums as well as remote areas of the country. Audrey participated in a ceremony to congratulate several men and women who demonstrated their newly learned reading skills. She also met a teacher, age sixty-three, who was considered a hero for her efforts in literacy. The leftist guerrillas didn't bother UNICEF's ambassadors on the trip; the right-wing death squads were inactive. Audrey took no notice of any danger and focused only on children and their issues.

On the final day in El Salvador, she took time to launch the 1989 State of the World's Children Report once again and then participated in more National Media Prizes. The minister of health appealed to the media to support the upcoming "days of tranquility" for the vaccination campaign so that all children, even in areas of conflict, could get protection against disease.

In fact, the tranquility during Audrey's visit might have been shattered at any time by sabotage or an accident. "Audrey was never concerned about her personal safety," said Horst Max Cerni. "She felt being on a mission for UNICEF and the suffering children in a particular country provided an unseen shield from dangers. All her missions were dangerous, starting with the flights, which sometimes involved small aircraft and unreliable local planes. On the ground, she was entrusted to the UNICEF people who, with the help of their government counterparts, had taken whatever precautions were necessary. In the case of Guatemala, UNICEF had worked with both sides of the conflict, especially during the days of tranquility, to allow children to be vaccinated. This truce had been reached because both rebels and government troops had children of their own. At Audrey's visit, I think the accompanying soldiers were supposed to give us a feeling of being protected, although an ambush could easily have taken place. We never had any incidents with our Goodwill Ambassadors, despite some scary moments."

After six days on the road in Central America she would make one more stop, this one in Mexico City for a two-day strategic visit that began Friday, February 10, 1989. Here she gave a television interview, and then she and Robbie traveled south to Acapulco and the State of Guerrero for a side mission to be captured by an ABC television crew for *The Barbara Walters Special* to be broadcast nationally in the United States.

From Guerrero Audrey and a team that included several health officials and the wife of the governor flew in a small plane to the mountain town of Tlapa. Then all piled into a helicopter and flew on to the small village of Chaucingo. As they circled in for a landing in rugged mountain terrain, it seemed the entire village had turned out to greet this woman whom most had never heard of, let alone seen in a motion picture. To the people of a remote mountaintop in Mexico, the white lady looked as if she needed a meal more than did those she had come to help.

She always scoffed at the idea of anyone knowing about a movie star in the developing world. However, she said of people in places like Chaucingo, "They're very happy to see me, because they know I come from UNICEF. And that they do know about. They don't know Paramount Pictures, but they do know UNICEF."

Banners thanking UNICEF floated in the air as the large crowd, including many farmers, all poor, escorted Audrey down a long farm-field hillside where she turned a valve inside a concrete enclosure to officially bring fresh mountain water to the village. Happy applause erupted and Audrey joined in.

Then a "band" began to play—some horns and some drums that the men playing them seemed only recently acquainted with—to signal that a ceremony would begin in the village center. Another similar band from a neighboring community joined the celebration in support of their own request for water.

Audrey cut a ribbon inaugurating the new water system, and for the first time in its long history, the village had clean drinking water.

She spoke into a microphone provided by UNICEF and made her speech in English for the sake of rolling cameras—at so remote a place, the local dialect rendered her Spanish problematic. She wasn't shy about borrowing elements of past speeches, as with this one that mirrored sentiments about Ethiopia. "You did all the hard work, and you, with your resources, with your effort, have provided water not only for yourselves but for the future and for your children—and especially for the little girls, who will not have to grow up to carry, to fetch water for hours, for miles, like their mothers had to do. For water is life, and clean water is health." The speech was then translated into local Spanish because nobody in this dusty corner of the world spoke any English at all.

After the ceremony she visited the village's new health center where she helped to demonstrate the mixing of oral rehydration salts against dehydration from diarrhea and gave oral polio vaccine to some babies. She was told that "health auxiliaries" trained here to visit homes in far-flung mountain communities where children previously hadn't been able to receive any kind of treatment.

The next day, after helping Victoria through a bout of altitude sickness, Audrey sat for a Central America post-mission press conference in Acapulco attended by thirteen journalists—a modest total given the crush of scribes and cameras that had heard her summaries after Ethiopia. As she learned in South America, even Audrey Hepburn couldn't keep mustering the press in response to UNICEF's drumbeat, especially discussing talking points like the 1974 Declaration of Cocoyoc—the result of an October 1974 conference in Cocoyoc, Mexico, attended by natural scientists, social scientists, and economists.

Nobody much cared about the Declaration of Cocoyoc in 1989; thirty years later its theme would become a headline for the earth—globally, governments were failing in efforts to satisfy fundamental human needs. "On the contrary, more people are hungry, sick, shelterless, and illiterate today than when the United Nations was first set up," stated the Cocoyoc panel in its abstract, which Audrey restated for the press. "At the same time, new and unforeseen concerns have begun to darken the international prospects. Environmental degradation and the rising pressure of resources raise the question whether the 'outer limits' of the planet's physical integrity may not be at risk." Added to the perils of a more fragile environment would be a doubling of the world's population by

2010. Audrey stated on behalf of UNICEF that without drastic intervention, children were in dire straits. And families. And indeed the entire globe.

She had begun to raise environmental issues that had long been on her mind; she had seen for herself the fragility of the planet and its populations on multiple continents.

In Acapulco she called for a renewed commitment to the health of women and children in Mexico and the setting of regional goals to reduce infant, child, and maternal mortality. She also made a special appeal for active participation in the upcoming vaccination campaign.

Then she gave a keynote speech to an international conference of chief executives of major companies. Her presentation centered on the effect of the debt crisis on children, and the need for greater international efforts to protect children and their families. Finally, she taped a long sit-down interview with Barbara Walters for the ABC television special; roll-ins showed her visit to the Mexican mountaintop village.

"I had been pursuing an interview with Miss Hepburn for years," said Walters later, "and she finally agreed to meet me on the beaches of Acapulco, Mexico, where she was doing some work nearby with underprivileged children for UNICEF." Walters called her "the very definition of class." They conducted the interview in overstuffed beach chairs by the windswept surf, with Audrey heavily made up to compensate for so many days in the field. Walters fired off her trademark blunt and probing questions; Audrey answered with her usual candor.

"I have this extraordinary thing that's happened to me," Audrey said with passion, "to be able to express my need to help children and to care for them in some way. I can personally do very little, but I can contribute to a whole chain of events—which would be UNICEF. And that's a marvelous thing. It's like a bonus to me towards the end of my life, and if this career has left me with something very special, it's the fact that it's left me with this, whatever it is, this voice, this curiosity people have to see me, to talk to me, which I can use for the good of children. What could be nicer?"

No, Audrey wasn't getting the media hits now that she had earlier in her stint for UNICEF, but she would always find ways to spread the message, this one in U.S. primetime to an audience of more than 100 million thanks to one extra stop on her Central American tour. In total she had spent nine days covering four countries in one of the world's hot spots of poverty and violence and managed to stay intact and on-message throughout. Her next mission would ratchet up the danger and increase the need for tunnel vision—but first, she faced perils of a different kind on Capitol Hill in Washington, D.C.

The Big Gun

Even Robbie didn't know what tasks Audrey had performed on behalf of the Dutch Resistance during World War II. He said in 1994, "She was rather amused by these gross exaggerations of her activities." There had been talk in the press and in biographies that she had run food and messages to downed Allied airmen, delivered a local Resistance newspaper called *Oranjekrant* to anti-Nazi operatives, and participated in ballet recitals to benefit Jews in hiding. It was all true, but to the end of her life she would hear her mother's voice saying, "You aren't interesting, dear. Don't call attention to yourself." And so she didn't tell Robbie—even Robbie—that she had served as a volunteer aid at age fifteen for the Resistance ringleader in Velp, Dr. Henrik Visser 't Hooft, and performed all the wartime activities described in print, and then some, at his behest.

The dangers of war were nothing new to Audrey Hepburn, which is why the Asmara, Ethiopia, hotel with armed guards in the lobby and no running water failed to faze her. Or artillery batteries, or army escorts in the field. And why she eagerly anticipated her next trip to war-torn Sudan.

The country south of Egypt and west of Ethiopia, Sudan was Africa's largest. Northern Sudan was Arab. Those in southern Sudan, which stretched down to Uganda, considered themselves African and most were Christians. Enmity between the north and south reached back generations to long before the incursion into Sudan by Great Britain in 1898 to block unification of Sudan and its northern neighbor, Egypt.

The usual mess resulted from colonial rule; the British had maintained a military presence with all its swagger and Christian superiority. In the 1950s revolution in Egypt meant an end to British claims on Sudan and they bowed out. Sudan established a parliamentary system in 1956, but volatility reigned into 1983, when a new military government proclaimed fundamentalist Islamic law. Civil war resulted between the Arab government and rebels in the south, primarily the Sudan People's Liberation Army, or SPLA. In 1986 a new Islamic government under Sadiq al-Mahdi came to power and attempted to put humanitarian reforms in place—but these didn't reach as far as the south because of the black skin of its inhabitants. Sadiq al-Mahdi fed weapons to any groups that would fight the black-skinned People's Liberation Army and then began to use starvation as a counterinsurgency weapon. A quarter-million Sudanese in the Christian south died of starvation in 1988 alone and more than two million fled their homes.

By April 1989 refugees from the south had made their way to the Sudanese capital of Khartoum where they were seen as squatters. Their black skin made them easy for the police to spot and round up. Thousands were trucked into the desert for dumping. Those that remained in Khartoum might be whipped if they approached food sources, their shanty towns routinely bulldozed. Sudan had become one of the nastiest and most desperate places on earth, so of course Audrey Hepburn needed to charge into the middle of it. But not just yet.

More than 6,500 miles to the west of Khartoum, Audrey stood with Jim Grant, Larry Bruce, and Robbie outside the U.S. Capitol in Washington, D.C., on a beautiful, breezy spring morning, some clouds but mostly sun and a temperature in the 50s. It was Thursday, April 6, 1989, and Grant was dog-tired after flying in from Sudan the night before.

The men watched Audrey smoke one cigarette after another as she barely concealed her fright. She wore a simple black dress, sleeveless yet, and was too slight a creature, as if the spring breeze might knock her over. It seemed a little bit hilarious: This rail-thin, terrified woman was the big gun of these brawny men, and they had unlimbered her from the caisson and were about to wheel her into position. She was their warrior who had been all over the world now—five continents and counting—in all conditions. She had mastered the fund-raising appeal and the after-action press conference using her warm and welcoming heart like a weapon in one holster and her Academy Award performance skills like a weapon in the other.

Today Grant and Bruce needed all she could bring to bear as the three of them entered a Capitol conference room to appear before the International Task Force of the U.S. House of Representatives Select Committee on Hunger. They had learned that the new Bush administration wanted Congress to cut UNICEF's budget by forty-four percent, from $60.4 million to $33.9 million. Why? Well, as part of an effort to increase military aid around the world by $334 million—in effect sending ten times more guns to countries that were already desperate for ten times more food; countries where guns had created hopeless situations for their populations, commonly with civil wars pitting the minions of Cold War powers against each other. The intended cut and its rationale infuriated Audrey, but Grant cautioned that UNICEF experienced these shifting political sands every year, and that funding from the U.S. government could never be assumed. But this year was the worst yet; hence a need for the big gun.

Audrey knew that appearances like this one meant everything, and she must not blow it for the children. "Speaking is something that is terribly important. And having to be responsible," she told

Dominick Dunne. "You can't just get up and say, 'Oh, I'm happy to be here, and I love children.' No, it's not enough."

Robbie said of Audrey's empathy, her ability to put herself into "the other person's skin," whatever color that skin happened to be: "It's perhaps what drew her to acting, or at least made her so capable as an actress. I don't know if she recognized that quality in herself, and therefore applied it consequently. It is also perhaps what drew her to UNICEF."

Now as she entered a Capitol conference room, the spirits of thousands of children entered with her, tens of thousands of specters swarming the hall behind their pied piper—all those she had encountered and kissed and hugged and dabbed with vaccines and swept flies from. Those who had lived and those who hadn't. She felt a responsibility to all; like never before she truly served as voice to the voiceless.

The polished-wood room that awaited her seemed oppressive at once, people crammed into every chair in the gallery save the ones reserved for the three from UNICEF. The din of chattering fell away as the meeting gaveled to order. She, Grant, and Bruce were fourth up behind representatives from the U.S. Agency for International Development, the World Health Organization, and the Carter Presidential Center. No cigarettes in here, unfortunately. Just waiting and listening, written speech gripped tightly in hand. Around her were many other representatives from relief agencies, all of whom heard an early warning shot against the administration's intended cut to UNICEF by Representative David R. Obey, a Democrat from Wisconsin. Obey called UNICEF "one of the most popular programs in the foreign aid bill." He said a little later, "The cut in UNICEF in the face of these military increases, it seems to me, is outrageous, and I think it's safe to assume that the subcommittee will not accept the recommendation made by the administration."

After three rounds of testimony, the UNICEF trio heard their names called and took their seats at a table before microphones where Audrey faced a long line of white guys who had grown up on Audrey Hepburn pictures—white guys and one forty-nine-year-old New Jersey Representative Marge Roukema, who seemed out of place among all these men in suits.

Representative Tony P. Hall of Ohio, a friend of Jim Grant's and champion of hunger relief programs, gushed to Audrey, "We are so very glad to have you, and certainly your commitment to this issue brings something very important in having you be able to go all over the world and speak. So we are so very glad to have you join this very important cause, Ms. Hepburn."

They had already jumped in her hip pocket. Her logical side knew that the nerves were nothing but insecurity from wounds inflicted by a father who left, a mother who belittled, a first husband who berated, and a second who strayed. But she was more an emotional creature than a logical one.

Now that she sat there, planted in one place at zero hour, she could tear into the cause. She began by stating how helpless she used to feel seeing news accounts of famine in Ethiopia, and children in the path of the guns of civil wars. Then she did something about it. "If I feel less helpless today," she said, "it's because I have seen what can be done by UNICEF, by many other organizations and agencies, by the churches, by governments, and most of all, by the people themselves."

She talked about Ethiopia, where the people built dams by hand; Ecuador and Mexico, where they built their own water systems; Guatemala, where mothers and children taught themselves to read; and El Salvador, where the fighting was stopped on days of tranquility so Salvadorans could immunize their own children. The common ingredient: UNICEF funding in all these places had helped the people help themselves.

"It would be nice to be an expert on education, economics, politics, religions, traditions, and cultures," she told them. "I am none of these things, but I am a mother and, unhappily, there is a great need for advocacy of children—children haunted by undernourishment, disease, and death, and you don't have to be a financial whiz to look into so many little faces with glazed, diseased eyes to know that this is the result of critical malnutrition, one of the worst symptoms of which is vitamin-A deficiency resulting in partial or total blindness, followed within a few weeks by death."

She spoke with the authority of boots-on-the-ground experience. She told them about the air travel in Hercules transports and small prop planes, the helicopter jumps onto mountaintops and jeep trips through deserts to reach the poorest of the poor. She talked about poverty "at the root of their suffering. The not-having—not having the means to help themselves and that is what UNICEF is all about, helping people to help themselves, giving them the aid to develop by allowing them to become self-sufficient and to live in dignity."

She spoke of the minuscule slice of the world economy that could end hunger if it were allocated, just a half of one percent, and it wasn't happening. This fact angered her. "When the impact becomes visible in the rising death rates among children, then what has happened is simply an outrage against a large section of humanity. So, Mr. Chairman, I am here today to speak for children who cannot speak for themselves, children who are going blind from lack of vitamins, children who are being slowly mutilated by polio, children who are wasting away through lack of water, for the estimated 100 million street children in the world who have no choice but to leave home in order to survive, for children who have no enemies but are invariably the first tiny victims of war, wars that are no longer confined to the battlefield, but which are being waged through terror and intimidation and massacre, children who are, therefore, growing up surrounded by the horrors of violence, for the hundreds of thousands of children who are refugees."

She pummeled them with example after example in country

after country, statistics at the ready. She pointed to UNICEF as "our most valuable arm against suffering in the developing world, and a truly effective arm for peace." She told them, "I pray that the lifeline that UNICEF represents and which you have always so generously maintained need not be diminished," and concluded with, "Every child has the right to health, to tenderness, to life. Thank you, Mr. Chairman."

As usual her speech had originated in New York—and as usual Audrey had torn the speech apart like a mechanic refitting an old junker with a new engine to put together a hot rod. "Sometimes she rewrote completely," said Christa Roth, "because it was very bureaucratic and very dull, the kinds of things they sent from New York. And she didn't just want to read that. So she used the facts and reworded it."

"I figure it out for myself," said Audrey. "I do it after breakfast, early in the morning, keep scribbling away."

In speaking for twenty minutes she had managed to take U.S. government representatives on a world tour inside feeding centers and refugee camps, health clinics and classrooms.

A silence followed. Her salvos had hit their mark. Jim Grant then read a statement presenting UNICEF's case from a more strategic perspective. He stated he had just returned from Sudan, which he called a "terrible disaster." He described a new initiative called Operation Lifeline that was about to commence. Operation Lifeline relied upon a cease-fire among the warring parties in the south of Sudan so a humanitarian relief effort could begin.

"I think we can succeed," said Grant, "but at the heart of whether we succeed or not is public opinion." He alluded to the woman beside him. "In the Sudan question, it's public opinion that's going to keep pressure on the two sides to allow the supplies to move. At the same time, of course, we need the support that comes from governments to do this. Ms. Hepburn will be going to Sudan next week. We have arranged a month of tranquility and the object is to dramatize it and to keep world public attention on it."

Givenchy's fashion-plate would be serving as boots on the ground in Khartoum *next week?* At any other time those present on the subcommittee might have balked at the notion, but they had just heard this dynamo speak.

In the question-and-answer session a congressman stated, "We need more Ms. Hepburns out there," and asked Audrey if she might be able to recruit others in the entertainment field to help with humanitarian efforts. She stiffened in her chair at the uninformed question, thought a moment, and said, "Thank you for saying that, but, you know? I don't think I need to reach out to the entertainment community. I am very proud of my colleagues, starting with Bob Geldof. So many of them do so much." Geldof had rocked the world of humanitarianism to such an extent that Audrey could only consider herself a Johnny come lately.

After a few more platitudes from panel members, including a moment of embarrassment when a congressman confessed to having a crush on Eliza Doolittle, Audrey and Robbie escaped the room as Grant and Bruce provided cover fire by answering more questions.

Next, she raced to meet a *Good Morning America* crew to tape a segment about Sudan and Operation Lifeline that would air on ABC the following Monday morning—when she already would be half a world away. Then she and Robbie sped to their suite at the Mayflower to shower and dress for a state dinner at the White House with 100 invitation-only guests to be received by President George H.W. Bush and First Lady Barbara Bush. Guests ranged from NFL commissioner Pete Rozelle to national champion University of Michigan basketball coach Steve Fisher to Bob Hope and yes, to Audrey Hepburn and Robert Wolders.

The next morning, Friday, April 7, Audrey slipped on a purple Givenchy dress trimmed in black and stepped into a cab with Robbie at a side door of the Mayflower for a hop back to the White

House for tea with Barbara Bush in the East Sitting Hall where they could discuss UNICEF in a quiet setting. Audrey presented the first lady with a copy of *We Are the Children*, a 1986 commemorative hardcover by Judith M. Spiegelman and UNICEF staff celebrating the first forty years of the organization. She asked the first lady for help publicizing the perils of children in the developing world. Their quick brainstorm resulted in Barbara Bush agreeing to invite children from Maryland and Virginia to the White House in costume as a kickoff for the "trick-or-treat-for-UNICEF" Halloween campaign that October. Audrey was giddy with delight at the idea and Bush's commitment to it.

Then Audrey and Robbie cabbed it over two blocks for a luncheon at the National Press Club where she delivered an address as Goodwill Ambassador and urged the large room of reporters to offer coverage of the desperate situation in Sudan where Operation Lifeline was set to commence.

She told the assembled group that Jim Grant had managed against all odds to negotiate a cease-fire that was about to go into effect between the government and rebels to allow food and other aid to flow toward hundreds of thousands of starving civilians in southern Sudan. She would be heading to Khartoum in a few days to witness the effort and do whatever she could to call the world's attention to yet another global crisis. The cease-fire was to last a month, and she said she could only hope and pray it would hold.

She described what she had experienced in the field: UNICEF's vaccination program to halt rising death rates from childhood diseases; the distribution of vitamin A capsules to prevent blindness caused by malnutrition; programs to carry running water to remote regions; population growth controls through family planning; and mobilizing support for children's rights by ratifying the Convention on the Rights of the Child.

During a question-and-answer period, a reporter asked what she thought of Pope John Paul II's opposition to all forms of birth control—how did that jibe with any effort to control population growth?

Her response was Audrey-practical. She sought, she said, "greater advocacy for children" but at the same time, "many women must be helped to have fewer of them."

The statement drew a chuckle, but reporters busily scribbled down her response. "Don't get me wrong, we do not preach contraception," she said. "We don't hand out pills and stuff like that. We educate women on how it's possible to space births. Where it's free in the country to do what they wish about it, there's no problem. [Otherwise] it's a very delicate problem." She paused. "I would say to the Holy Father too, that many, many, many, many women must be helped to have fewer children."

Of this appearance, a writer for the National Press Club said, "While some cynics in the press dubbed her 'Mother Teresa in designer jeans,' Hepburn's speeches, which she wrote herself, displayed a sincere and passionate commitment to UNICEF's goals." Beyond that, members of the international press on hand that day understood that retired movie stars had no business in the south of Sudan, which was, without question, heating up into about the most dangerous place on earth.

The Adventurer

Summer 1985. Vero Roberti lived a life of adventure. Roberti had always been different from others in his family of pharmacists. He grew up a sweet young man who followed in the family tradition and became a chemist. The only problem: Vero's passion was writing, not chemistry, and he followed his heart and obtained a job at the Roman office of *Il Resto del Carlino*, a Bologna newspaper and one of the oldest in Italy.

At the outbreak of World War II, Vero became a war correspondent for *La Stampa*, Turin's main newspaper, which assigned him as the embedded reporter on Italian warships in the Adriatic and Mediterranean. Several clashes with the British fleet followed, which Roberti would record in a landmark book, *La Guerre sul Mare 1940–1943*, in which he would document a war that had been censored from the Italian people and was, he said, "criminal and useless fought by Italian sailors against the greatest aeronaval power in the world."

After Italy's defeat in the war, he became an active member of the anti-Fascist navy operating against the German occupation force fighting the Allies. Late in the war he was among a group who stopped the Germans from destroying the Emerald Meadow radio tower as they abandoned Rome.

Then, as a two-man demolition team, Roberti and his partner

guided a small boat carrying a bomb to the hull of the Italian air-craft carrier *Aquila*. The Germans intended to sink the *Aquila* in the middle of shipping lanes to slow down the Allies, but the an-ti-Fascists had other ideas; they sought to "safe scuttle" the *Aquila* away from shipping channels, and Roberti's bomb succeeded. But in the detonation he received a head wound that left him partially paralyzed for the remainder of his life. For these and many other acts of heroism in the war, Roberti—although a civilian—received a Silver Medal for Military Valor and a War Cross for Military Valor.

After the war he resumed his career at the Milan newspaper *Corriere della Sera* and served as a foreign correspondent in London, Geneva, Moscow, and Hong Kong while also writing a number of books for the Italian publisher Mursia. A small sampling of Vero Roberti's adventures included interviewing Nikita Khrushchev in the Kremlin, meeting a young American malcontent named Lee Harvey Oswald in Moscow, shooting the only film footage of the funeral of Russian novelist and Nobel Prize winner Boris Paster-nak using a film camera hidden in a briefcase, and getting close to and writing about Malaysian pirates on the South China Sea.

Of all his adventures, none may have held more importance than the time he lay in a bed unconscious after surgery and former movie star and current Italian housewife Audrey Hepburn saved his life. Or rather, helped to extend it. In exchange, Vero Roberti placed UNICEF in Audrey Hepburn's sights, if indirectly.

Vero Roberti the adventurer became Audrey's father-in-law in 1969 when she married Andrea Dotti. Vero was the second hus-band of Andrea's mother, Paola Bandini. In the summer of 1985, Vero lay in a small hospital on the outskirts of Rome, incapacitated at age sixty-eight by a worsening of his old war wound.

Audrey loved Vero for serving as her safe harbor within the Dotti family given the volatile and controlling nature of Audrey's mother-in-law. Paola not only controlled the family's fortune as heiress to a food empire; she also had been a world traveler as Vero's wife and companion. And now, with the love of her life struck down by stroke, Paola "lost her mind," as Luca described it. She placed Vero in a "shit hospital" and headed for the seashore.

But to Audrey, Vero was more. He was a handsome man with silver hair, and in Vero's eyes she had always seen wisdom and kinship from the war. Both had fought the Nazis, Audrey and Vero, and she could look in that face and revere this man for being what neither of her parents had been. Vero had navigated the war never violating his principles. He had been so brave, as a journalist on the front lines in naval engagements and then as a member of the anti-Fascists fighting the Germans at exactly the point in time when she worked for the Resistance. Perhaps the same day that Audrey and her family had been liberated in Velp, Vero was steering a mine into that aircraft carrier and sinking it to foil Nazi plans.

Such a career he had gone on to enjoy, and through all his travels he always talked about the place he longed to visit, Easter Island. He had managed to miss Easter Island, and now it seemed certain he would never get there.

Audrey and Luca gazed upon Vero, immobile in a hospital bed days past surgery, in a small room he shared with another patient. In short order the visitors noticed what seemed to be indifferent care. Fifteen-year-old Luca sat in a chair between the two patients; Vero's roommate lay unmoving. So unmoving, in fact, that Luca grew suspicious. The more he studied the man, the more he came to a conclusion. "Mummy, that man is dead."

Audrey dismissed the idea. "No, he must be sleeping," she said.

They watched the man for any sign of life. Slowly Audrey grew concerned as well. Finally, she eased her way over and lightly touched the man and, yes, *morto*.

The lack of urgency from staff upon learning that a patient had died or, more precisely, their lack of attention to this patient when he was alive, weighed on the minds of mother and son after leaving the hospital.

"Obviously, people are there to die," said Luca of the place entrusted to care for his heroic grandfather. Luca pleaded with Audrey to find a better place.

Audrey fended off his concerns with a mother's practicality. "Your grandmother had to find whatever she could find," Audrey explained. "It's very difficult during the summer," she reasoned with her son. And that was true enough—the harsh Roman summer and its high temperatures put hospital space at a premium, and Audrey understood how dear that space could be. But to appease Luca, who loved his grandfather, she agreed to make a call to a better facility located closer to the family.

Mrs. Andrea Dotti made the call the next day and was told, "I am sorry, signora. We have no space available. Call back in September."

"No, no," Luca said when he heard this outcome. "Nonno deserves better!" Again, Audrey tried to explain that only so much could be done, only so many beds could be occupied in the summer. Luca couldn't bear it another moment. There had remained a great unspoken here—Vero wasn't just another anonymous patient. Vero was a nationally known journalist and author, and a member of the family of Audrey Hepburn, the world-renowned actress.

"For once in your life, Mummy," Luca pleaded to his mother, "use your bloody name!"

The idea rubbed against every attitude passed on by Audrey's mother the baroness. Ella had preached that her daughter must not "fiddle or fuss" about herself. "Think about others first. Don't show off. Don't make a spectacle of yourself."

The practical Dutch never treated noble lineage the way the British did. A Dutch baron more often than not stated his title with a laugh and a dismissive wave of the hand because it didn't really mean anything. The van Heemstras had evolved that way—yes, they had noble blood and yes, the nobility gravitated to one another, but that was the extent of it. Here and now, Audrey saw her son hurting. Adolescence had hit him hard and he had been lost, and it warmed her heart to know that Luca cared about his grandfather. To Luca, Vero was bigger than life. A hero. And so she yielded.

"She went the extra mile, violating her beliefs," Luca said. She called the hospital again, this time as international movie star Audrey Hepburn. "You know?" said Luca. "Suddenly, there was room."

An ambulance moved Vero Roberti to the better facility closer to his family where he received excellent care that extended his life by almost two years. Luca and Vero went on spending time together. And Audrey Hepburn made the great concession that in certain rare cases, yes, she could allow her name to be used in a righteous cause.

She shared the revelation about Luca, his passion and advice, with Robbie. When Robbie had arrived on the scene and moved into La Paisible in 1980, Audrey—a total square and strict parent—had changed.

"My mother became super cool," said Luca. No longer did she have to wear the pants in the family because buttoned-up, old-fashioned, by-the-book Rob Wolders, the quiet Dutchman, could do it for her.

In the Roberti situation, Robbie admired Luca for his wisdom, and acceded to Audrey's wish that her reaction to Luca's outburst about using her name be kept secret. It touched her heart that he did it, but he must not know of his impact—the teenager couldn't grow to rely on his mother using the weight of her name for his benefit.

Luca wouldn't learn until long after his mother's death what an impression those words had made on her. For once in your life, Mummy, use your bloody name! As with ballet, as with acting, as with parenting, Audrey would prove a quick study, and in just a couple more years, she would master the art of using her name in righteous causes.

Tuesday April 12, 1989. Audrey never felt a cause to be more righteous than the one that took her to a Sudan that dripped with blood, yes, and also with history. "Some places we went to over the years were run-of-mill, but this was one of the truly exotic places we'd heard about as children—Khartoum," said Robbie of his destination with Audrey after Washington, D.C.

Khartoum and the Arab uprising of 1885 had been the subject of one of those sprawling Hollywood Cinerama epics of the 1960s that reconfigured all the elements of *Lawrence of Arabia*—British hero leading a foreign army, deserts, and battles. Movie lovers certainly remembered the climax of *Khartoum*: Mohammed Ahmed al-Mahdi, chosen as the messianic savior of Islam, ends the siege of Khartoum by sending his army to crash into the ancient city, overwhelming its defenders. Charlton Heston as Maj. Gen. Charles "Chinese" Gordon walks out to meet the attackers on the steps of his palace. Gordon has been a friend to the Sudanese and they respect him. As he stands there, one of al-Mahdi's followers throws a spear into Gordon's chest; he falls into a throng of a thousand Arabs. Yes, the name Khartoum did indeed bear the weight of a significant history and unending troubles.

On the flight in, Audrey had been reading the New York packet about Sudan. The mission this time was clear: Operation Lifeline Sudan, or OLS, must make progress before the rainy season would take hold in the southern Christian and black part of the country; the previous year a quarter of a million people had perished in the rainy season. In the town of Aweil, 8,000 had died. In Abyei, all the children under age two were lost in a measles epidemic. In all, 6,000 had died of starvation in Abyei. Fighting in the south between government troops and the Sudan People's Liberation Army had driven another 350,000 into exile in Ethiopia looking for food and, above all, for peace.

Despite the gloom of the reports, on final approach to Khartoum Audrey expressed optimism to Robbie about Operation Lifeline Sudan and the possibilities of giving these people some relief. She had already run herself ragged in D.C., and her schedule wouldn't let up after their three days in Sudan, which left Robbie in his usual place: worrying about her health because she wasn't about to.

First up after landing, Audrey and Robbie were driven to the presidential palace for a meeting with Sadiq al-Mahdi, prime minister of Sudan and great-grandson of Mohammed Ahmed al-Mahdi, General Gordon's foe from the 1885 siege. Robbie said Sadiq "didn't usually deal with UN people, but he wanted to see Audrey, and he was gracious to her."

Audrey had good reason to pay a deferential social call on Sadiq given the importance of OLS as negotiated by Jim Grant. She described the operation: "There were months and months of negotiations and finally, permission was granted, and there are eight peaceful corridors allowing trucks, planes, boats, and trains to get through, with either the government or the rebels guaranteeing their safety." And Sadiq was the government. The fate of two million Sudanese hung in the balance, and all her activities, including ultimately a visit to the besieged city of Juba far to the south along the White Nile, would be under Sadiq's watchful eye. He announced cheerfully during their meeting at the presidential palace that his minister of social welfare and the governor of the large central region of Kordofan would be accompanying the UN team on all their visits in Sudan.

After leaving the prime minister, the UNICEF party, including local field representatives, a photographer, and video crew along with Audrey and Robbie, traveled by motorcade from the section known as Khartoum North over a bridge crossing the Blue Nile and down through the heart of Khartoum to its southern suburbs. There they pulled up near a large gathering of dignitaries at the edge of the lazy and expansive White Nile, its waters having crashed down through mountains to reach Lake Victoria before beginning the long passage north to Khartoum.

A hot breeze blew off the surface of the water as Audrey exited the car and the group headed toward water's edge where a 200-foot rusting barge sat loaded, she was advised, with 100 tons of food and medicine to be sent 450 miles up the White Nile to the besieged southern city of Malakal. This was the kickoff of Operation Lifeline Sudan and the shipment of 12,000 tons of food by the end of April, and Audrey was here to see it off.

The Goodwill Ambassador said a few words, as did the other officials, and after a short delay motors sputtered to life and the barge, whistle blowing, crawled away from the pier as Audrey and the others applauded. But already there were murmurings in the crowd—the Sudan People's Liberation Army had begun what they stated would be ninety-six hours of shelling of the city of Juba, the most important city on Audrey's agenda. She would be there, according to the schedule, in less than forty-eight hours, and the city would be shelled two days beyond that, placing her mission in jeopardy as the fragile thread of peace negotiated for Operation Lifeline Sudan threatened to snap.

They would have to head south and take their chances. The UNICEF party stepped onto an aging White Nile tour boat that now flew the UN flag for a cruise south to the city of Kosti, where Audrey saw off another caravan of eighteen trucks of supplies from Rabak Station.

Their next stop would be at a sprawling refugee camp called El Mereim.

"It's wrong to think we'd go to a place like that [Sudan] and immediately be immersed in misery," said Robbie. "There was a period of assimilation." As usual, he and Audrey had been greeted warmly on arrival in-country. They accepted flowers and heard the good cheer of Arab trilling; the meeting with Sadiq had been cordial and the launch of the barge and the truck caravan hopeful. But now the real work began, and the heartbreak, as they walked into the camp and the heat of the day hit them along with the overpowering stench of thousands of starving humans suffering dysentery and diarrhea and crammed into a small parcel of desert.

Oh, dear God, the children here; little dark-skinned bags of bones, bellies distended, eyes bulging and gray. They were everywhere she looked, in all directions, some in the arms of their mothers and some alone in the sand. It was Ethiopia all over again as the displaced had managed to reach the edge of civilization and safety from civil war—only to find themselves in conditions without food or medicine or hope.

She knelt beside a boy of perhaps five in his mother's lap and reached out to gently take a small ebony hand between two fingers. With her other hand Audrey fanned away flies. "They have nothing left—not even their bodies," she would tell the press. "They are so emaciated. It seems that all they have left are their souls."

She stood up, shaken, and wandered a few steps, forcing a smile and waving to some distant faces peering over a fence. Then she knelt with another mother and child. This little girl seemed a bit better off, and Audrey stroked her little upturned palms with hands that seemed giant in contrast. In the field she would always battle the helplessness she felt within, the knot in the stomach. She was here to do something, but calling attention to a problem wasn't solving the problem, and Audrey felt a deep burning need to help NOW. End their despair NOW.

Audrey the realist took the victories where she could find them, one by one, minute by minute. Some of the older children looked much healthier. They crowded around and adults led them in boisterous songs as Audrey stood there and forced a smile. She saw a teetering little boy and picked him up in her arms, as usual shocked by the lack of substance to him. The urchin looked into her eyes, then tucked his head into the crook of her neck and she snuggled him tight as the singing and chanting went on. Their faces were so black and so beautiful and so thin.

Then she and her party climbed into Range Rovers and rode to a landing strip nearby. They crammed themselves into two Beechcraft King Air Turboprops, those specialty short-takeoff-and-landing planes she knew so well by now, and off they went, speeding west over a vast stretch of empty, sun-burnt landscape. She would record hundreds of hours of flight time in her UNICEF career relying on planes with one engine to get her to the most remote spots on earth.

After an hour in the air heading west the planes banked to port and touched down on a dusty earthen landing strip south of Muglad, a town surrounded by endless brown desert. They had seen their destination from the air, another sprawling refugee camp that looked like they always looked, with acres of shanties hastily thrown together from anything available, whether corrugated metal or cardboard.

Here she wandered inside a hut and came upon a teenage boy lying on a dirt floor. A translator said the boy suffered from acute anemia, respiratory problems, and edema due to malnutrition. That particular combination of issues caught Audrey's attention. "That was exactly the same way I finished the war," she said, "at that age, with those three things. I thought, how strange to hear those same three things."

At that moment a commotion raised outside the hut. She could hear the sound of a truck laboring into range and shouts and cheers rising up. Audrey would call it a "moment of glory for me" as "a big UNICEF truck came by full of food and medicine."

Reality crashed down a moment later when they stumbled upon a family of three newly arrived, a "father, mother, and a child," said Audrey. "The father was the worst of the three; the nurses had to help him straight away. But while we were watching, the mother and the child died. That same night, thirteen people died of thirst. There is water, but there isn't enough, the camps are so huge."

Later, as she related this story of a moment in time in Muglad, her interviewer indicated that the situation seemed too enormous, too hopeless. Audrey went on the attack: "Can we let them die of thirst, simply of thirst? I don't think so, otherwise we might as well as tell everyone to stay at home." She thought a moment. "It's against nature. Should Médecins Sans Frontières stay back home? But there are all these people who are giving all their time, their lives if you like. Ought they to go back home? It's unthinkable. It's unacceptable."

During their hours in the camps, Audrey kept wondering how far they would get as they drifted toward southern Sudan and the combat that raged in defiance of the OLS cease-fire. In Muglad she learned the answer. Communication reached the UNICEF team that the Sudan People's Liberation Army refused to guarantee the safe passage of UN planes to the planned next stop at a camp an hour south by air over mountains near the city of Aweil.

Robbie said, "From there we were supposed to go with the Moslem minister of health into rebel country, the city of Juba, which was totally surrounded by government troops."

Sadiq's promises had turned out to be as empty as those of the SPLA, and to Audrey it seemed Operation Lifeline Sudan had failed as quickly as it had begun. Frustration and anger boiled up inside her at the selfishness of men who would use the denial of food and medicine as a weapon in war. And a war for what? Because the government says prayers to one god and the southern Christians say it to another? Because one faction's skin is light brown and the other's dark brown?

She talked it over with Robbie, and they reached quick agreement: They would, they said to the UNICEF team, continue with the mission at whatever personal cost—and they would respect anyone else's right to turn back now. "The UN officials overruled us," said Robbie. Their decision took the minister of health and therefore Sadiq's government off the hook for any more revelatory bad press about conditions in Sudan. She had been drawn here in particular because of the void of information about conditions in-country.

"No one knew because of the total silence that there was a civil war going on," she said, and now both sides wanted to keep it that way, despite Operation Lifeline Sudan. Two days on the ground had accomplished something; she had seen the war and its catastrophic results with her own eyes. "In fact, I'm a witness, a witness to the situation of the children and their needs," she said.

As the UNICEF team accepted their fate and piled into the UN turboprops, Audrey's temper boiled, and on the flight northeast back to Khartoum she began formulating a plan. Robbie could feel the wheels turning in her mind. To hell with safety—one way or another, war or no war, she would complete her mission and get to the Christian south of Sudan.

Back on the ground in Khartoum on Thursday, April 13, with Luca's voice in her ears saying, "Use your name! Use your name!" Audrey Hepburn did just that. She knew she needed to extricate herself from the sphere of influence of Sadiq al-Mahdi and so she used her name to find a Red Cross plane willing to fly them out of Sudan, due south to Lokichoggio, a town inside Kenya near the border with southern Sudan. UNICEF went along with the move. The long flight would be conducted largely overnight and, said Robbie, "It illustrated Audrey's determination."

Audrey embraced this first true secret mission, and her actions revealed the dangers inherent in travel into the war zone. Detlef Palm, a UNICEF official working closely with UNICEF's Cole Dodge on Operation Lifeline Sudan, got word in the rebel-held town of Kapoeta that Audrey was coming and scrambled to prepare. "For a full day ahead of the visit I met with the area commander and the spokesperson of the Sudan People's Liberation Army, [and] plotted a route that Audrey could take," said Palm. "I probed the flight conditions by sticking my finger into the mud of the airfield, sought assurances that nobody would shoot down the aircraft, and that no guns would travel in the UNICEF car."

Meanwhile, "They sent one of the rebel leaders to Kenya to fly us back into Sudan," said Robbie.

"We flew down into rebel country," said Audrey. "There of course are areas that are terribly inaccessible and haven't had any help yet, and that is the drama."

Or rather, just part of the drama. When Audrey and Robbie crammed into a Cessna with some journalists for the night hop over the border to Kapoeta, each was handed a flak jacket that they slipped over their arms and fastened. No, no, sit on them, they were told, in case bullets or rockets came up through the fuselage.

Much of Detlef Palm's efforts focused on cajoling individuals in the rebel group to keep fingers off triggers. "Everyone was informed that the plane would be coming. The SPLA had assured us of security; it was in their interest that nobody got hurt. I was sent in advance to help make sure that no idiocy would happen during her visit—the SPLA would make an effort to prevent any irate rebel from misbehaving; or that no stray cow would run across the airfield upon approach, and so on."

The Cessna touched down safely, unimpeded by mud or cattle. Palm arranged a meeting between Audrey and Lam Akol, a Ph.D. chemical engineer and senior SPLA official. James Duku, head of the Sudan Relief and Rehabilitation Association, also sat in.

As for the discussion between the Goodwill Ambassador and the rebel leader, "both knew the symbolic nature of the visit," said Palm, "and that any perceived closeness of the UN and the SPLA was to be avoided. Audrey, the entourage, and all of us were treated well by SPLA/SRRA that time. I don't know what she learned other than what she had been briefed about in Nairobi or Lokichoggio. But seeing, smelling, and touching is always different from listening to a second-hand account, and the visit must have made an impression."

She witnessed for herself the cumulative effect of Africans under constant and vicious long-term attack from the Khartoum Arab fundamentalist regime. Most galling of all to Sadiq were SPLA victories in the south, which only ratcheted up attacks from the north and increased the suffering of civilians caught in the middle.

Detlef led Audrey on a tour over narrow roads that included a bombed-out clinic and destroyed water pumps, and she met with women and children in desperate need. At one point, as they sat in a Land Cruiser between two SPLA trucks, the roar of a machine gun just a few yards away deafened the passengers. One burst, then another. "Audrey sits next to me on the passenger seat, looks at me," said Palm. "When the machine gun fires for the third time, I can see, from the corner of my eye, the head of a guinea fowl flying off its trunk."

Audrey and Robbie didn't want to push their luck. They asked that the airstrip be radioed and the Cessna warmed up for the return to Lokichoggio and then on to Nairobi. In three hours on the ground in the south, they had accomplished all they felt they could while remaining in one piece.

Chicken or Fish?

Summer 1985. Hormones had hit Luca Dotti a year earlier and the good boy his mother had known, the shy, quiet, and studious one who was never an issue and earned good grades—well, he had vanished. By age fifteen, Luca zipped around Rome on his Vespa—not quite to comic effect as had his mother and Gregory Peck thirty-two years earlier. Luca took up smoking; he took up girls. In Hollywood Sean had earned a credit as associate producer on a Kubrick-inspired indie called *Strangers Kiss* and now was working as a producer on *Good to Go*, a predominantly black-cast thriller to be shot on location in Washington, D.C. Serious, quiet Sean had also become what Audrey called her "best friend."

But, oh, Luca. Audrey split time between La Paisible and Rome for her son's sake—a son who saw the world through fifteen-year-old eyes. "Being a selfish bastard, I didn't know I had a very privileged life in the sense that I had a house and food and clean clothes and somebody to cook for me and my friends when I showed up at home," said Luca. "I was the little emperor. I thought that life was good—I had my Vespa, I could see my friends whenever I wanted. I didn't have to call home every five minutes. I had basically all I wanted; my freedom."

Never fond of school, Luca began to cut class, and then real life hit him out of nowhere: The family hero, his grandfather Vero

Roberti, was cut down by his old war wound and Luca considered it his mission to visit Nonno as often as possible. School be damned. To pass the time, Vero lay abed and told Luca stories about his life, about the war on the Adriatic, about serving as a foreign correspondent to the Kremlin, about making his way inside pirate havens on the South China Sea.

For the Dotti family, it was a beautiful thing, this bonding of Vero and Luca. But not so beautiful when Luca's school in Rome called and informed Mrs. Dotti that her son had been expelled. Audrey had already worried that drugs would be next for Luca, and she went full-blown mother on him. Full-blown square. She enrolled him in the Swiss boarding school Collège Alpin International Beau Soleil in Villars-sur-Ollon, located southeast of Lake Geneva in the foothills of the Swiss Alps and two hours by train and bus from La Paisible. After all, boarding college had helped Sean to become a responsible and successful adult.

Collège Alpin wasn't exactly Elba or the Château d'If, but Luca, the emperor, felt appropriate levels of culture shock in this spot of the Alps that also served as jet-set jumping off point for the world's finest ski resorts.

"Most of the people there, unlike me, were not there because they were little bastards," said Luca. "They were there because they had lost their parents in war. They were coming from Lebanon, and Iran, and Iraq—the other side of the world. Everybody had tragedies. I was calling home to talk with my mother to tell her how life was in boarding school. The others, sometimes they called home to see if everybody was alive and not hijacked, bombed, or killed. That gave me an immediate perspective. Of course, you get to boarding school and the food is horrible. The bed is terrible. You're living in school, so you're not allowed to do this and you're not allowed to do that. You're allowed to basically study and study and behave and behave."

He studied and he behaved. Well, he studied. When in his

first term the principal called Mrs. Dotti to report the outrage that Luca had kissed a girl, Audrey calmly asked about Luca's grades. Was her son studying? "Oh yes, his grades are excellent," said the principal.

"OK, Madame, please understand this," said Audrey. "You are to take care of Luca's scholastic education, and I'll take care of his life education," and she hung up the phone.

Luca would learn of the incident later and feel astonishment that his by-the-book mother had stood up to so powerful a figure as the principal of an international college. And for the first time he realized his mother the square and the nag could also be, at least once in a while, a badass.

April 1989. Back safely inside La Paisible, the tense and danger-filled trip to Sudan made by his badass mother would filter back to Luca as a placid adventure. "My mother came back with little stories of the people and the rotten food. She never was dramatic about it.... She saw some terrible things but she was always very positive."

Then Rob told Luca the story of the flak vests they were told to sit on during the nighttime plane ride into the south. Luca suddenly understood, this was a war. Appropriately alarmed, he said to his mother, "What the hell are you getting yourself into on the road for UNICEF?"

She went palms-up. "Yes, there are bullets; it's a war zone."

As Luca phrased it, "Her response was like, 'Yes, there are mosquitoes; we're in Florida.'" Danger was part of the experience.

But her message to the world about Sudan was anything but benign. She stated it was imperative to "bring pressure to get the government of the Sudan and the rebels to set up a cease-fire. A cease-fire has just been agreed on now for a month, and of course I hope it's the start of a lasting peace, because after all, what the trouble is, in the world and for the children, is wars—the wars in Sudan, Central America, Lebanon, Mozambique. There are thousands and thousands of children who are refugees. All the donations can be destroyed by war. Too much money is given to governments for arms. Just imagine what it would be like if this money could be given to the poor, and as a result to children. The Sudan, and I believe Ethiopia too, spend a million dollars per day to carry on their civil wars, and I can see what could be done with that money."

During their secret passage into the south, she was able to have more candid conversations "without that corps of journalists along," said Robbie; "we could speak our minds more bluntly to the leaders there, and we did. It produced some results." Audrey had implied she would seek to bring global pressure on Sadiq to stop waging an Arab war on the Christian south of Sudan.

She would always claim to be apolitical, but she employed in the field for UNICEF a certain type of cunning she had learned in hard years with those who had dominated her. First it had been Ella into the 1950s, and then Mel Ferrer through 1967. Andrea hadn't dominated, but she spent years trying to conform to Italian life. The end of that marriage made Audrey determined to become her own person—a person in charge, making her own decisions and asserting herself by managing people and situations.

In 1980 while making the film *They All Laughed*, director Peter Bogdanovich noticed that when Audrey didn't like the dialogue, she never said so. Instead, according to Bogdanovich, "What she'd do in her own sweet way [was] simply change the line. She'd say, 'Oh! Terribly sorry, Pete-ah. I thought that was the line.' I caught onto it after a while. I'd say, 'That's not the line.' She'd say, 'Oh, isn't it? I'm so sorry. I'll say the line—what is it?'"

Luca and Sean shared nostalgic memories of their mother's talent for appearing to seek consensus while doing anything but. "She was the best at getting you to vote for something, and then convince you of what she had already decided," said Luca. "Sean and I talked about the example of, 'What would you like to have for dinner?' And I would say chicken. She would say, 'Oh, chicken is great! But I went to the market and they had a deal on salmon, so we're going to have salmon.' She was never bossy or pushy, but she knew what tools and weapons to use to get things her own way."

Sean explained, "She would always say, 'This is what I would do if I were you. You're free in the end to make your own decision.'" He added, "Then comes in the little Jewish gene, where she'd say, 'It'd kill me if you do it, but in the end you can choose, but this is what I would do.'"

She used not spoonfuls of sugar, but ladles of it. She would charm reporters, or misdirect them, or talk around a subject as necessary, especially when a subject got too personal. And now she turned these skills to diplomatic work.

"Everyone loves children," she would say, wide-eyed. "And even in the worst case, when we talk about regimes, there is no regime that systematically wishes to kill or harm children. And so that's the most important weapon, for everyone loves children, and everyone wants to help them."

Of course, this wasn't the case at all. Many regimes fighting civil wars sought to smother rebel groups by whatever means; starvation could prove an effective weapon. Establish blockades, poison wells, hijack food caravans—whatever it took to win. But by bringing the issue out into the light of day, Audrey challenged oppressors to justify killing children, or their mothers for that matter. She could sit wherever—Paris, New York City, or Stockholm—and put Sadiq al-Mahdi in the cross hairs for policies that resulted in dead children in southern Sudan.

The Sudan mission ended in a way she couldn't have predicted, with a secret mission, but the job had gotten done in a better way than if she had indeed flown back to Khartoum and then headed toward home. She had done it her way, Robbie had backed her up, and she had gathered new ammunition for her campaign to see the cease-fire extended beyond that mere month.

Less than a week after leaving the south of Sudan, she delivered a report to the UNICEF executive board in New York—a large international body with translators—that captured her frustration and horror at what she had seen. She spoke of a population that "has been uprooted and displaced in living fear of four threats, all of them deadly: the government troops, the rebels, armed bandits, and famine. I have seen hundreds of thousands of men, women, and children in the camps I visited, both in the government north and the rebel-held south—camps and now overcrowded towns where hundreds of newcomers [arrive] every day after months of walking. Many die on the way—phantoms carrying their sick, transparent babies—but reaching their destination urged on by the one human quality which is the last to die—hope."

Still, she couldn't let her disgust at both sides in the civil war dominate the report to her bosses. She changed course while managing to continue the attack on the warring factions: "Even if this mammoth Operation Lifeline Sudan were only to achieve half its goal, due to the countless odds it's up against in a vast country with no infrastructure, few roads to speak of, and no communication system, it will have succeeded, not only in saving thousands of lives, but together with the government, the rebels, the brave, tireless NGOs—pilots, truck drivers, loaders, and operation officers— it will have given the Sudan hope and the United Nations will have shown the world that only through corridors of tranquility can children be saved. And only through peace will Man survive."

She would continue to pound her convictions home in a series of April and May 1989 interviews, including her first appearance on CNN's *Larry King Live* on Wednesday, April 19, joining King in the Atlanta studio via satellite from New York. Dressed in black Givenchy with a soft, ruffled neckline, she was slotted into the last segment of his show—the movie star to keep people tuned in. Fluff. She had to know it but she didn't care; the message was the message. King had mastered the nine-to-ten slot, so she'd play by his rules. But in, oh, forty-five years of interviews, hundreds and hundreds of interviews, she had seen and heard it all. Word was out about this guy: minimal preparation, ace ad-libber, and gargantuan ego.

At exactly twenty-one to the top of the hour the segment began, and his over-the-shoulder shot revealed a solemn Audrey Hepburn on the large monitor sitting before the king of interviewers as he hunched low at his desk, his trademark pose.

"Look at that face!" he cooed on sight of her. In no way could King, then in year four of his unprecedented CNN broadcast run, expect what would unfold in the ensuing sixteen minutes.

Audrey launched on King like a famished lioness. Her speech forceful, she began by describing Sudan as "one of the worst tragedies the world has ever known." She compared it to the Ethiopia of 1985 "but it's worse, because it's no natural calamity; it's a man-made disaster to which peace is the only answer. Sudan is the biggest country in Africa. They've had a civil war for the last six years—a war between the north, the government, and the people of the south, Christian. It's not a religious war, but this is all part of the complex situation." Every word choice spoke of mastery of the political situation.

By coincidence, CNN that night had brought on board new affiliates in countries around the world, and Hepburn pounded home her message about millions of people displaced by the war, "half of them children." She caught King flat-footed. Now he fumbled for what to say next and asked what viewers could do. The Goodwill Ambassador said, "Viewers mostly, in this case, can bring pressure on their governments to bring pressure on Sudan to make peace." In several moments of searing television, the world saw a hostile Audrey Hepburn battling King for the floor. When she found a clear opening, she said, "We have the resources, we have the time, and we must have the love to take care of these millions of children!" She went hot on her mic to say the word millions. King stumbled backward through her assault—this wasn't the puff piece he expected, which served to sharpen her temper and message. She spoke of the frail little children, "their lovely black heads almost blond from anemia." The situation was, she said, "apocalyptic."

King included a Q&A in his show. Audrey had been so forceful that by the time this portion commenced, a woman calling in from New Jersey began by saying, "Miss Hepburn, please don't get mad because my question isn't about UNICEF!" Audrey's tensed muscles slackened, as if only this second she realized she had mauled her host. She eased into a serene smile that gave Larry King quarter. After another couple of questions, King wrapped up the segment and Audrey closed with another sweet smile.

"Have me back again, will you, Larry?" The battered host stammered that he would. How many times had she been condescended to in her career? Heck, almost always. But she must court this powerful man to get her message heard around the world at every opportunity.

With the mission, press conferences, and interviews concluded, Audrey and Robbie arrived back home in Tolochenaz toward the end of April, after three weeks on the road. Luca said, "My mother went into Sudan, talked with these war lords, and risked her life on so many occasions. But then when we were at home, she was busy asking me about how art school went and was I happy with my girlfriend. It tells you about what kind of person and human being my mother was."

Intermission

Summer 1982. The apples didn't fall far from the tree with Luca Dotti. Luca's father Andrea remained in many ways a big kid, and Luca's paternal grandfather was, after all, the adventurer-journalist Vero Roberti. Luca's maternal grandmother, Ella van Heemstra, had contributed to Luca's imaginative upbringing by telling ghost stories and buying him comic books and models of Universal monsters like Frankenstein and Dracula.

Audrey appreciated Luca's interests and imagination—the admitted "square" would always require a hard sell for any kind of movie Luca wanted to see. *Star Wars* was a non-starter because of its concept: freedom fighters battling an evil empire. She had been a freedom fighter and battled an evil empire, so no thanks. Been there, done that. *Close Encounters of the Third Kind* qualified in Audrey's mind as science fiction, and another no. *Raiders of the Lost Ark* and Nazis with melting faces? Forget it.

So when *E.T. the Extra-Terrestrial* hit Italian cinemas that summer, twelve-year-old Luca faced the long walk once again. After the usual debate and his promise that even though this could be thought of as science fiction she would love it, Square allowed Luca to drag her to the theater, not exactly kicking and screaming, but close to it.

"I have no interest in little Martians," she sniffed.

Cut to a Roman theater twenty minutes into the picture. When E.T. waddled into Elliott's bedroom, Audrey was hooked. "My mother starts jiggling, crying, laughing, loving, killing my hand," said Luca. "At movie's end—I have remembered this all my life— she said, 'This man is not just a director. He's the best storyteller I have ever experienced!' For the public, Steven Spielberg was very well known, but for my mother it was a discovery."

May 1989. La signora was resting. The missions hit her ever harder, in part because she bit into them like a police dog, no longer as acquiescent as she had been that first year. All the Sudan post-mission stops were behind her and finally she had made it back to La Paisible.

As was her custom, Rucchita Orunesu spent time in the garden prior to the return of her mistress: "I made it a point to bring in bouquets and arrange them around the house when I knew she was coming back from a trip because I knew how much she loved flowers."

"And she mastered the art!" confirmed Luca of Rucchita's efforts. "Mum didn't like flamboyant anything so she had the smallest possible vases that would accommodate five, three, or sometimes just a single rose. That's the way she liked things, unadorned and sparkling in their singularity."

This time, a bug had hitchhiked back home in Audrey's system, causing symptoms resembling influenza. She would admit to losing ten pounds by the time Sudan was behind her; it was weight she couldn't spare.

Luca had arrived in Tolochenaz from London where he had begun graphic design studies, and Sean and his wife Marina flew to Geneva from Los Angeles. It would be an occasion: Audrey was about to turn sixty years of age on May 4.

"It was Mum's idea to have a restorative birthday at home, a simple day of rest with her family," said Luca.

Instead, chaos knocked on the door of the house early that Thursday. Unannounced to Audrey, Connie Wald had flown over from Los Angeles for pickup at the Geneva airport by Doris Brynner; movie star and jet-set personality Capucine arrived as well. The latter arrival placed all, especially Audrey, on high alert because Cap could be described as merely "volatile" on her best days. The renowned beauty lived in nearby Lausanne. Now past sixty, the looks she could see fading year by year contributed to sometimes violent depressions and, frankly, Audrey's empathic nature made it difficult-going-on-impossible to be around Cap.

Surprise!

Putting it diplomatically, Luca said Connie, Doris, and Cap "had very different personalities; one reason Mum preferred seeing them individually."

With a quiet birthday no longer on the agenda, replaced by a surprise party with VIPs, "Giovanna was quite tense," said Luca, as she proceeded with her chosen menu of the day, boeuf à la cuillère. Engracia the housekeeper was assisting. Giovanna slaved over the recipe many hours. But in the presentation phase, in the presence of three women closest to la signora, Engracia stumbled while carrying the dish Giovanna had spent the day preparing, which ended up in Marina Ferrer's lap. The resulting diplomatic incident among staff produced injuries that would never quite heal.

Almost 6,000 miles away, a major motion picture for Amblin Entertainment geared up to begin location production in Montana, U.S.A. The project had begun as a running gag between director Steven Spielberg and actor Richard Dreyfuss on the set of *Jaws* in 1974. They had surprised each other back then with a shared intimate knowledge of the 1944 MGM wartime romantic drama *A Guy Named Joe*. The picture starred Spencer Tracy and Irene Dunne and concerned a bomber pilot dying during the war only to be sent back to earth in spirit form to guide rookie pilots to success. Spielberg credited *A Guy Named Joe* with pointing him toward a career in film; Dreyfuss bragged about seeing *A Guy Named Joe* more than thirty times because of his endless admiration for Spencer Tracy, and so Spielberg and Dreyfuss spent many moments between takes on *Jaws* trying to out-geek each other with lines of dialogue from a picture made long before half the crew had been born.

The experience during production of *Jaws* had led Spielberg by the end of the 1970s to embark on a remake of *A Guy Named Joe*, updating the plot from pilots confronting death during wartime to pilots fighting wildfires in California. Any Spielberg/Amblin production would be big-time, and for this one he sent film crews to cover the Yellowstone wildfires of September 1988 and the Redding fires in Northern California in October and November of that year. In 1989 his set design team converted the sleepy airstrip at Libby, Montana, into a full firefighting air base and flew in a fleet of aircraft, including a Super Catalina PBY, two A-26 tankers, a Beech 18 smokejumper, a Twin Otter, a Decathlon stunt plane, a DC-4, a C-119, a Huey helicopter, and, finally, a vintage World War II B-25 twin-engine bomber (like those in *A Guy Named Joe*) to serve as an air camera platform.

Spielberg brought to bear a fortune for his *A Guy Named Joe* remake, which carried the working title of *Always*. Then again, he could afford it. By summer 1989 Spielberg reigned as king of the movies after more megahits than he would even bother to stop and count. But for the record they included *Jaws*, *Close Encounters of the Third Kind*, *Raiders of the Lost Ark*, *E.T. the Extra-Terrestrial*, and *The Color Purple*, all of which he directed, and *Poltergeist* and *Back to the Future*, which he produced. He carried with him at all times a passion for the motion picture art form and the enthusiasm of youth—he was only forty-two as cameras rolled in Montana and Washington for *Always*. And with him would be, of course, forty-one-year-old Richard Dreyfuss in the role of the pilot who dies and returns to earth—the part once played in *A Guy Named Joe* by his hero, Spencer Tracy.

As Audrey clawed her way to health in the wake of the dangers of both Sudan and her birthday and tended her garden and enjoyed June in Switzerland with Robbie and their Jack Russell children, Spielberg's *Always* took to the skies over the U.S. Northwest. In the story guided by Spielberg, hotshot pilot Dreyfuss is killed in an air crash and finds himself dead, the news broken to him by an angel from the Other Side named Hap. It was a part handcrafted for another golden age Hollywood actor Spielberg and Dreyfuss knew well, Claude Rains, who had played such a role not once but twice during the 1940s. But Claude Rains was long gone, and Spielberg turned to the best available godlike actor in Hollywood at the time, Sean Connery, to play the angel who welcomes Dreyfuss to death. Spielberg and Connery had agreed on the idea during production of a Spielberg-directed film now in release, *Indiana Jones and the Last Crusade*. But as of June 1989, with *Always* in full swing, Connery had begun making another powerhouse property, Tom Clancy's *The Hunt for Red October*, and no longer could fly to Nowhere, Montana, to play a spirit guide in what amounted to a cameo part totaling two scenes.

Spielberg found himself in a jam, with his major motion picture—which also starred Academy Award nominee and future winner Holly Hunter—in the can except for the angel scenes. He thought some more about his concept and reconsidered the definition of godlike in Hollywood. The answer was as obvious as the day's headlines, with Audrey Hepburn just back from another humanitarian mission, this one to Sudan.

Spielberg sat down and composed a short note to an actress he had long revered. "Dear Miss Hepburn," began his typed note on Steven Spielberg stationery. "Being a long-time admirer of your films—among those high on my list, *Wait Until Dark* and *Two for the Road*—I thought of you in connection with a movie I am presently directing, *Always*, and thought you might be interested in the role of Hap—or, Hep if you do the part."

He described his production and the fact Hap had been conceived for a man but "would be much more poignant played, not by a man, but by a woman." He concluded by saying, "In any case, whether or not you would decide to join our family in the last weeks of production, it is a tremendous thrill for me to make this offer. Either way, we will meet some day."

The fuse lit in the western United States burned steadily eastward across the continent and then the Atlantic Ocean. Detonation took place inside La Paisible after a phone call when Audrey came crashing down the steps shouting, "Luca! Luca! Luca!" They met at the bottom of the staircase.

"You remember that director from *E.T.*? The one who I said was a genius storyteller?"

"Yes, Mummy. Steven Spielberg."

"He wants me in a movie!" she exclaimed.

"That's great!" he said. "What's the part?"

"It doesn't matter what the part is!" she exclaimed. "He wants me!" As her words hung in the air, her face darkened. "But I'm old. I'm retired." She paused. "What should I do?"

Luca responded instantly: "It's Steven Spielberg. Take the part!"

Audrey would say later, "We had just come back from this harrowing trip.... I was going to stay here quietly [at La Paisible] and rest, but this was even better because we left everything behind, got in a plane, ended up in Montana, then in Spokane—much like Switzerland."

In the American Northwest with its wide blue skies, breathtaking mountains, rugged waterways, and lush pine forests, Audrey and Robbie were greeted with reverence by the Amblin crew and then met the bearded genius, Steven Spielberg. Audrey found in Steven not the oppressive filmmaker, the Orson Welles, she expected. Spielberg appeared to be, of all things, nervous. Funny how the most powerful moviemaker in the world could end up with the jumps in a moment like this. She should have been the one with the jitters, but like it or not Steven Spielberg was enamored of her. The notion didn't exactly rate the evening news. Larry King professed his love for her on CNN. Johnny Carson pronounced on the *Tonight Show* that he was in love with her. Columnist James Brady stated, "I have been in love with Audrey Hepburn for many years." Former U.S. President Jimmy Carter would stand before Audrey at a gala one evening and declare in his quiet Georgia drawl—as wife Rosalyn and hundreds of others looked on: "I have admired and loved you at a distance."

But of course, nobody really fell in love with her, she knew. They had been snared by Princess Ann or Holly Golightly, or by a troubled nun or a widow tracked by killers, or the many other idealized women she had portrayed up there on the screen. How or why it happened she couldn't understand, but she would admit privately it delighted her, seeing the adoration in these men's eyes, and here was another one, Spielberg, the genius of the day no less, who had clearly coached the crew to expect royalty to arrive in Montana. As she shook hands with the director and he called her "Miss Hepburn," she realized they would have to come to a meeting of the minds, and fast.

She offered a deal to Spielberg: She would be just plain Audrey when they weren't rolling and Hap during takes. No special treatment needed. Okay?

Audrey and Robbie retired to a house rented for the duration of their stay. "Spielberg and Dreyfuss came to this lovely house in the woods," said Robbie, "and they sat around and talked about what she was going to wear. I even went into the little town, Libby, to see what was in the shops there. All they had were hardware stores that also sold clothes. They finally decided on a simple turtleneck instead of wings."

The night before she was set to shoot, a not infrequent rainstorm soaked eastern Washington, including the exterior location that had been specially prepared. A forest fire had burned all but a green patch that would be Richard Dreyfuss' character's "launch pad" to the hereafter. The area was soaked and incompatible with Hap's wardrobe of a white sweater and white pants. The line producer's solution, agreed to by the director, was to sit Audrey in a chair and let four grips carry her to the green spot.

Halfway to the designated area, Audrey began to giggle and then so did the crew—after agreeing that no special treatment would be needed, now bearers were conveying her to the location like Cleopatra going to meet Caesar.

Upon the picture's release Audrey participated in the publicity campaign, where she was asked over and over to describe the part she had played. An angel? A spirit? An alien? "Nobody knows what I am, even Steven Spielberg!" said Audrey. "I would say I'm a spirit more than anything. But not an extraterrestrial. No, it's just plain old me with a sweater on. I played a tiny part, but it was great fun and I loved doing it."

Before flying off to the set of *Always*, Audrey had been inspired to write a letter to Shahida Azfar, a UNICEF representative in the new country of Namibia, formerly South-West Africa. Luca had been among a group of friends invited there for a country visit by the son of Italy's recently appointed ambassador to Namibia.

According to Audrey's letter about Luca, "She wanted him to see UNICEF's work there so he could better appreciate her work with UNICEF," said Shahida Azfar.

Luca at nineteen was more interested in seeing "zebras and lions" than UNICEF projects, but he did honor his mother's request to visit the UNICEF office in Namibia's capital city of Windhoek. And that summer Luca received quite an education in Namibia and one that directly related to his mother's work with UNICEF; just not in the way Audrey had intended.

Throughout Luca's life his friends had come from many countries, and he made no distinction between skin colors. His mother had always been color-blind; the one time he dared tell a joke at the expense of an ethnic group, she had scolded him for it.

"I don't think that was a conscious decision on her part, to treat each and every person in an identical fashion," said Robbie. "It was just her natural tendency, her love of people; she would find as much fascination or as much reason to show her devotion to—I don't know—someone of greater or lesser stature."

It was the only reality Luca knew as he set off on his Namibian adventure.

Namibia had been declared independent of South Africa mere months earlier, and the country Luca visited was eerily quiet. "I learned very quickly: There is a separation [apartheid] still going on," said Luca. "Everything economic was handled by whites—stores, agriculture, industry—all this was firmly in possession of the white. The blacks were submissive. They were silent. They looked under pressure—even sad. You could feel strongly the fact that for centuries they were slaves. It's a blankness in their look, a silence in their behavior, the way they walk." They existed in a void, as if awaiting direction.

Luca was appalled. "I grew up with people from all over the world. There was never the question of race. I always regarded racism as a terrible thing from the past, and at the same time as not such a big problem today. In Italy, in Rome, there was never the need in my family to explain there was no difference between white and black. It was just a fact." But in Namibia, blacks weren't considered to be human; not like whites. "It was terrifying because it was normal to them."

When he returned from his adventure at the end of the summer, he explained, "I realized what my mother had meant when she said, 'Giving a little can make a huge difference,' because I finally saw it with my eyes. It can be a well. It can be a water pump or a canal—something that enables people to help themselves; like the mother who has to walk six hours to find water for her family and carry it back. With a well she doesn't have to do that." The people in Namibia needed such an extraordinary level of help now, not just wells and water pumps but a way beyond generations of horrifying, systemic racism. For Luca, after Namibia his mother became truly badass, and her UNICEF career and the trips and exhaustion and ducking of bullets made perfect sense. From the opposite perspective, Audrey could smile at the realization: My adolescent has received an important dose of reality. Over one summer, Luca had become a man.

Robbie called the ten days with Spielberg and the crew of *Always* "a fantastic experience for Audrey." In the American wilderness of Washington and Montana, Audrey went back to basics with a small corps of filmmakers, getting to know one another and working for the pure passion of creating art. She could lose herself in the enjoyment of work and in her off-hours commune with nature. She found it necessary to allow herself the luxury of working for Spielberg because UNICEF was out there always demanding her attention. She rationalized the luxury of a Spielberg shoot by donating her million-dollar salary to the cause, and that made the Montana lark okay.

In the evenings, Audrey and Steven got to know each other. She told him about the war as she knew it, and her memories of seeing Jews loaded into rail cars at the Arnhem Central Station— she had lived very close by. Or trains heading east from Amsterdam and Rotterdam would pass through Arnhem. She recalled vividly a little boy with red hair on one of these trains and wondered what became of him. Spielberg found the war fascinating and had already worked it into the plots of his Indiana Jones pictures. He told her he held the rights to a book called *Schindler's Ark* about a German industrialist in Poland who saved the lives of Jews destined for gas chambers in concentration camps. It wouldn't be commercial—Spielberg knew that going in—but he had to make it one day, this three-hour public service announcement about the danger of organized evil.

Audrey had made another dear friend. Later, she would receive a letter of thanks from Steven, along with a gold bangle bracelet engraved on its face "Audrey" and inside "You are my inspiration, Always."

She would tell Jane Pauley of the *Today Show* of her week and a half with the genius, "I had the best time. I had a ball. Working with Steven is what I expected it to be. He's just the sensitive and humorous man I expected."

Back at home in September, Audrey and Robbie celebrated her film work by inviting Leendert de Jong of The Hague Film Office and his partner, Michiel Brouwer, to visit. The pair stopped by on their way to the Venice Film Festival.

"Every morning we had breakfast with Audrey and Robert, and they were dressed in their bathrobes," said Leendert. "We walked the dogs in the garden, drank coffee, and discussed how we would fill the day in which, among other things, groceries had to be bought."

Audrey had her established routines that mustn't be messed with. "Boring for you, so don't go along," she advised her guests.

"At dinner, Hollywood was discussed with care," said Leendert. "When I dropped the word 'star,' referring to her status as an icon, I was kindly corrected. She did not consider herself a 'star' at all. That name applied to actors like Elizabeth Taylor. She considered herself more as an 'actor by chance,' as luck would have it, 'nothing more, nothing less.' I understood what she meant ... but still. When we asked if she ever met Montgomery Clift, she replied with a sigh: 'Oh yes, what a lovely man,' and disappeared into the kitchen."

De Jong said that, according to Audrey, if she talked about her career it would invariably mean gossiping about the colleagues she had worked with. "'That was something she tried to avoid," he said.

As Leendert and Michiel prepared to head on to Venice, Audrey spent time in the kitchen preparing "CARE" packages for the road. "We were given two paper bags, including one from Chanel," said Leendert. "When we stopped for lunch, we opened the bags to find our names written on a card: 'Michiel (no butter),' 'Leendert (with butter).' Beside the bread was a real glass from her cupboard, a bottle of water, and an orange."

Another commuter passing through Geneva was John Isaac; John's older brother Sam lived there. Audrey had insisted that John alert her via telephone if ever in the area—a fact he mentioned to his brother. "We had a slight age difference, like six years," said John, "so he always acted like an older brother, kinda bullying me in his own way."

John did as instructed when in the area and called La Paisible, where Robbie answered and relayed the message to Audrey in the bathtub. "Ask him to come and have a beer with us!" she called out from the bath.

Sam drove John to Tolochenaz, where Robbie invited them to relax in the living room. "Audrey came and sat on my lap," said John. "My brother was sitting next to me and his jaw just dropped. And Audrey had her arm around me, and I introduced my brother Sam. She told him, 'Sam, promise me one thing: When your brother comes to Geneva, you promise me that you will share him with us.' That was one of the first times my brother was in awe of me."

Turning Point

December 1971. The former East Pakistan had become inde-pendent amid rivers of blood after acts of genocide committed by West Pakistan. The resulting conflict touched off the Indo-Paki-stani War and created the eighth-most populated country in the world, Bangladesh.

Situated on the troubled continent of Asia, with the Vietnam War raging in all its horrors on the one hand and the Cold War raging with its spy vs. spy global chess match on the other, the new independent People's Republic of Bangladesh had become nothing but a headache for U.S. National Security Advisor Henry Kissing-er as he entered the White House Situation Room under the West Wing the morning of December 6. Twenty-two members of the interdepartmental Washington Special Actions Group (WSAG) crowded into the cramped room with him. Wood paneling and a drop ceiling gave the Situation Room a claustrophobic feel as the most important members of the group found seats at the confer-ence table for eight and the others sat in an outer circle. Kissinger took the dad chair at the head of the table. The subject was South Asia.

The topic got round to the newly independent Bangladesh, which had torn itself away from the iron grip of a Pakistan that wasn't even its natural neighbor—northern India separated West

Pakistan from East Pakistan, once known as Bengal and under British rule back in the day.

Kissinger favored Pakistan strategically, had no use for an independent Bangladesh, and advised President Richard Nixon accordingly. Now chaos reigned in the new country as Kissinger had predicted it would and sitting in the WSAG meeting, he heard words that infuriated him—there might be instability caused by famine within a year in the former East Pakistan. He turned to Maurice J. Williams, deputy administrator of the U.S. Agency for International Development, or USAID, and chairman of the Interdepartmental Working Group on East Pakistan Disaster Relief.

"Will there be a massive famine in East Pakistan?" asked Kissinger in his quiet and monotone German accent that made will come out "vill." Kissinger couldn't bring himself to call the country by its rightful name.

"They have a huge crop coming in," answered Williams.

Kissinger's job required a thorough understanding of Asia and its challenging seasonal weather—just a year earlier a cyclone had killed half a million people in then-East Pakistan and India's West Bengal. "How about next spring?" he asked.

Williams shrugged. "Yes, there will be famine next spring unless they can pull themselves together by the end of March."

"And we will be asked to bail out the Bangla Desh from famine next spring?" He forced himself to use the words the Bangla Desh.

Williams knew one didn't sugar-coat things for Kissinger. "Yes."

Kissinger said gravely, "Then we had better start thinking about what our policy will be."

"By March the Bangla Desh will need all kinds of help," said Williams, parroting back the security advisor's name for the country.

Under Secretary of State for Political Affairs U. Alexis Johnson cut in: "They'll be an international basket case."

Kissinger looked at him coldly. "But not necessarily *our* basket case," he said.

As with all such meetings, the minutes carried a top-secret designation. But then United Features Syndicate reporter Jack Anderson began poking around into the way Nixon and Kissinger made decisions during the Indo-Pakistani War that year. Anderson obtained a leaked copy of the minutes of the WSAG meeting, among other documents, and the description of Bangladesh as an international basket case made it into print and stuck in the political consciousness where it fueled arguments to "unmake" Bangladesh. Kissinger hadn't been the first person to describe Bangladesh as an "international basket case." He had merely piled on. But it didn't matter. From 1972 on, Bangladesh became known as an international basket case thanks to a meeting run by Henry Kissinger.

Seventeen years later, in 1989, Bangladesh made it onto Audrey Hepburn's radar and became what Luca called a "turning point" for his mother, who had read an interview with Henry Kissinger in the *International Herald Tribune* that renewed his attacks on Bangladesh. "His language was really harsh," said Luca. "Like, 'There's nothing we can do; we can let them die. It's so bad; it's so corrupt; it's so poor.' That infuriated my mother—the idea of a politician with so much influence taking for granted that you can forget a corner of the world and leave it for dead. And Kissinger used the term basket case again referring to Bangladesh. That infuriated her."

Ten days in Montana with Steven Spielberg followed by two weeks at La Paisible had wound Audrey up for action and she committed herself to a Bangladesh mission.

While at home she watched news broadcasts with interest to learn about the new non-Communist government in Poland, an effort spearheaded by forty-five-year-old labor activist Lech Walesa. There was talk now about countries of the Soviet bloc falling like dominoes—who would have thought it? But these days she was sending herself back to school, with mornings at the dining table poring over UNICEF packets regarding Thailand, which she would visit briefly, and Bangladesh, which would command a longer stay and all her energy.

Sifting through the UNICEF documents she again came across the words "basket case" in describing Bangladesh, with their attribution back to 1971 and America's old war hawk Kissinger. Audrey was having none of it.

Both Luca and his big brother Sean understood the toughness of their mother. In Sean's eyes, she was like "a steel fist in a velvet glove."

Her UNICEF schedule, a five-week monster, would begin in mid-September in the Netherlands, then hit Chicago, then New York City for the United Nations Ambassadors' Dinner, then back to the Netherlands for the annual televised Danny Kaye fund-raiser. Then she would ping-pong back to the States for television appearances and then head west to Australia.

Assigned to escort her when she landed in Australia Monday, October 9, 1989, was Ian MacLeod with the Australian Committee for UNICEF. "I was certainly skeptical about her to start," said the athletic young MacLeod, "especially since so many at UNICEF headquarters were sending messages about what her personal needs were, what she ate and drank, how important it was to have flowers in her room, to have them [Audrey and Robbie] whisked through customs into a VIP lounge at Sydney airport." MacLeod pegged Audrey as "another superstar out to promote and pamper herself, all in the name of the world's poorest children."

What MacLeod saw at the gate didn't match that expectation. She arrived in a polo shirt, cotton slacks, and sneakers, hair in a ponytail and Robbie in tow. "It was like having your favorite aunt arrive," said MacLeod. "No airs, no pretenses; just an incredible amount of grace, sincerity, and love."

After a wardrobe change MacLeod took them for an afternoon meeting with Australia's highly educated and equally hard-nosed Prime Minister Bob Hawke, then in his sixth year in office. The hero of the working man, Hawke met Audrey at Kirribilli House, a steep-pitched, nineteenth-century clapboard house with brilliantly green terraced lawns that overlooked Sydney Opera House across the harbor. There amid the jacaranda trees Audrey made her usual plea for Australia to maintain funding to UNICEF despite the many demands on government purses.

Hawke had become savvy in part through decades of experience—he had risen to power in 1983 at just about the time young superstar Princess Diana emerged onto the world stage during a tour of Australia with Prince Charles. And now here came Audrey Hepburn, a superstar every bit as charismatic. So, the silver-haired Hawke listened intently to Audrey's pitch, then grabbed his nine-month-old grandson and kissed him for a flock of news cameras as the UNICEF Goodwill Ambassador looked on in bemusement, a smile carefully painted on her face.

Yes, Audrey Hepburn had drawn the press to Kirribilli House, and yes, the prime minister had commandeered said scribes for his own purposes and upstaged her. "Why pay for re-election ads when they come free?" asked the *Sydney Morning Herald*. But one rolled with the punches when one pitched for UNICEF and the episode would prove worth the investment—Hawke didn't increase funding to UNICEF, but then he didn't ask for a reduction, either.

The next morning, Wednesday, October 11, Ian drove Audrey to a live broadcast of the popular *Midday Show*, seen across Australia on 132 stations and hosted by beloved TV personality Ray Martin. Luckily, Martin gave Audrey free range on the subject of children and even managed to interject the fact that he found her more attractive than reigning global sexpot Joan Collins.

Afterward the UNICEF group headed for a National Press Club appearance in Canberra, which would have amounted to a one-hour hop by plane except for an airline strike and no UN planes available. Instead, it became four hours by minivan with MacLeod driving. Audrey would so love the vastness of the country and the nature she saw as they rode southwest through a valley near the Blue Mountains that she began to envision a family vacation to Australia that would include Sean and Luca.

"We picked up Robert Wolders and a UNICEF colleague, Robert Nestdale, at the hotel and departed for Canberra," said MacLeod. "We were all a bit hungry and in need of a pit stop about 100km out of Canberra and so stopped to fill the petrol at a roadside diner in a small country town called Goulburn. 'Audrey Hepburn having a hamburger, French fries, and mineral water at our diner?' was the obvious but unspoken question going through the minds of the two ladies behind the counter whose TV set was still tuned to the station where she had appeared on the *Midday Show* some four hours earlier."

MacLeod's mad dash to Canberra proved successful and Audrey addressed the National Press Club luncheon, where she again appealed to reporters to give their attention to stories about children in dire need. She would target the press at every opportunity because she knew they were growing ever more weary of her message.

"It was a flawless performance, in matter as in manner," said Marion MacDonald of the *Morning Herald*, "and at the end there was a kind of silence more resonant than applause." MacDonald knew how unusual it was for her colleagues to actually stop eating to listen to a guest speaker. Finally, a woman stood to break the silence and asked the first question of Audrey Hepburn. "I think you've moved all of us very much," said the woman. Audrey smiled serenely, and then the smile froze in place at what came next: "So, what was Rex Harrison really like?"

It happened often. Too often. Come to think of it, it happened all the time. Questions off the all-important topic. Questions not thought out. Questions reflecting the cynicism of the day. Like the time she sat down for a fifteen-minute television interview and the very pleasant woman interviewer with a big blond helmet of hair sprayed into place began the session by harping on Audrey's weight and lack of "bosoms." Through it all: Be polite, keep smiling, and one way or another, get around to the subject of the children.

After the National Press Club luncheon she and Robbie prepared for the black-tie UNICEF/National Arts Week Ball, a $100-a-ticket fund-raiser for UNICEF held at the Sheraton Wentworth Hotel. "How many stars would offer to iron your shirt before you all go out to a gala fund-raising dinner?" said the now-starstruck Ian MacLeod.

Audrey delivered her message before a sellout crowd, saying "I am here to speak for the children who cannot speak for themselves. Let us never forget those children who do not know peace, who do not know joy, who do not smile, and who are terribly silent. Children should not be silent."

Aside from such awkward moments as being asked about *My Fair Lady* after laying her heart bare about children in need, Australia proved a big win for the cause. The next stop in Thailand would maintain that high energy level as Audrey focused on the subjects of street children and education. Upon landing in Bangkok, the UNICEF team for Thailand met Audrey and Robbie. The group included Jack Glattbach, the field officer who had recruited her in Macau; Steve Umemoto, regional field director; and Celita San Agustin, senior administrative officer.

UNICEF had arranged a meeting for Audrey with a woman she was anxious to spend time with, humanitarian Prateep Ungsongtham Hata. Prateep had grown up without a birth certificate in a Bangkok slum and at sixteen began a kindergarten in her home to care for abandoned street children—Audrey was shocked to learn that in Bangkok alone, 30,000 girls under sixteen years of

Above: Audrey poses with agent Kurt Frings at Connie Wald's house in the early 1980s. (Family photo; Audrey Hepburn Estate Collection) Below: La Paisible, Audrey's home at center, overlooks Lake Geneva and the Alps beyond. (Family photo; Audrey Hepburn Estate Collection)

Above: Ella, Baroness van Heemstra, walks with Audrey in Rome in October 1959. (INTERFOTO/Alamy Stock Photo) Left: Giovanna Orunesu with Audrey at La Paisible. (Family photo; Luca Dotti Collection)

Above: Doris and Victoria Brynner with Audrey and Andrea in the mid-1970s. (Family photo; ©Doris Brynner Collection) Below: Peter Ustinov, Engracia de la Rocha, and Audrey celebrate Christa Roth's birthday. (Photo by Robert Wolders; Audrey Hepburn Estate Collection)

Above: Audrey's first trip to the field in March 1988 calls the world's attention to famine in Ethiopia. (Photo by John Isaac; ©UNICEF/John Isaac) Left: Audrey's view of dam building. (GKB Collection) Below: Audrey sits by a basin of captured rainwater at the dam site. (Photo by John Isaac; ©UNICEF/John Isaac)

Above: Audrey sits in the co-pilot's seat of the C-130 Hercules cargo plane that ferries the UNICEF team and supplies to the Asmara war zone in northern Ethiopia. (Photo by John Isaac; ©UNICEF/John Isaac) Below: Robert Wolders, Audrey, and Lawrence Bruce sit amidships during the flight. (Photo by John Isaac; ©UNICEF/John Isaac)

Above: Audrey meets with Barbara Bush at the White House to influence presidential action and presents a copy of *We Are the Children*, a look at UNICEF's first forty years. (Photo by Vince Manning/GKB Collection) Below: A week later, Audrey is in Sudan during Operation Lifeline. After photo ops in the calmer northern areas, she and Robbie will travel by stealth into the war-torn southern region. (Photo by Jeremy Hartley; ©UNICEF/Jeremy Hartley)

Above: In Sudan. (Photo by Jeremy Hartley; ©UNICEF/Jeremy Hartley) Below: Oblivious to the fact she is ruffling the feathers of experts, Audrey attempts to adjust lighting at the Givenchy exhibit at The Hague in November 1988. Her friend Hubert de Givenchy intervenes to gently tell her to stop as event organizer Leendert de Jong looks on. (Photo courtesy of Peter van Mulken)

Left: Audrey's father-in-law, famed Italian journalist Vero Roberti, in the late 1960s. (Family photo; ©Luca Dotti Collection) Below: Audrey and Luca at Connie's house in Beverly Hills, December 1985. (Photo by Camilla McGrath; ©Camilla and Earl McGrath Foundation)

Above: At the airport in Bangladesh, a weary Audrey says to John Isaac, "Let me rest on your shoulders, Johnny." (Photo courtesy of John Isaac.) Below: At a session of the UN General Assembly convened to adopt a Convention on the Rights of the Child on November 20, 1989, Audrey looks adoringly at UNICEF boss Jim Grant as he shakes hands with Jan Mårtenson, Under-Secretary-General for Human Rights and director of the UN Geneva Office. Horst Max Cerni, UNICEF Public Affairs Officer (holding earpiece), sits directly behind Audrey. (©UNICEF/NYHQ1989-0746crop/Isaac)

Above: Michael Tilson Thomas kisses Audrey's hand during the "From the Diary of Anne Frank" tour. (Audrey Hepburn Estate Collection) Below: The garden at La Paisible includes an orchard and vegetable garden in addition to flowers. Increasingly, the garden becomes Audrey's refuge during the UNICEF years. (Family photo; Audrey Hepburn Estate Collection)

Above: Connie Wald remains one of Audrey's closest friends for more than twenty years. (Photo by Camilla McGrath; ©Camilla and Earl McGrath Foundation) Below: Prince Sadruddin Aga Khan influences Audrey's opinions of humanitarian causes and the environment. He's seen here with his Belgian Shepherd Arak in the early 1990s. (Christopher Pillitz/Alamy Stock Photo)

Above: In the mountains of northern Vietnam, Audrey dons Tày traditional dress in a photo op that becomes famous. (Photo by Peter Charlesworth; ©UNICEF/Peter Charlesworth) Left: By the latter half of 1990, Audrey, seen here with Vietnamese children, is running out of gas and recruiting others to carry on her work. (Photo by Peter Charlesworth; ©UNICEF/ Peter Charlesworth) Below: With the help of an interpreter, Audrey meets with famed General Vo Nguyan Giap. (GKB Collection)

Above: According to photographer Peter Charlesworth, General Giap "turned into a kid in a sweet shop, all giggles and smiles" with Audrey. (Photo by Peter Charlesworth, Getty Images) Right: Peter Ustinov, Audrey, Rob Wolders, Luisa Mattioli and her husband, Roger Moore, at the 1991 UN Convention in Geneva. (©UNICEF) Below: Robbie and Audrey brave the press on arrival at her Lincoln Center Tribute in New York City, April 1992. (Peter Warrick photo/GKB Collection)

Above left: Audrey speaks to a shy blind girl in Baidoa. (Photo by Robert Wolders; ©Robert Wolders Estate) At left and above right: The situation on the ground in Somalia overwhelms Audrey, whose stamina is now failing. (Photos by Betty Press; ©UNICEF/Betty Press) Below: Adrenalin kicks in when she meets the newly arrived Pakistani contingent of UN peacekeepers and insists on shaking the hand of each at Mogadishu Airport. (Photo by Betty Press; ©UNICEF/Betty Press)

Above: UNICEF team members, including Mark Stirling at right, don Mae Wests and helmets for a quick helicopter flight to the U.S.S. *Tarawa*. (©UNICEF) Right: A teary Audrey kisses the cheek of *Tarawa* Capt. Nigel Parkhurst as Capt. Braden Phillips looks on. The men of Phillips' amphibious squadron have just donated more than $4,000 to UNICEF. Below: On the hangar deck, Audrey delivers an impromptu address to the troops. (Both photos, Nigel Parkhurst Collection)

Above: Audrey hides the abdominal pain she is feeling as she poses with Tito Puente and Ralph Lauren at the Casita Maria event October 27, 1992. (MediaPunch Inc/Alamy Stock Photo) Below: Roger Moore, recruited by Audrey, plunges into his role as a UNICEF ambassador and continues on for more than twenty years. (Photographer: Peter Bischoff, PB Archive, Getty Images)

age were working as prostitutes. In her dynamic way, Prateep was keeping a few vulnerable girls safe. Her ongoing effort resulted ten years later in her earning the Magsaysay Award, comparable to the Nobel Prize of Asia. With it came a $20,000 grant, which she used to start a foundation to educate street children. She was now rightly known at the tender age of thirty-seven as the "Slum Angel of Bangkok."

Prateep led Audrey on a tour of her school and children's center located within Bangkok's largest slum. Audrey told the press of her kindred spirit, "I am full of admiration for this marvelous angel, as she is called. I've seen many of these people. They are the ones that make a big, big difference."

The meeting earned global recognition and increased donations for Prateep's cause. "She is proof that where there is determination and love, there is a way," said Audrey, who went on to other school visits and photo opportunities with children in her two days in Thailand.

Then it was on to the land made famous in the west by George Harrison's "Concert for Bangladesh" at Madison Square Garden in 1971 and infamous by Henry Kissinger.

Audrey felt a certain triumph when they finally touched down in Dhaka on Thursday, October 19. "Everybody was calling Bangladesh a 'basket case,' said her UNICEF mentor, John Isaac, who had been assigned to take photographs on the Bangladesh mission. "But when everybody else was throwing up their hands, Audrey said, 'I want to go there and be with them and promote their cause.' I thought that was amazing."

They set to work at once, promoting UNICEF's immunization program against six killer diseases: tetanus, measles, poliomyelitis, whooping cough, diphtheria, and tuberculosis. This time the information packet had educated her that each year 10,000 children are crippled by polio in Bangladesh and 40,000 go blind due to vitamin A deficiency.

The most famous moment of the tour occurred at their first stop in a Dhaka slum—slum improvement was another UNICEF project. As usual, children had been encouraged to go greet the white lady. "She smiled at the children, and some of them came forward to stroke her arm and hold her hands as we walked," said Cole Dodge, UNICEF field rep for Bangladesh.

At that instant, Audrey caught sight of a tiny little girl sitting quietly by herself. The girl was maybe five, with a full head of black hair. She wore a yellow dress and sat unmoving, even though she seemed fearful of the commotion about her. As children swooped around Audrey, seeking to gain her attention and hold her hand, Audrey said of the girl, "Why doesn't she join the others?" Then Audrey realized what was going on and seized the important moment—the little girl suffered from polio.

"None of the rest of us had taken notice of that child," said Dodge in astonishment.

Audrey reached out and picked up the girl in the yellow dress and held her. For reporters and cameras, she found a stoop and sat with the girl in her lap and held out limp legs. John Isaac realized the importance of the moment and captured it. Audrey called this a tragedy, a tragedy that could have been prevented through immunization. She cited the statistic that polio hit 10,000 children a year in this country and urged the international community to support UNICEF's immunization campaign so others wouldn't be struck down like this little girl.

While in the slum, Audrey told a local reporter, again with Kissinger in mind, "In our part of the world, we know much about you by just floods and tragedies that struck Bangladesh. But there is also a lot about your people, your poetry, and the beauty of your country."

The UNICEF party then set off for the farthest reaches of northern Bengali country, near the border with India. "She traveled to every little corner," said Isaac.

Audrey felt confident, she told her friend, that way out here, no one could possibly know her. Then Isaac overheard one man say to another, "I think that is Miss Hepburn."

"When I told her that," said Isaac of the conversation he had overheard, "she turned around and asked, 'Do you know me?' The guy said, 'I have seen *Roman Holiday* ten times!'"

On the road, Isaac was reminded of the Audrey from Ethiopia—she gravitated to the sickest, weakest children, those struck down by hunger and disease, with no thought to her personal safety despite the rise of AIDS in the Third World. Said Isaac, "She never asked the authorities, what kind of disease are they suffering from, and that really made a big impression on me about how she was selfless, and all she wanted to do was take care of the kid."

Wherever she went, Audrey carried extra positivity with her in a conscious attempt to prove Kissinger wrong about Bangladesh and its hard-pressed people. "One time she was speaking to a crowd of orphan children," said Isaac. "They were all listening to her intently. One girl broke from the crowd and came up to where Audrey was sitting and hugged her and they were sharing a very private moment. I was right next to Audrey and decided not to disturb them by trying to take a photo. Later, Robert Wolders asked me why I didn't take their photo. While I was explaining to him the reason, she told Robert that she was happy that I didn't take the photo. It's a contradiction. Yes, there were times I decided not to take a photo."

Team spirit among the UNICEF party remained high as the tour continued into days three and four. "We came across a man in a village who had a dog that would jump into his arms as he had his arms open," said Isaac. Audrey had been missing her dogs because of their extended time away, and seeing the closeness of this man and his dog delighted her. "She was so thrilled to see that and talked about it later that evening."

Circling back to Dhaka, Audrey and Robbie visited a poster

exhibit on child health, then attended an immunization event in which two national celebrities participated: Actresses Babita and Shabana held infants in their arms while Audrey administered oral polio vaccine. Photos of the three beautiful women fussing over babies shot around the world.

In her post-mission remarks, Audrey once again took a shot at Kissinger for the way he looked past the beauty and accomplishments of the area and "cruelly condemned" Bangladesh. She then launched into a fierce defense of the eighteen-year-old nation and the accomplishments of its people, which she had witnessed by being there. Once again the people had proven that with a little help, like that provided by UNICEF, they were capable and willing to help themselves.

Then it was over and the warrior had conquered another country. "Audrey had no color, no race," said John Isaac. "She went to Bangladesh at a time when the main crisis was over, but it was still an ongoing thing. 'I want people to be reminded,' she said." Isaac went on, "Today, we forget what happened yesterday with all the satellite technology. Today you are here, tomorrow there, the next day, somewhere else. How soon people forget the previous tragedy. But she never did."

Audrey's visit to Bangladesh proved a shot in the arm, literally and figuratively, for a beleaguered country. And she had fought the good fight against a cynical Cold Warrior.

The fifty-four articles of the Convention on the Rights of the Child, first suggested in Poland, took ten years to write. Early in 1989 the United Nations Commission on Human Rights approved a draft of the document, which gave children in any signatory country a bill of rights and built on the 1959 Declaration of the Rights of the Child, which the UN General Assembly had adopted November 20, 1959.

Despite the 1959 declaration, Audrey had seen children without rights everywhere she traveled as an ambassador. In Ethiopia they didn't have the right to eat. In Ecuador they didn't have the right to a home. In El Salvador they didn't have a right to be educated. In Sudan they didn't have the right to live in peace, and in Thailand they didn't even have a right to childhood. She had seen injustices toward children in every country, so many injustices, which gave Audrey a stake in the game when it came to an international document laying out children's rights.

Three weeks after the adventure in Bangladesh, on Monday, November 20, 1989, she sat on the dais next to Jim Grant in New York City facing the UN General Assembly. It was the thirtieth anniversary of UN adoption of the Declaration of the Rights of the Child. This day the Convention on the Rights of the Child would come to a vote. She shook, visibly shook, because of the part she would play this day. After an introduction by Bob McGrath, better known as Bob Johnson on *Sesame Street*, Audrey hunched over the microphone placed in front of her at the table.

"I would like to read to you something very, very important and it moves me deeply to have this privilege," she began. "The preamble to the Convention on the Rights of the Child: Every child shall enjoy the following rights, without any exception whatsoever, and should be entitled to them without distinctual [sic] discrimination on the basis of race, color, sex, language, religion, or politics. The child shall enjoy social protection and be given the opportunities, facilities, and means to enable development physically, mentally, morally, and spiritually in conditions of freedom and dignity.

"The child shall be entitled from birth to a name and nationality. The child shall be entitled to grow and develop in health and should have the right to adequate nutrition, housing, recreation, and medical services. The child who is physically, mentally, or socially handicapped shall be given special treatment, education, and care. The child needs love and understanding and should have the right to grow up in an atmosphere of affection and security. The child is entitled to receive education and an opportunity to develop abilities in order to become a useful member of society. The child shall in all circumstances be among the first to receive protection and relief in times of emergency and disaster.

"The child shall be protected against all forms of neglect, cruelty, and exploitation and shall not be admitted to employment before an appropriate minimum age. The child shall be protected from practices which may foster racial, religious, and other forms of discrimination and shall be brought up in a spirit of understanding, tolerance, friendship among peoples, peace, and universal brotherhood.

"These rights were put into words thirty years ago. Today and now, on this anniversary day, they have become part of the most comprehensive treaty for the protection and support of children in history. Thank you."

The document that had taken a decade to write was adopted by the General Assembly in two minutes. Jim Grant pronounced, "For children, this is the Magna Carta."

Now if only adults would stop engaging in civil and uncivil wars and using famine as a weapon. Fat chance. Audrey's work would go on. Only problem was, she was beginning to run down, to wear out.

Reunion

She had been born in another part of Europe but moved with her family to the Netherlands before the war and spent all those years under Nazi occupation. She feared the green police—the Dutch Nazi police in the green uniforms—and experienced too many heart-stopping close calls. She had no idea her fame would reach every corner of the world and endure long past her death.

That was Audrey Hepburn. That was also was Anne Frank. They were born less than six weeks apart in 1929, Audrey in Brussels and Anne in Frankfurt, but they became Dutch girls before Hitler invaded the Netherlands. As a Jew, Anne spent most of the war in hiding with her parents, sister, and some friends while Audrey lived a less chaotic time until her world exploded with the battle of Arnhem.

Both girls were picked up by the green police—Anne with her family at the beginning of August 1944 and Audrey by herself in March 1945—but while Audrey made a clean getaway, Anne and her family did not, and all but Anne's father died in concentration camps.

That Audrey would end up in Amsterdam at age sixteen living in the same building with the editor of Anne Frank's papers seemed more than coincidental. And when Audrey was handed and then read the manuscript called *Het Achterhuis*—the title Anne had chosen for the book she hoped to publish from her diaries of life in hiding from the Nazis—it simply shattered Audrey. Their stories were so parallel; same country, same adolescence, same Germans, same war.

"I almost had a nervous breakdown," Audrey admitted. "It destroyed me because it was such a parallel—this is where the war comes out. Was it all fear and starvation? No. But ... enough hardship to appreciate everything that I have. She reported practically day by day ... including what she ate and I was eating too. So many things. Apart from that, reporting what she heard. They had a radio; we didn't. We didn't dare because our house had been searched. It's an extraordinary chronicle of an adolescent, her trouble with growing up inside, her becoming a woman. Much of that I suffered from to the same extent. I was living with a grandfather, my mother, my aunt, locked into the German occupation, very limited movement, not being allowed to let off steam. The way she reports that is so full of feeling."

But the diarist's timeline had stopped while the dancer's had gone on. Survivor's guilt didn't have a name in 1946, but Audrey experienced exactly that, and teenage Anne hung around in the back of Audrey's mind for more than four decades.

Their fame grew in parallel. As Audrey began to land small parts in British motion pictures and television shows, *Het Achterhuis* was selling out six Dutch editions, prompting Otto Frank to say, "If she had been here, Anne would have been so proud." Anne had proclaimed in the diary her dream to become a world-famous author from its publication. The U.S. edition, *Anne Frank: The Diary of a Young Girl*, saw release by Doubleday in June 1952 and shot straight to the top of bestseller lists amid critical acclaim as Audrey completed her run on Broadway as *Gigi* and packed for international travel to film *Roman Holiday*.

In 1957 director George Stevens asked Audrey to portray Anne in the 20th Century Fox adaptation of the Pulitzer Prize-winning stage play, *The Diary of Anne Frank*. Stevens cajoled Otto Frank into a meeting with Audrey in Switzerland to add his request that she portray Frank's late daughter. "He came with his new wife, who had lost her husband and her children [in the Holocaust]," said Audrey. "They both had the numbers on their arms. He was a beautiful-looking man, very fine, a sort of transparent face, very sensitive. Incapable of talking about Anne without extreme feeling. I had to ask him nothing because he had a need to talk about it."

But Audrey told Otto and his wife that she would be unable to portray Anne. "I could not have suffered through that again without destroying myself," Audrey admitted.

When asked about turning down the offer, she said, "It's a little bit as if this had happened to my sister. I couldn't play my sister's life. It's too close, and in a way, she was a soul sister perhaps. I couldn't exploit her for what I considered entertainment, the suffering and experience she had gone through."

Thirty years passed after Audrey had met Otto Frank. She signed on with UNICEF and began tying as many activities to UNICEF as possible—the Film & Fashion festival plus exhibit in The Hague, for example, and trips to Los Angeles that combined fund-raising with visits to Connie, Greg and Veronique Peck, Jimmy and Gloria Stewart, and other Hollywood friends.

Before she had appeared in *Always* for Spielberg, she engaged in conversations with Geneva and New York about ways to raise money to feed the "bottomless basket" of a UN organization that enjoyed no UN funding. She heard that Michael Tilson Thomas, a gifted American conductor, pianist, and composer, had approached UNICEF about lending his talents and those of his Miami, Florida-based New World Symphony. Audrey thought back to her earliest activities for UNICEF—the concerts in Macau and Tokyo. When she heard about Tilson Thomas, she thought it indeed "would be nice if we could do something beautiful with music instead of all these endless galas."

But what would the 'something beautiful with music' consist of? She searched the corners of her memory and her heart. As always in such musings, the decades would propel her back to Arnhem. "Everyone suffered in the war years," she said. "What food there was went to the Nazi soldiers. The civilians lived as best they could. The children, of course, were hungry. When there is a war, the children are the first victims. I find that now everywhere I go."

But even in the worst war-torn situations, in Ethiopia, in Sudan, in Central America, as in the Netherlands of 1944 and 1945, "the children have a marvelous resilience and courage that is wonderful and inspiring"—a set of characteristics that took her thoughts about working on a new fund-raiser involving symphonic music in an unexpected direction. Her soul sister, the girl she couldn't portray on Broadway or on-screen, came once again crashing through any walls Audrey had managed to put up in defense of her own sanity. What if she could read from Anne Frank's diary in a symphony setting? Of course, the idea terrified her—standing at the front of a concert hall speaking Anne's words. But as always Luca's voice sounded in her mind: You have a name, Mummy! Use it!

Luca's advice became so ingrained that she would confide to her friend Dominick Dunne, "I'm glad I've got a name, because I'm using it for what it's worth. It's like a bonus that my career has given me, with which I can still do this."

On another occasion, she told Eleanor Ringel of the Cox News Service, "When I was acting, I did very little publicity. I've always been shy and rather introverted.... Now I'm delighted to do publicity, because it's for the children. That's what enables you to have the strength, if you like, to do a lot of things you wouldn't do for yourself. It's the cause more than the confidence."

Audrey's idea of reuniting with her soul sister for the cause went to Michael Tilson Thomas in Miami—he responded with an enthusiastic yes and the three-way collaboration began, with performance dates under the working title "Concerts for Life" set for March and April 1990, just seven months away to accommodate the schedules of a Goodwill Ambassador, a conductor, and an orchestra comprised of young musicians from across the United States.

She found the appeal of reading Anne's writings to raise money for UNICEF irresistible—not that diving back into the diary would be easy. "I could not play Anne Frank, but I can read her words," she reasoned. Besides, she said, "Anne Frank's words—she herself a child—will be used to bring solace to children. It would have made her very happy."

Hepburn and Tilson Thomas agreed she would make selections from the diary and forward them to the composer, who would approve or reject them and, once a final script had been developed, create an original musical score to back up the theme of each diary passage. Along the way, Audrey fretted that the experiment might not be workable, that an orchestra might overpower two mere Dutch girls. But she pressed on, helped in part by excitement expressed in major U.S. cities that agreed to stage the performances.

"We discovered there were a number of passages we both agreed on," said Tilson Thomas, "and I asked Audrey to make me a tape of her reading those sections. I listened to that and started to think about how the music would work—to put order into it, how it would flow. But so much of the music, I realize now, was influenced by hearing the way she read, her voice, her personality. The piece is as much about Audrey as about Anne Frank."

After Audrey's return from Bangladesh, she traveled to Zurich where Michael and the London Symphony had stopped on tour. He and Audrey met at a piano, where he played through his creation composed in two hectic months.

He would admit, "I never expected the piece to be so tonal, so simple, so Jewish, so naïve and adolescent as it has demanded to be. It is as Anne describes herself—'a little bundle of contradictions.'"

And Audrey's reaction to what he had created? "She was blown away," he said. "She had no idea what it was going to be like. I think she was terrified it would be some giant, bizarre, dissonant, horrible thing."

Listening to a twenty-five-minute symphony played merely on piano revealed to Audrey the enormity of the composer's talent, and his connectedness to Anne and the project. The experience in Zurich cemented the three-way partnership between Audrey, her soul sister, and Michael Tilson Thomas.

At the beginning of January 1990 Audrey went public with the project at a press conference in Miami, the composer's home base. She was asked again why she once turned down the role of Anne Frank but now agreed to take on something similar. "I'm just re-laying her thoughts," said Audrey. "I'm reading. I still wouldn't play her. It would be like putting me back into the horrors of that war."

The project to benefit UNICEF, she added, would be an entirely new approach to the young girl's diary. "If the words of Anne Frank have lived this long without it, they will live forever with this music."

That was on the one hand. On the other, the idea of reading the passages into a microphone live and keeping up with Tilson Thomas working behind her produced anything but goodwill in the ambassador's mind. The woman who had charged into war zones and mine fields, who hopped on single-engine planes to fly to mountaintops and stayed in hotels without running water and had recently heard the rattle of machine guns near her ear, wondered if she was heading straight toward disaster.

"She was nervous to do something like this live," said Tilson Thomas. "It was a huge act of daring and devotion on her part."

Flash forward to the tumultuous evening of Monday, March 19, 1990, backstage at the Philadelphia Academy of Music, a magnificent, cavernous concert hall built in the 1850s—ancient for the United States, almost new for Europe. Audrey had passed a milestone without knowing it; fewer than 1,000 days remained in her life.

Within the concert hall's backstage labyrinth, Audrey smoked half a pack of cigarettes as she powered through new limits of pre-performance nerves. Out there in the main hall, her friend Michael led his New World Symphony through the Academic Festival Overture by her personal favorite, Brahms. Any other time, she would have been overjoyed to listen to it. But just now the stage fright clashed with heartbreaking news from Switzerland that had just shot around the world: Capucine, her tortured friend of many years, had finally succeeded in killing herself by jumping out a window of the apartment building in which she resided in Lausanne. Audrey would admit that "I've just been crying a great deal because I've lost a very dear friend." She found the distraction of this night a blessing.

The music ended. Grand applause echoed through the hall and its corridors underneath. Then Audrey accepted Robbie's advice to "break a leg," placed herself in the hands of the fates, and walked hand in hand with her soul sister out onto the stage. As she set up shop at the podium and donned her saucer-sized reading glasses, she looked back at a maddeningly calm, confident Michael Tilson Thomas. Around him his young people, many of whom she now knew by name, busily arranged their music. Out ahead in the dark amid stately pillars and gilded adornments sat 2,400 patrons of the arts on a main floor and three balconies. It was all too much for one human. But. This audience had purchased tickets in the range of $25 to $75 each. Hundreds of donors had paid $250 to $500 to rub shoulders with Audrey and one another at the pre-event cocktail hour. Tonight's gate for UNICEF would total north of $350,000.

And so she knocked it out of the park. And then did it again two nights later in Chicago, where, reported Howard Reich's review in the *Tribune*, "The power of Frank's words, which capture the horrors of war with a child's eloquence, seemed all the more poignant in Hepburn's soft and lyrical reading." As in Philadelphia, the audience sat quietly at the conclusion of the work, and then built into a thunderous, continuous standing ovation.

Audrey pounded a third home run in Houston before the Concerts for Life series concluded on Wednesday, March 28, at the United Nations General Assembly Hall, described by James R. Oestreich of the *New York Times* as "an inspiring setting with horrendous acoustics."

Audrey could count the experience in four cities a personal triumph of commitment over fear, and another million dollars for UNICEF. Critics admired the originality of the concept and the passion of the talent involved, but reaction to the music came in mixed. Certainly there were bugs to be worked out, but Audrey and Michael so loved the experience of working together that they vowed to give it another go in years to come, this time recording the performance for audio and video release, because finally, after forty-four years, Audrey and Anne had found a way to co-exist. To work together. To create together. Audrey Hepburn and Anne Frank were one.

The Recruit

Evenings with Anne Frank had been a gauntlet that Audrey had forced herself through, emerging at the other side a little bloody but intact. The day after that last performance with the awful acoustics, she reported to Ralph Lauren's New York City headquarters for a costume fitting. She had agreed to host the six half-hour episodes of a television series called *Gardens of the World*, an offshoot to a book of the same name edited by Penelope Hobhouse and Elvin MacDonald, with a very brief foreword written by Audrey.

When an invitation came for Audrey to host the series, she considered the assignment to be what she called a "holiday"—the series producers would fly Audrey and Robbie around the world during two months and shoot in upwards of sixty gardens both famous and obscure. Thirty years tending the grounds of La Paisible had made Audrey what she called "a garden nut, like everybody else. I loved the idea."

While she appeared for UNICEF motion picture and still cameras out in the field wearing a pullover shirt and jeans, now she knew she had to dress the part of a garden host, and that meant calling Ralph Lauren for help. Not that she needed his advice; she only needed access to his racks, which had resulted in ego bruising for the legendary designer. "She knows who she is and what she wants," Lauren snapped as Audrey chose twenty-four outfits for two months of work. Yes, Lauren had an ego; yes, Hepburn did too. Reporters wanted to know why she had defected to Ralph Lauren and away from her supposed best friend Givenchy. She responded, wasn't the answer obvious? Ralph Lauren was daytime wear; Givenchy was for evenings.

As she sat for a *Gardens* promotional photo shoot dressed in a few of the Ralph Lauren outfits, she muttered forebodingly to the photographer, "The old girl's tired. Remember that, please."

The next day, March 30, Audrey and Robbie jetted from JFK to Schiphol in Amsterdam to shoot the first episode, "Tulips and Spring Bulbs" at multiple locations in the Netherlands, from the tourist mecca, the sprawling Keukenhof Gardens near Amsterdam, to Hortus Botanicus in Leiden, Hortus Bulborum in Limmen, and Het Loo Palace in Apeldoorn—just up the road from Arnhem and Velp, where she'd spent the war. She was suddenly as far from the extreme poverty of Ethiopia, Sudan, and Bangladesh as she could possibly imagine.

While in the country of her youth, Audrey received a surprise announcement by the Netherlands Flowerbulb Information Center that a white tulip had been named in her honor. The "Audrey Hepburn" celebrated "her career and longtime work on behalf of UNICEF." She joined rare company, including Marie Curie, discoverer of radioactivity; Dwight Eisenhower, liberator of Europe; and John F. Kennedy, Audrey's one-time romantic interest and martyred president—all had had tulips named in their honor.

Other *Gardens of the World* shooting locations in the nerve-wracking production schedule for her "holiday" stretched from the Dominican Republic to Japan. Stops included La Roseraie de L'Haÿ-les-Roses south of Paris; Hidcote Manor and Mottisfont Abbey Garden in England; Giardino di Ninfa, Villa Gamberaia, Villa Lante, and Villa La Pietra in Italy; Château de Courances and Versailles in France; even George Washington's Mount Vernon in

Virginia. She attacked each location with an almost manic vigor, while on the side nursing field producer Julie Lieferman through a prolonged viral outbreak.

"She ended up being my caretaker," said Lieferman, whose role was supposed to include pampering the star, not the other way around. "When she got comfortable with you and cared about you, she had this need to fuss over you, do things for you."

The Anne Frank project and now this garden job confirmed something Audrey could never say publicly: She had burned herself out on missions to the Developing World. She had reached her limits of endurance and the warrior felt compelled to assume a defensive posture against an unexpected threat, UNICEF itself, an organization that was, she realized, quite capable of devouring its own.

She confided to Alan Riding of the *New York Times* International Bureau, prophetically so: "My dream has been to have my own say over my own time.... There's a lot to do around here [at La Paisible], to take care of my life, go where we want when we want, to have this freedom from duties and obligations because, much as I love doing this for UNICEF, it's exhausting and it creates enormous stress. I'm under constant stress, and that I have to one day stop doing, or I will end up with an ulcer. Because it's a huge responsibility. Lots of work, lots of physical work, traveling, fund-raising, but also lots of preparing. You can't just know where a country is on a map. You have to know its history, its problems, what can be done, what has been done. Because once you have been to these places, you have to face the press and they ask lots of questions and you have to make keynote speeches to whomever and raise awareness and funds. So it's a big job."

In the same conversation, sitting at La Paisible with Riding, she admitted something that shocked even herself: "I'm running out of gas."

The clues to her burnout were evident. To syndicated colum-

nist Bridget Foley of the Fairchild News Service Audrey had blurt-
ed out, "I'm scared," and then reiterated of her UNICEF work,
"It's exhausting." Foley's piece about production of *Gardens of the
World* ran in many papers around the United States.

Luca said, "My mother was pushing the envelope, doing things
she never did before. She knew these things were bad for her," but
the need to fight for the voiceless by far outweighed any notion
she entertained to take it easy. She knew she was a fuse, and she
was lit, and burning fast. But she could also see she was making a
difference, as when she learned that Capucine had left part of her
modest estate to UNICEF because of Audrey's work. It was a magnificent gesture by Cap and a surprise, and another sign to Audrey
that she must keep going despite the relentless anguish she felt in
the field as each interaction drained her, drop by drop.

Former UN High Commissioner for Refugees Prince Sadruddin Aga Khan had witnessed Audrey's conflict in conversations in
their homes—both lived near the lake, Audrey above its northern
curve and Sadri below its southern tip.

Born in Paris of a French mother and Prince Aga Khan III,
who was Iranian, Sadruddin received his education at Le Rosey
and then at Harvard. He considered himself a citizen of the world
and had over the years become known as "a man for all nations."
He had been involved with the United Nations Refugee Agency,
or UNHCR, since 1958, working from the Palais des Nations. In
1966 he became the UNHCR high commissioner, overseeing a
staff of 700.

He spoke elegantly, thoughtfully, and quietly. His accent resembled Audrey's—both had lived in and represented several nations. And both, whenever it was needed, displayed an iron will and
disregard of personal fear. Sadri had influenced Audrey to become
involved with UNICEF and now regretted it for the desperate
dedication with which she served the cause and for the toll her
service had taken.

"I think she was extremely distraught to see the poverty, the enormous gap, between the affluence of the rich countries and the conditions in the poor countries," said Sadruddin. "You know, having a close knowledge of the affluence of the United States, standards of living in places like California, and then suddenly to be placed in the situation of the Sudan, or whatever, was a tremendous shock for her. I think that left her very much torn and very despondent. And at the same time she felt that somehow you could turn things around, and our hopes hinged on children, so if we couldn't do something for children then we would have failed; our generation would have failed."

In a report to the United Nations the previous June, she had stated, "I must admit to you that the magnitude of the task that UNICEF has undertaken sometimes overwhelms me and I am saddened and frustrated when I stop to think of what we cannot do—like change the world overnight—or when I have to deal with the cynics of this world who argue is it morally right to save the lives of children who will only grow up to more suffering and poverty due to overpopulation."

Those cynics had wounded the warrior, as had bureaucracies that often, or almost constantly, interfered with professionals in the field from UNICEF and the non-governmental agencies who worked tirelessly on behalf of children. Audrey could retreat to La Paisible and take breaks; those on the front lines never stood down and she credited their dedication at every opportunity.

Out of instinct or perhaps desperation, Audrey contacted an old friend from Gstaad to see if he might be interested in co-hosting the annual Danny Kaye International Children's Awards in the Netherlands the coming September.

At two years Audrey's senior, Roger Moore knew her from way back in 1950 when both kicked around London film and television studios looking for work. Each landed a bit part in the 1951 Coronet Films production *One Wild Oat*. From there both ended up in Hollywood, where Moore landed at MGM and then Warner Bros., appearing on the big and small screens before finding international stardom as The Saint, Simon Templar, in a long-running 1960s television series. When Sean Connery had bowed out as James Bond in 1972, Moore stepped in for the next seven entries in the series, finally walking away at age fifty-seven with *A View to a Kill* in 1985. Since then he had appeared in a few lesser pictures but began hinting he was ready for charity work; he'd done some small favors for UNICEF dating all the way back to the early 1980s. Audrey, her energy for the field waning, took notice from his statements about a desire to do something "worthwhile." If Moore did indeed have the motivation to lend his name to charitable causes—a name certainly equal to hers thanks to his stints as 007—then maybe Roger Moore and not Audrey Hepburn could be slotted into UNICEF field assignments and she could take the step back that her body told her she needed.

She confided to a reporter for the *Haagse Courant* August 26 while preparing to tape the Danny Kaye broadcast, "I'd like to go on forever helping the kids who really need it as best I can, but of course there are limits to my physical capabilities."

Roger Moore received her invitation with gallantry. "When one of the world's great beauties calls you and asks if you would like to go somewhere with her," said Moore, "what do you say? No? Of course not! You ask where and when." When the press wanted to know what his role on the Danny Kaye program would be, he applied the kind of droll humor that marked his rendition of James Bond: "I am to memorize and announce a great number of unspeakable Dutch names." And what qualified him for work with children? "I suppose it's because I'm in my second childhood."

On Saturday, August 25, 1990, Audrey showed Roger the UNICEF ropes in Amsterdam. He observed the way she diverted questions about her Hollywood days toward responses about global children's issues during the pre-event press conference. The next day they taped the Danny Kaye awards final round featuring the performances of talented children. "I couldn't quite believe that I was onstage co-starring with the wonderful Audrey Hepburn. I felt so honored and humbled that she had asked me—little realizing that she was, in fact, intent on recruiting me."

As the show taped in late September, Audrey and Roger stole glances in the direction of Iraqi dictator Saddam Hussein, whose army had just invaded and occupied neighboring Kuwait. "I am depressed by this crisis around the Persian Gulf," said Audrey, "because in the end children will be the victims there again."

After the taping, which would be broadcast in a dozen countries, Hepburn and Moore traveled to Geneva together and she provided a tour of the UNICEF office in the Palais des Nations. Audrey spent time providing tips to the newbie, about the importance of the packets of information from New York City—make sure to read everything before the trip. She told him that the simplest things mean the most in remote areas where there was no knowledge of Roger Moore or James Bond. They may never have heard of you, Roger, but they'll remember you when you turn a tap and bring water to their village.

The way Moore told it in his memoir, "In Geneva I talked with Sir Peter Ustinov—a longtime ambassador—and lunched with one of the great minds of UNICEF, the executive director, James Grant. I knew that I wanted to help, but how? Mr. Grant asked me to meet him in New York, at UNICEF headquarters, to discuss just how I could help. Audrey smiled, knowing her job was done."

Mission accomplished; she had found her successor. As she told Alan Riding of the *Times*, she wanted "to do as much as possible in the time that I'm still up to it." Time was running out and yet, another mission beckoned with another dragon to slay.

Conqueror

Vo Nguyen Giap and Audrey Hepburn both had learned the ways of the soldier in World War II, Audrey in the Netherlands as a teen in the Resistance battling Germans; Giap as a teen in the rugged northern mountains of Vietnam battling Japanese. Giap would always hold in high esteem the people of this region. A decade later he had become a military leader of the Viet Minh resistance against French colonial rule and would help expel the French from Vietnam in 1954. Another decade later he commanded the North Vietnamese forces resisting American aggression in Southeast Asia. For Gen. Vo Nguyen Giap, the war in Vietnam boiled down to an exercise in respect. The U.S. imperialists didn't respect Vietnamese people, history, traditions, or territory. In Giap's view the imperialists sought only to create another colony out of a land that he believed could never be tamed. He saw the South Vietnam government as a puppet of the Johnson and Nixon administrations in Washington.

"Since the Saigon 'government' is drowning, the United States intervention is a rescue operation," he wrote in 1968. "The more the Pentagon increases its forces in South Vietnam, the more the drowning government founders and sinks, dragging its rescuers with it into the disaster. This is the most tragic defeat for the Americans."

History proved him correct. By October 1990 America had spent fifteen years and counting trying to accept the fact that it had fought in and been driven from Vietnam. The war had touched off a revolution in the United States unlike anything seen since its Civil War. Even in 1990 you were a hawk or a dove, a conservative or a liberal, a square or a hippie.

Hollywood had done its part to explore the trauma produced by an unwinnable war that many of its citizens found unjust. The psychological adventure picture *Apocalypse Now* appeared in 1979 and *Platoon* in 1982—between those two releases the concept of post-traumatic stress disorder was defined. The TV series *M*A*S*H* that aired from 1972 to 1982 really dealt with Vietnam, although it pretended to focus on Korea, and *China Beach* about a Da Nang evac hospital premiered in September 1988 and was doing quite well going into its third season in September 1990.

In the States, twenty years had passed since the murder of four antiwar protesters—students—at Kent State University in Ohio; eighteen since Hollywood actress Jane Fonda toured Hanoi in protest of U.S. policy in the war; fifteen since America had watched news reports of desperate helicopter flights carrying Americans and South Vietnamese out of Saigon hours before its fall. Vietnam had torn a gaping wound into the soul of the United States, and by autumn 1990 that wound had barely begun to scab over.

Audrey's personal connection to the Vietnam War took the form of Ella's late-in-life charitable work in the 1970s on behalf of wounded Vietnam vets in San Francisco. "Maybe it wasn't the best idea because back then we were supposed to forget about Vietnam, even—unfortunately—those who had been wounded," said Audrey.

For all her assertions that politics held no interest for her, Audrey Hepburn took on Vietnam as another personal cause, another political battlefield, much like Bangladesh. She found the facts about the health of the Vietnamese people shocking and unacceptable: In the most remote areas of the country, where ten million people or a sixth of its population lived, goiter and mental impairment had hit about four in ten because of a lack of iodine in the soil, the plants, and the animals. Malaria was bad too and the number-one killer of children. All the while, an embargo by the mighty United States had passed its fifteenth year against the Communist government of Vietnam. The embargo had cut off not only trade but also humanitarian efforts by other Western countries.

"European countries were ready to restore aid, but the U.S. was still holding out," said Jack Glattbach, who had first put Vietnam on Audrey's radar.

The poorest of the poor Vietnamese citizens lived hundreds of miles from city centers—they were the people who cared nothing about politics but suffered because of Washington's embargo. The people sought only to survive, to care for their families and children. To Audrey, this was Henry Kissinger all over again, the haves of the First World dictating to the have-nots in the Third. It was time to act. She should have limited her schedule; she really should have. But no, again she packed an agenda and off they went.

Her warpath this time took her west from Switzerland to the United States and a visit with Connie Wald, followed by a Friday, October 19, 1990, address to the International Women's Forum meeting in Beverly Hills. She spoke about UNICEF and the just-completed United Nations World Summit for Children, the largest-ever gathering of world leaders on the topic that had become Audrey's passion.

She would point to the fourteen million children dying each year around the world. But to her the Summit, which signed on UN member nations to pledge for children's rights, meant a chance for change: "People will look back and say, 'How was it possible that we allowed these massive deaths of children, 40,000 a day?' Like once upon a time the world accepted slavery, there will be a day when this no longer will exist, and we have now reached a point where that possibility has really opened up. Because we're not just individuals trying to save a child here and there. Each government is going to be held responsible. And I don't care how many people say, 'Ah, but they just came to New York for publicity, to sign a declaration because it looks good.' That's fine with me, too! Because they're going to have to look awfully good when they come back in two years' time and report on the achievements in their country. And then they'll really look good when they say the immunization has been completed, there's less malnutrition, there's less child death, and so forth."

From Beverly Hills she and Robbie headed west again to New Zealand where she had been declared a "1990 Living Treasure." In central Auckland they celebrated Universal Children's Day in the company of 7,000 school children. From New Zealand the next stop was Sydney for fund-raising events to benefit desperately poor children in Malawi in southeastern Africa. Her impossible goal of raising $2 million in a day was accomplished by ten that night during dinner at Parliament House.

Two mornings later, on Friday, October 26, 1990, they landed in Hanoi, the capital of Vietnam, and were received by Glattbach and UNICEF field officer Jean Dricot. Audrey's mission: immunization, education (given that thousands of underpaid Vietnamese teachers had resigned, creating a crisis for the children), and nutrition in the battle against iodine deficiency. Or, as she said it plainly enough, "Vietnam has had great difficulties, especially because of the U.S. embargo, and that's why they need us."

She also took a swipe at Bush administration doctrine: "I have a vision of Vietnam no longer associated with war, in which differences between governments need not result in indifference toward children."

On Thursday, November 1, she dressed in her UNICEF uniform—a purple Izod pullover shirt, khaki pants, and tennis shoes—and headed with Robbie, Glattbach, and Dricot to a local army base. With them was contract photographer Peter Charlesworth, a tall, curly-blond Brit who worked for *TIME* magazine and at thirty-three had already covered conflict in Lebanon, the fall of Ferdinand Marcos and rise of Corazon Aquino in the Philippines, and the June 1989 Tiananmen Square protests.

Charlesworth had heard that not all UNICEF Goodwill Ambassadors lived up to the goodwill part and initially kept a distance from Audrey Hepburn as a result. But the morning they arrived at the army base to fly to the farthest reaches of the remote north, fog kept the team grounded.

"Audrey was sitting smoking a cigarette on one of the white-washed stones that marked out the helipad when she called me over," said the photographer. "I half expected her to snap at me or moan about the delay, but instead she told me to sit down next to her. Then she smiled."

"I know it may seem a bit vain," she told him, "but I just wanted you to know that I look much better when you show my left side profile. I know you won't always manage that but I thought you should know."

Peter said she then "chatted away, not in the least perturbed by the long delay, let alone the prospect of flying over rugged mountains in a rather old and battered Sikorsky helicopter."

Finally, the all-clear was given and the UNICEF team, which included two veteran TV cameramen, piled into the large Sikorsky transport copter and lifted off heading north to Hoàng Liên Son province in the mountains, up near the Chinese border. It was home to the Tày ethnic minority, Vietnam's largest, the people General Giap admired. The Tày had settled in the mountain country from Thailand somewhere around 500 A.D.

Mid-flight Audrey was invited forward to watch progress through the cockpit glass. The nature lover thrilled to the sights below—terrain that seemed more green, more lush than any garden in the world. How could vital nutrients, or anything else, be in short supply down there in Eden?

They flew into a tiny target in a vast mountain range, and she and Robbie were reminded of Mexico—the village, the banners, the people, with drums this time instead of a brass band. The helicopter came in for an easy landing on a cleared ridge line, and under the spinning blades Audrey descended the steps off the open door and ran at a crouch with the grace of a ballerina and the youth of a girl to village leaders awaiting her. And below, down a long hill, a crowd of a few hundred milled about, waiting. Here and now she experienced only exhilaration for the job without the fear or frustration or weariness that had plagued her back home.

In the midst of the village, which was composed of thatched-roof bamboo huts, she exchanged the usual greetings and received the usual flowers. An umbrella popped open and someone held it above her head to shield her from the heat of the midday sun. Moments like these overwhelmed her. Too many faces, too many people to meet and hands to shake. Too many words she couldn't understand spoken in her ear by locals, too much commotion—this time up-tempo traditional dances performed by local teens. She had learned to remain poised, smile, and just do her best to keep up. Through all the villages in all the countries on all the continents, her best had been good enough so far.

Once again, the locals had no idea who she was, but they loved that something different was happening, an outsider come to visit, a helicopter, excitement, drumbeats, and best of all, UNICEF caring about their commune in their mountain valley.

Children continued to hand her flowers until she held a bouquet too grand even for hands she had always considered to be giant. These children seemed happy enough, but already she could see that the poverty was extreme, as if she had gone back 100 years in time during the length of that helicopter ride.

Inside an immaculately kept communal building, refreshments had been provided along with local fruit. Here she said for the cameras, "This is a great honor for me to be here, and I was told yesterday that I was going to see one of the most beautiful places in Vietnam." She paused for translation and added, "—and also the hardest to get to!" She smiled and made the motion of a spinning helicopter blade. "But I've come to Vietnam not to speak, but to learn."

UNICEF team member Jean Dricot led her on a tour of the village. First, she saw the commune's water system that captured mountain water and channeled it into village huts using gravity, flumes, and tubes of bamboo. The people had constructed the elaborate system with know-how provided by UNICEF. "Marvelous," Audrey murmured with a smile.

Then she visited the school and performed for the cameras, handing out UNICEF lesson books and book bags to elementary school-age students who showed pride and excitement to receive them.

In the next communal building, the health center, she received a traditional skirt and blouse of the Tày people. When she said, yes, she would be honored to wear the outfit, excitement mounted and several girls and women, also dressed traditionally, helped Audrey slip the garments over her clothes.

For the woman who had spent decades concerned about what she wore and how she looked, dressing Tày was quite a concession, and she waited patiently as the women fussed until the garments were fastened and final.

"Now I want a baby on my back," Audrey kidded when dressed as a Tày woman. The girls and women surrounding her chattered with great energy about the white lady dressed in their attire.

She knew the resulting photos would be newsworthy and caught Charlesworth's eye, gave him a wink, and nodded toward the door. He said, "I left the wooden house and, looking around, quickly worked out where the next shot should be. I turned to the left down the village pathway to wait."

From his chosen spot, Charlesworth's heart sank: "A crowd of minders, Vietnamese health care workers and UNICEF staffers poured out of the house and crowded around Audrey as she came out. I inwardly cursed, thinking that any kind of meaningful picture was surely gone. She stopped, looked around, and instantly turned into director mode.... She turned to see me waiting, nodded, and then facing the throng spilling out of the house, she held up her hands and shooed all of the grownups back inside."

Audrey called, "This is about the children; please can all of the grownups wait here!"

Charlesworth said, "She grabbed the hands of two girls and led all of the kids down the path towards me. The perfect long lens shot of the Pied Piper with her gaggle of delighted children."

Resulting photos of Audrey Hepburn dressed in Tày clothing and leading a procession of hundreds of young villagers down the hill and along a valley path back toward the helicopter would be among the most famous ever taken during her UNICEF years.

She would say later, "To me, I was very touched because somehow it was symbolic because not only had they received me as a woman and a mother, but I felt as though by putting the dress on me they were entrusting me and regarding me a little bit as if I was one of them, therefore, a Vietnamese mother."

That evening, back at the hotel in Hanoi, Audrey and Robbie sat with Jack Glattbach and Tarique Farooqui, UNICEF Field Representative for Vietnam. Glattbach explained to Audrey "how UNICEF was lobbying governments to adopt policies which really help children, often against the effects of 'structural adjustment' policies, and Vietnam's special problems with aid, and more."

Audrey riveted her attention on the conversation because this was her private secret mission: Calling attention to outrageous U.S. policy intended to force a country to submit that had long ago been driven to its knees and was too proud to reveal it. Of course, she couldn't address the Bush doctrine directly, but was there a way to call attention to a kinder, gentler Vietnam that no longer posed a threat to the United States?

When the UNICEF men asked if Audrey could highlight UNICEF's accomplishments in the mountain country, yet stress how much more could be done, she hesitated because she didn't want to fumble the opportunity—the stakes were too high. She said she wanted to get it just right "and if I don't understand it, I can't speak it."

Glattbach said, "The next morning Philippe [Decaux, UNICEF cameramen] heard that one of the big U.S. TV networks was interested in footage of the visit, but it had to include a strong element of Audrey talking 'straight to camera.'" The UNICEF party was already back in the field on a visit to another village when the tip came in, and Audrey seized the soapbox moment to get word out about UNICEF's goals and the real Vietnam.

The camera team sat her by the doorway of a wooden health center with Glattbach beside the camera, prompting her with questions. First, he asked why she had come to Vietnam.

"Well, the real purpose of course is to come and see their children and to see for myself what their needs are," she responded. "But the purpose is also to come and understand better a country which I know a bit about, but not enough. And I think the rest of the world doesn't know enough about Vietnam. There's been a silence about Vietnam and perhaps therefore some misunderstanding. Vietnam is a country, and a country with a lot of children. And that's an image I'd like to take home."

"What would you say has impressed you since you've been here?" Glattbach asked.

"Well, yesterday, we went into the mountains quite far to a rural area where not many people can get to because it's so far away. But unlike so many other small rural areas where I've been to in other countries, it's rural but not forgotten. And that was terribly encouraging because there is a health center. There is a women's education center. There is a school. And they lack of course. The school lacks books, which UNICEF is trying to provide. They lack medicines, which UNICEF is providing. But the infrastructure is there. What's extraordinary about Vietnam and its people is that unlike some of our countries, there may be a deficit of resources but not of will. That is not always true about our countries. We have the resources but not always enough human will."

"What will you do when you get home?" Jack asked.

"Tell people about the real Vietnam, not the one we associate perhaps too much with war—with the tragedy of war. But tell them about their courage, about their ethic. Children really do come first in this country, perhaps more than any other country I've visited."

Glattbach would say later, "In one take, watched by a few hundred Vietnamese villagers and with absolutely no 'fluffs,' she spoke four minutes to camera and covered every major point from the discussion she 'didn't understand.' It was one of the best summaries of what UNICEF is doing I've ever heard."

ABC News ran the interview in prime time in the United States and it got, said Glattbach, "incredible TV pickup around the world."

That day she visited a number of villages and their health centers, community centers, schools, women's education centers, and women's organizations. She pumped water from a new well, witnessed immunizations, and held babies—quiet babies, crying babies, and screaming babies. "I love to hold babies," she admitted at one point.

The people seemed happier here than in any other country she visited on any mission; really delighted at the attention she paid them. The children had a vitality missing in so many other parts of the world, and she gained energy from every stop along the way. And yet, their poverty stunned her.

"The country is suffering with such hardship, which is due to many reasons—forty years of war," she would tell Joan Lunden a month later on *Good Morning America*. "They're isolated from the world. They're cut off. There's no economy to speak of for whatever reasons there are. The result is always that the children are the ones who are undernourished, and many areas of the country, especially in the north—in the mountains, in the rural distant areas, which are very hard to reach—people are really suffering enormous hardship."

The mission culminated with a meeting between the UNICEF Goodwill Ambassador and Gen. Vo Nguyen Giap, hero of three wars. Like Ulysses S. Grant of the American Civil War, Giap had thrown as many men as had been needed against his enemies, accepted horrendous casualties, and prevailed to become a national hero and one of the most revered generals in history. Now gray-haired but still wearing a red-trimmed green army uniform, he served as deputy prime minister of his country.

Peter Charlesworth snapped pictures of the meeting between the dignitaries and through his viewfinder saw that "the great warrior, often credited as having masterminded victory over the United States in the Vietnam War, turned into a kid in a sweet-shop, all giggles and smiles. Audrey's warmth instantly charmed him."

Audrey felt the same way—she found Giap a quiet man with a friendly face, hardly the ramrod-straight commander she expected. When they stood together and shook hands, she towered over him.

She told the general through an interpreter about her visit to the far north, to Hoàng Liên Son province, and all she had seen, and about being dressed as a traditional Tày woman.

Giap smiled warmly and wistfully. He said in his language, "This is something most moving to me since you have come all the way from a very distant place and this is a very isolated province of my country." He spoke carefully to the interpreter seated behind them. The young man relayed the message to Audrey, and then Giap went on. "I have gotten very deeply attached to the mountains and people. I learned to speak the language of the minority people who presented you with the traditional dress. And we thank you very much for visiting this place." He paused and added, "The most difficult part of my life was spent up there in the mountains and I know how difficult life is there. But I love deeply the nature, the mountains, and the land. And the people are very good at heart."

Audrey said in her best Audrey Hepburn, "They are very courageous people. I have on my many missions for UNICEF before visited rural areas in the mountains because invariably the poorest are also often forgotten, which in your case is not true." She commended him for what the mountain people *did* have because he had encouraged UNICEF to help, which resulted in health centers, schools, and so much more for the benefit of the children and their mothers.

He smiled again, a bashful, dazzling smile. "On behalf of the people of this country, particularly the people in the mountains and the children, I want to thank you very much for your visit." She couldn't have asked for a better conclusion to a mission.

"We have both fought many battles for children," the UNICEF warrior told the general. "I just hope we will be as triumphant as you have been, and conquer all the children's diseases."

One other Audrey-as-director moment struck Charlesworth. "When she suggested that we go outside for a photo on the steps of the rather formal government house, the Vietnamese security guys were all shaking their heads and mumbling apprehensively to the effect that this was not on the schedule. But the general was having none of it. He smiled and said, 'What a good idea!' and he took Audrey's arm and led her to the front door."

The next day she held a press conference in Bangkok to debrief the mission. "I would like to give a much more accessible, human picture of Vietnam than just the Vietnam War," she said. "It's a ghost that has to be laid to rest."

"Yes, she did get involved a little bit in politics, but in a way which I feel came off very well," said Geneva PR liaison Christa Roth. "That was always her doing—that never came from us [at UNICEF]. Her speeches that they wrote in New York never had anything like that in them." Roth laughed and added, "And that's why she so often wrote her own speeches."

Her inability to toe the UNICEF mark—or unwillingness to always do things the UNICEF way—became an accepted fact of life for an organization that had grown to rely on her fund-raising ability. "Sometimes it annoyed her, all the little bureaucracy we have to go through between you and UNICEF and the local government," said John Isaac. "She was saying that in many ways; [there is] so much red tape here and there. A lot of the time she would want to just go and do it without all this bullshit. I was very impressed with how honest she was and straightforward. Nothing was roundabout and all that fake politeness."

Just a day after Audrey said the ghost of the war should be put to rest and concluded a very public, very successful visit to a belea-guered but proud country, U.S. Senator Claiborne Pell, chairman of the Senate Foreign Relations Committee, joined with seven of his colleagues in echoing Audrey's pronouncement about the trade embargo. The senators sent a bipartisan letter to President Bush calling for its end. That wouldn't happen for another three years, and only after a change of administration that brought in Bill Clin-ton. But Audrey had made her point and called attention to an outdated relic of the Cold War that had become an embarrassment of U.S. policy at the expense of millions of innocents.

Jack Glattbach said, "Audrey belongs in the ranks of our great Goodwill Ambassadors—Ustinov, Attenborough, and all. Beyond the talents and skills which have brought them fame, they all have special qualities of intelligence and humility, which can translate major issues of the human condition into terms we can all under-stand. Great human beings."

This Iron Will

Beginning in 1971 when the Pakistani army tried to quell a Bengali uprising that led to the founding of Bangladesh and the slaughter of more than a million people, while many millions more fled Pakistan, Prince Sadruddin Aga Khan—articulate, poised, and fearless—waded headlong into the refugee situation as an advocate for those in peril. Crises drew him like a magnet and there he would be, boots on the ground in some beleaguered country standing in front of a group of refugees, demanding rights for the "stateless."

He left his post as high commissioner for refugees in 1977 but retained his passion for those displaced by dictatorship and war. He became especially sensitive to Western powers meddling into the affairs of the poorest countries.

For most of his life, Sadri kept a residence in the Swiss village of Collonge-Bellerive near the southern tip of Lake Léman. He was thus Audrey's "neighbor" in what mutual friend Anna Cataldi called "a small society that lived on the lake." But that lake was vast and separated Tolochenaz to the north from Bellerive to the south by a forty-five-minute drive each way—only fifteen minutes by speed boat, if one was handy.

"Whenever we had an opportunity of getting together, we would meet at either her place or my place," said Sadruddin. "And we used to see each other quite frequently, time permitting."

Over the course of their friendship, Sadri's views on super-powers imposing their will on poor countries and his passion for championing underdogs became a part of Audrey's belief system. He saw in the world a disturbing trend toward the United States and Soviet Union and radical leaders alike stirring up trouble, displacing populations, and in that process destroying family units. In fact, the prince saw that the refugee situation would curse future generations; the scenario continues to play out in the 2020s all around the Western world as fleeing Third World populations flood into the West, bringing reactionary right-wing leaders to power and closing borders to the people most in need of sanctuary from terror.

The prince wrote in 1981 that it was "my considered opinion that if we are to succeed to spare future generations the spectre of millions of uprooted people, more is required than reports and resolutions, however pertinent and useful they may be."

So effective was Prince Sadruddin in educating Audrey on social issues that she would go on to make almost identical statements to the press and stand firm on issues of social justice and human rights. Audrey also shared Sadri's dim view of the Western world dominating Third World countries for economic or political gain.

The personalities of Audrey and Sadri meshed perfectly. "He had a great sense of humor and was fun-loving," said his colleague Diana Miserez of the United Nations Refugee Office, who would go on to become his biographer. At the same time, she added, "He was extremely broad-minded, as exemplified by his work methods—consulting everyone concerned with a situation, even the most junior."

His mentorship gave Audrey's views remarkable depth. "The Third World is a term I don't like very much, because we're all one world," she said. Like Sadri, she insisted on use of a different term: Developing World. They didn't always talk politics. The two globe-traveling friends held in common a passion for gardening, a love of animals, and a growing concern that the industrialized countries were slowly killing the environment and putting the planet in peril.

"Sadri was a very good person," said Anna Cataldi. "That's why when Sadri tried to persuade Audrey to do something [with UNICEF], she took that seriously because she respected Sadri. At first she didn't want to; she was reluctant."

"We exchanged views quite frequently on her work, on UNICEF, on the UN, her trips, her impressions from the field, contacts with children and all that," said Sadri.

She found what she had witnessed in the field terrifying. Children remained the focus, but by now she mentioned the environment often, and sought to raise awareness around the fact that based on where she had been and what she had seen in the past three years, humans were systematically killing their planet. She had heard Sadri speak of it for many years, and now she knew he was right.

"She was very close to nature, which is not something a lot of show business people have," Sadri stated. "She really was an environmentalist, a conservationist at heart, and I think the poverty and devastation that she saw in Africa with all the forests gone to waste, the enormous erosion of soil in places where she went for the kids, was something that profoundly affected her as an environmentalist."

Audrey saw the rape of the planet as a spiritual issue because of the importance of nature in her belief system. She had grown up in the Netherlands with the Calvinist van Heemstras and with Ella's Christian Science, elements of which she had long ago incorporated into her own belief system. But organized religion, she said, "has no importance at all to me." She described herself as aligning with animism, with a belief in the connectedness of all things. She saw God especially in nature, and the lack of connection of humans with their planet alarmed and frightened her.

Luca said, "My mother understood the link between man, nature, ecology; everything is connected. Beyond the wars there is a disruption of the natural order. She always said to me, 'Nature is above the humans. We are not ruling the planet; we have to be *with* the planet.'" She sensed time running out for landmarks like the Great Barrier Reef and built Queensland into her dreamed-of trip to Australia with the boys.

To the United States Congress in Washington, she stated: "We are dealing with a far more ominous threat than sickness and death. We are dealing with the dark side of humanity—selfishness, avarice, aggression. All this has already polluted our skies, emptied our oceans, destroyed our forests, and extinguished thousands of beautiful animals. Are our children next? ... It is no longer enough to vaccinate them or give them food and water and only cure the symptoms of man's tendency to destroy everything we hold dear. Whether it be famine in Ethiopia, excruciating poverty in Guatemala and Honduras, civil strife in El Salvador, or ethnic massacre in the Sudan, I saw but one glaring truth: These are not natural disasters but man-made tragedies for which there is only one man-made solution—peace."

At the end of 1990 she said, "Some twenty years ago, I think people thought we were rather flaky when we talked about acid rain and the planet and the destruction of our world. Now, politicians, governments are desperately having summits of their own to save the planet."

But by this stage in Audrey's UNICEF career, something besides her passion struck Prince Sadruddin—he had become alarmed by what he perceived to be a decline in her vitality. "If she hadn't had this strength, this inner strength, this philosophy, I don't think she would have kept going. She would have just given up." He saw her now as "a very frail person" with, unquestionably, "this iron will."

Vietnam had been a success on many levels, but she began 1991 by guarding her health. Robbie had been gung ho for UNICEF while Audrey was gung ho; now she hung back and he followed her lead. Neither had any intention of hurrying into the field again, which didn't mean she would step back from fund-raising for UNICEF. Quite the contrary.

The year 1991 would become Audrey Hepburn's renaissance in U.S. popular culture. She started the year by shooting a PBS *Great Performances* episode called "The Fred Astaire Songbook" in which she served as host for a loving look at not Astaire's dancing, but rather his light but pleasing singing voice as he performed songs by the Gershwins, Cole Porter, Irving Berlin, Jerome Kern, and Harold Arlen, as seen in clips from many of his popular Hollywood pictures.

Audrey and Robbie had planned to return to the States for several UNICEF engagements, which coincided with the outbreak of the Gulf War that resulted from the aggressions of Iraq's dictatorial leader, Saddam Hussein. Flying commercial became an issue because as Robbie said, "There was great fear of terrorism."

The couple decided to proceed with their plans and fly to Los Angeles for visits with Sean and Connie. From there they expected to begin UNICEF activities. "We were due to fly to Atlanta on a commercial airline," said Robbie. "But we were much more concerned than most people were about this being the absolute schism between the Arab and non-Arab world. We had a dark view of the whole situation."

At Connie's house they met up with Anne Cox Chambers, chairperson of an upcoming $150-a-plate, black-tie UNICEF benefit at the Swissôtel in Atlanta that would feature former President Jimmy Carter. Chambers offered to fly Audrey and Robbie on her private jet, and because of the security issue, they accepted the offer. They arrived Monday, February 18, 1991, so that the next evening Audrey could hear Carter's pronouncement, "I have loved and admired you at a distance" as he introduced Audrey to speak, and then handed her the 1990 Child Survival Award.

On Thursday, February 28, she and Larry Bruce visited the Pier 1 Imports Houston Street store in Fort Worth, Texas, and received a check in the amount of $772,675.94 from Pier 1 President Marvin Girouard. Pier 1 had been selling UNICEF greeting cards in its 570 U.S. and Canadian stores, and this check represented the take from that effort. She accepted the large presentation check, looked down at it, and murmured, "Three-quarters of a million dollars!" Then she giggled. "Regardless of what you think about movie stars, I've never held a check for three-quarters of a million dollars. Think of what this will do!" Then she told them exactly what it would do: buy vitamin A to prevent blindness and distribute oral rehydration therapy to fend off dehydration—just a few pennies could protect a child from each, and here was three-quarters of a million dollars.

Saturday, March 2, in Dallas she received the U.S.A. Film Festival's Master Screen Artist Award at another UNICEF fund-raising dinner. Then she and Robbie flew to New York City where she fulfilled a charity auction commitment to a "Breakfast at Tiffany's" fantasy prize where she popped into Tiffany's and shared a Danish with the lucky winner. The next day Cartier honored her for the PBS premiere of *Gardens of the World*, which aired that week. She signed copies of the Hobhouse book containing her foreword, with the queue of her fans extending outside for blocks in the winter air.

"I had to leave out the back because of the crowds," she said later. "I feel bad because all those people were left standing there in line for so long."

The same evening she and Gregory Peck co-hosted a *Roman Holiday* bash for 400 at the Equitable Center to benefit UNICEF's New York Metropolitan Committee. In her speech she referred to this first big picture of her career as "the longest holiday ever."

Audrey seemed to appear on every society page, and *Gardens of the World* played multiple times a week on PBS. Her library of feature films already circulated across the explosion of U.S. cable channels. "The Fred Astaire Songbook" premiered March 9, also on PBS.

Shadowing her throughout was author Dominick Dunne who gathered material for a May 1991 cover story in *Vanity Fair* magazine that would serve as the most thorough and accurate examination of her life to date as she approached her sixty-second birthday; he covered the war years, her rise to fame, her marriages, sons, divorces, and relationship with Robbie. And now, UNICEF.

Audrey considered Dunne a pal and they gabbed about a variety of topics that did and didn't make the article, like her secret obsession with Jaguar automobiles. She didn't drive after a fender bender in Hollywood had turned ugly, but she loved the look of Jags and had to resist Luca's entreaties to buy one. In the end she couldn't make the purchase because there wasn't room for groceries in a car like that. But she could still enthuse about Jaguars with Dominick, who understood all too well.

With the lines of fans at Cartier on his mind, Dunne asked, "Does it surprise you the incredible excitement that you still cause?"

"Oh, totally," she responded. "Everything surprises me. I'm surprised that people recognize me on the street. I say to myself, 'Well, I must still look like myself.' I never considered myself as having much talent, or looks, or anything else. I fell into this career. I was unknown, insecure, inexperienced, and skinny. I worked very hard—that I'll take credit for—but I don't understand any of it. At the same time, it warms me. I'm terribly touched by it."

Judged by many now as the world's most beautiful woman, she really did believe what she had told Doris in 1961—Audrey Hepburn was a fraud created by careful makeup. From the moment she shot up to five-seven as an early teen, she hated the way she looked. "I was an Amazon," she groaned. And the litany of flaws she could list proved unending. Big hands, bigger feet, crooked teeth, the shoulders of a linebacker, the square jaw that had become a nickname, and eyes too small. But for Dominick Dunne she boiled it down to not having much in the way of "looks."

Dunne nailed her personality in three sentences: "In hotels, she presses her own clothes, does her own hair and makeup, and answers her telephone without disguising her voice or pretending she's her maid. She makes no late star entrances. In fact, often she's where she's supposed to be before the key people arrive." All were habits, Audrey stated, drilled into her by Ella, which invited Dunne to seek her confirmation that she and her mother had been close.

Audrey iced over instantly and failed to meet his gaze as she considered the question. Then she elegantly danced all the way around it—a ballerina to the end. Even six years past Ella's death, the wounds she'd inflicted had not healed and never would.

Uppermost in Audrey's mind with Dominick Dunne was UNICEF. As she sat with him, conflict raged in Iraq and Kuwait. It had been seven months since Saddam Hussein invaded Kuwait and less than two since the beginning of Operation Desert Storm. Yes, Kuwait had been liberated, which evoked in Audrey memories of the day the Canadian Polar Bears entered Velp with all the joys that freedom brought. But after the defeat of Iraq by coalition forces from thirty-five nations, both Iraq and Kuwait lay in ruins.

She was quick to report that UNICEF had gotten into Baghdad on February 16 with fifty tons of medical supplies. She could relate to Dunne reports from Baghdad back to the UN that stated, "There is no electricity, no water, no sanitation, no heating. The water purification plants are closed down. The sewage system is backed up. People are both bathing in and drinking from the Tigris River." She told him that now epidemics of cholera and typhoid were feared—she'd already given him too much gloom and doom for his profile, so he left that part out.

The release of the May issue of *Vanity Fair* with Audrey's portrait on the cover—beaming, dressed in pink and holding a giant bouquet of tulips—made news in itself for the light shone into the corners of the mind of an omnipresent yet reclusive and private superstar.

Dominick Dunne noted in his article that she was about to be celebrated by the Film Society of Lincoln Center in New York with a gala and presentation of its Living Legend award in April. Since 1972 the Film Society had chosen one legendary star per year for an evening retrospective. To date honorees had included Charlie Chaplin, Fred Astaire, Bob Hope, John Huston, Laurence Olivier, Elizabeth Taylor, Bette Davis, and James Stewart.

Audrey said, "If they feel the body of my work is enough to be given an evening like this, well, it's absolutely marvelous, but it's also absolutely terrifying."

Two thousand admirers showed up to fill Avery Fisher Hall at Lincoln Center, with thousands more lining Broadway and Columbus Avenue as Audrey and Robbie made a grand entrance. She wore a white Givenchy evening gown topped by a sparkling gold-and-aqua bolero.

Inside she met up with Greg Peck, then just past his seventy-fifth birthday but as tall and elegant as ever, his once chestnut-brown hair now gone white. They had adored each other since first meeting in Rome thirty-nine years earlier.

In his speech before a crowd that included Audrey's directors (Billy Wilder and Stanley Donen), co-stars (Alan Arkin and Anthony Perkins), UNICEF co-workers (Harry Belafonte), and friends (Richard Avedon, Ralph Lauren, and Hubert de Givenchy), Peck said, "It was my good luck during that summer in Rome to be the first of her cinema swains, to hold out my hand and help her keep her balance as she did her spins and pirouettes and made practically everybody in the world fall in love with her." At which point she threw him a kiss from a box at the side the stage where she sat with Robbie.

Peck got a good laugh by noting that "they all lined up to work with her, fellows like Bogart, Holden, Gary Cooper, Cary Grant, and Fred Astaire—fellows like that."

Billy Wilder spoke of the *Sabrina* set: "Suddenly there was that dazzling creature, looking like a wide-eyed doe prancing through the forest. It took exactly five minutes for everybody on that set to fall in love with her."

Lincoln Center proved to be the apex of a life's arc that had been launched from quaint pre-Depression Brussels and ascended upward through the clouds of war to a sweaty ballet stint in Arnhem, two-shows-a-night in London burlesque, lucky breaks, heartbreaks, love affairs, awards, marriages, miscarriages, sons, hits, misses, retirement, divorce, and a warrior's comeback. It was a life renowned for its lack of tantrums, backstabbing, cheating, lying, and self-aggrandizement—so much so that this was her Karma: Thousands gathered to love and pay homage to Audrey Hepburn.

She could but go along for the evening's ride, and after an obligatory standing ovation as the Givenchy gown she wore gave the illusion that she had floated to the microphone, she thanked the body gathered to pay her tribute. Specifically, she appreciated the directors, producers, leading men, and everyone else involved in her pictures who "gave so much to a skinny broad and turned her into a marketable commodity."

Even on this evening of all evenings, when she stood on top of the world, adored by everyone in sight, thousands of worshipers dressed to the nines, she experienced the disquiet of the empath. The broadcast media had been crackling about a new threat to children, and headlines in major newspapers screamed Somalia on verge of man-made disaster. "What happens," the press asked, "when a country totally breaks down?"

An idea began to form during this U.S. visit—she didn't know if she could get into Somalia, which had become a void after the overthrow of dictator Mohamed Siad Barre. All the men country-wide, even teenagers, belonged to one clan or another, the media said, and they all carried guns. The overwhelming majority of the six million citizens of Somalia were living in despair—and of course the children suffered worst of all. Audrey didn't consider it a matter of wanting to go to Somalia. She had recently told a reporter, "I won't be doing a field trip for some time because I got awfully tired last year," and who could possibly want to go to the most dangerous place on earth? But she needed to go, and that was a different matter entirely.

She's Real

The congratulations for a lifetime of positivity traveled back with Audrey and Robbie to La Paisible, where she alternated between resting and fighting the good fight for children. At the end of May 1991 she delivered one more UNICEF benefit performance of "From the Diary of Anne Frank" at London's Barbican Centre. Michael Tilson Thomas had recently been named principal conductor of the London Symphony Orchestra, so the fit was natural.

Audrey and Robbie crossed the Atlantic to New York City on Saturday, June 1, 1991, and she presented at the Tony Awards the next day. At the Plaza Hotel, John Isaac paid a visit.

"She showed me a video that she and Robert Wolders acquired, I don't know from where," said Isaac. "I was in her room in her hotel, and she showed some of the video she had gotten from UNICEF about the Somalian situation. So we saw it and she was appalled. She said that's something she wanted to do [go to Somalia]."

Following an appearance on *CBS This Morning* June 3, Audrey and Robbie traveled to Washington where she once more presented to Congress, this time addressing the Senate Appropriations Subcommittee on Foreign Operations to request additional funding for UNICEF, her third appearance on Capitol Hill in three years. She still worked through nerves and still stormed into battle with Jim Grant and Larry Bruce at her side. Senator Patrick Leahy, Democrat of Vermont and committee chairman, made it standard practice to say no to celebrities when they requested a platform in the Senate to testify. He sought to avoid grandstanding and the needless spectacle that accompanied it. This time he said yes to Audrey Hepburn because "she's real," due to a UNICEF resume akin to a red badge of courage for travel to parts of Africa he considered "godforsaken."

In her testimony, Audrey asked the committee to help stop Africa's wars and the "silent, invisible catastrophe" that resulted from them. "Never before have so many people needed so much help at one time," she stated, with reporters spying the carefully handwritten notes she had prepared in advance as she held them in trembling hands. Wherever she spoke, the notes were written in her careful pen, large and spaced wide so she could easily find her place.

Afterward, Patrick and Marcelle Leahy took Audrey to lunch, where an unusual "number of senators found reason to come by the table to say hello," Senator Leahy reported.

And yet, despite the awe of Audrey and fierceness of her message, Senator Nancy Kassebaum dared voice the thought: "She looked very frail."

From Washington, Audrey and Robbie flew to Atlanta for a date with Larry King on CNN June 5. It had been twenty-six months since her previous appearance, the one that took King's measure. To his credit, with Audrey sitting on the other side of the desk, he played it straight, using roll-ins of Audrey in the field and before the U.S. Congress as he said, "For millions of poor and hungry kids, she is their only hope for help. Audrey Hepburn is a one-woman crusade whose grace, style, and commitment epitomize her title, UNICEF's Goodwill Ambassador."

She kicked off by correcting him—she was one of several Goodwill Ambassadors and she named the others. Soon she found

her message. "Adults make war," she told him, "and children die."
In effect, the next twelve minutes with King represented Audrey's
greatest hits.

One moment she said, "As Maria Montessori once said—the
great children's educator—how strange it is that there isn't a science of peace. There's a science of war; nothing comparable to the
science and strategy. There are colleges of war. Why can't we study
and really have a science of peace?"

And next she said, "Where does prejudice start? It starts in the
cradle. We are the guilty ones. We teach them to hate. We teach
them intolerance and racism and all of that. Children—if you leave
them alone, they'll play with each other regardless of what color or
creed or anything."

When King announced a caller with a question from Sarasota,
Florida, a boy said, "Hello, Audrey, this is Oliver."

Audrey thought a moment and became startled. "Oliver?
You're kidding!" It was the son of Robbie's sister Margreet.

Rob's youngest sister, Claudia Deabreu, said her mother and
another sister "were glued to the TV" in Rochester, New York,
watching the *Larry King Show* and were as startled as Audrey to
hear Oliver's voice. Claudia said that Oliver was "a very forward
little boy. He saw the number on the screen and wandered into the
kitchen to make the call. He wanted to talk to his aunt."

"What could kids of my age do for UNICEF?" he asked.

Before a coast-to-coast audience, Audrey responded, "Well,
darling, what you've been doing in school—I know you all know
about UNICEF and you've been talking about UNICEF and
what's terribly important is what I said earlier: to never never let
yourself grow up believing that anybody's different from anybody
else. We're all the same. And [we need to] love each other and do
what you can for your neighbors." She knew the importance of
the national spotlight and would drive home the message of skin
color at all opportunities. Skin color shouldn't have mattered but

did matter, because so many in the Developing World wore darker skin and their needs were especially desperate.

In search of a refuge, Robbie took Audrey into upstate New York to visit the Wolders family in Rochester. The Rochester area had become another home away from home in recent years—like Connie's house in Beverly Hills. Audrey and Robbie stayed at his mother Cemelia's house, with the homes of sisters Grada and Claudia close by. Audrey loved the quaint Rochester area, known for its three waterways, Lake Ontario, Irondequoit Bay, and the Genesee River.

"Audrey would be doing her thing in the kitchen," said Claudia, "and not want my mom to lift a finger." Claudia found in Audrey "another sister" and the Wolders girls and Audrey would rush to the new, bustling Irondequoit Mall, where Audrey excelled at shoe shopping.

The year 1991 had come in a torrent. Audrey said of Rochester, "We were desperate for a moment of peace, so we came here to be with family." She boasted of "great sleep and a peaceful time" in out-of-the-way Rochester. "It's like being in the country," she said. "It's so green and beautiful and peaceful."

Even here, speaking to a reporter from the *Rochester Democrat*, she turned the theme of the story to UNICEF. "Perhaps people in Rochester will help UNICEF by raising money, making contributions. A town in Florida—Fort Lauderdale—handed me a check for $750,000 for UNICEF." By this time, delirious from the road trip, she made odd connections. She noted that the "town" of Fort Lauderdale had donated when it was really a major retailer, Pier 1. But to Audrey, a town's donation was a town's donation. And she brainstormed with the reporter, "You could set up a UNICEF committee in Rochester. People could buy UNICEF greeting cards. They were a source of income for us last year. I even drew a card—I'm no Picasso," she said, adding, "but I drew it anyway and autographed it. And UNICEF got $25,000 for it in an auction."

She gave her last breath of the day to interviews tied to UNICEF, no matter whether they made sense or if they scrambled the facts like eggs. She had worn herself out and needed to head back to La Paisible and recharge. Meanwhile, her new recruit, Roger Moore, headed into the field for his first UNICEF mission retracing Audrey's path through Latin America to check progress on water and immunization projects. Moore, every bit The Saint, dug into field work with the passion of his mentor Audrey.

"Just a week ago, I got to 'introduce' running water to a Guatemalan village," he said in Dallas, after having just completed two weeks in the field. "That is, I was privileged to turn on the tap, which the community had built with UNICEF assistance. It's been a fascinating time. I knew all about the conditions from reading the official statistics, but I've really wanted to go and put some faces to those statistics." His famous face darkened as he related his experience to Michael Price of the *Fort Worth Star-Telegram*. "It's painful, some of it, to witness. How do you overcome conditions like that—the malnutrition, the infant mortality? Well, you assist the poorer countries toward self-sufficiency."

Moore met up with Audrey on Sunday, September 1, to tape their second Danny Kaye International Children's Awards show together in the Netherlands. Also appearing were Natalie Cole, Luciano Pavarotti, Whoopi Goldberg, Ben Vereen, Michael Caine, and Peter Ustinov.

Backstage, Roger told Audrey of his tour to places she had visited eighteen months earlier—Guatemala, El Salvador, Honduras, and Costa Rica. She peppered him with questions about progress made since she'd been there, remembering the critical needs in each country, and especially the situation in El Salvador, where she had heard that peace talks between the government and National Liberation Front were making great progress. Was this true? Had things improved?

"She was an extraordinary, warm, and passionate lady," said Moore.

At the end of September 1991 she returned to the place where she had been "Mrs. Dotti," Rome, for a speech before the Mayors as Defenders of Children group. A week later she and Robbie flew into JFK in New York, where Audrey appeared with former President Jimmy Carter at the United Nations to host certification of a six-year report by the World Health Organization on immunization and the world's children. The report proved encouraging, Audrey announced—eighty percent of children worldwide had been immunized against six common and sometimes deadly diseases. A decade earlier the number of immunized children had been only twenty percent. But her appearance with Carter held an unpleasant surprise: The UN failed to get word out about its two star headliners and their announcement of the immunization report; only eight reporters showed up to cover it—none from U.S. newspapers. The only coverage the president and former movie queen could land in American print was a photo as they administered a vaccine to a child in the Bronx, which ran in a few newspapers as filler without mention of the WHO report.

The media called it "compassion fatigue," and Audrey had become familiar with the term and seen it firsthand. Usually compassion fatigue referred to the emotional distress and physical toll on caregivers, but Audrey had been warned that the public could burn out on one fund-raising appeal after another and just stop listening. Apparently, so could the media, and was the international flight from Switzerland worth the expense and effort if the media really had grown tone-deaf to her message? She knew you won some and lost some, and took the same approach she did when asked why give money to UNICEF when not all of it reached the children? It was a question asked and answered much too often. Her back would straighten and she would go to the attack. "Yes, money is sometimes diverted," she would admit, "but some does reach the children. And that makes every donation critical." So, she and President Carter didn't attract a roomful of reporters and cameras. Yes, but eight did show up, from Swiss, Australian, French, and British TV stations and also ABC and CBS in the States, which meant Carter's and Hepburn's statements about the immunization report would reach millions worldwide and result in donations to UNICEF.

In November she and Robbie returned to Helsinki where she served as a judge and presenter at the Ten Outstanding Young Persons of the World Awards, and in December she spoke before Wiesbaden, Germany's UNICEF working group of volunteers that had been raising awareness and funds since 1965. Days later she traveled to Brussels to launch the 1992 "State of the World's Children" report. All the while she avoided field work because she claimed she just couldn't face it at present—but she was merely kidding herself because the constant travel on UNICEF's behalf battered her physically and emotionally.

"What kills me is the jet lag," she said. "You come and go, and just when you're adjusting, you start again." More than that, food on the road could never be as healthy as fresh fruits and vegetables from her own garden. And the hours were too long no matter how often Robbie insisted she rest.

She knew she must save some reserves for the big prize. She knew she would get there, somehow. Some way.

Good Ol' What's-Her-Name

Of all the Third World hot spots she might visit, one continued to blaze like the fires of hell. The executive director of the
human rights watchdog Africa Watch, Rakiya Omaar, noted in an
op-ed on January 2, 1992, "In Somalia now, it is easier to obtain
lethal weapons than an aspirin or something to eat." She went on
to say, "Somalia was once important as a Cold War pawn in Africa.
But now it is just an impoverished country trapped in a spiral of
war; it is not an attractive candidate for the attention of the United
Nations or any government."

Audrey and Robbie began 1992 as they had closed out the previous year—with travel, this time a U.S. fund-raising tour of three
cities arranged by UNICEF USA. She followed the worsening Somalian situation from the road. On Thursday evening, January 23,
she appeared at the Fairmont Hotel in San Francisco for "a gala
tribute to Audrey Hepburn," a $200-a-plate, black-tie dinner and
dance benefiting UNICEF. In an interview designed to lure people
to come see the woman of "UNICEF legend," a reporter asked
her, "Is this the most rewarding role you've ever played?"

She blanched, took a breath, and said sweetly, "I'm not playing
a role. Roles are imaginary and fantasy. There's no fantasy to this.
It's tough, heartbreaking reality."

Reporters often failed to take into account the dangers of her missions, but this one asked about them. Audrey replied, "What's uppermost in your mind is getting there and hoping you're going to see something that you can do something about." And she let slip the warrior's reality. "Then there's the nitty-gritty of bumping around in jeeps and helicopters, in and out of civil wars."

Larry Bruce and others from UNICEF had flown in for the event and would follow Audrey on to Chicago and Miami, the other stops on the tour. Punctually at 7 p.m. Audrey swept into the Fairmont Hotel penthouse suite with her entourage for a pre-event cocktail party. She wore exactly what her audience would expect, a black crepe Givenchy gown, with Robbie in an obligatory tux. Energy crackled and Audrey expected another successful evening for UNICEF, but perhaps because she hadn't sugar-coated the message in the sprawling *San Francisco Examiner* Q&A of twelve days earlier, when the group transitioned downstairs to the grand ballroom for dinner and speeches her gaze settled on a half-empty room and once again she faced two possible realities. She was witnessing compassion fatigue among the elite, or Audrey Hepburn had traded on her name once too often and people were beginning to tune her out. Or both.

The evening included a video about Audrey's career and UNICEF years, songs performed by a children's choral group, and speeches honoring the Goodwill Ambassador before Audrey delivered her keynote, hitting all the messages she knew by heart. Then it was time for San Francisco Mayor Frank Jordan to present her with a key to the city. "The speech was going well," related *Examiner* reporter Mandy Behbehani, "until the affable mayor called Hepburn 'Katharine.'"

Mortification gripped those in attendance, particularly local philanthropist Athena Troxel, who had chaired the dinner. But the warrior who had plunked herself down on a flak jacket in Sudan to protect against stray bullets wouldn't be nicked by a stray 'Katharine' at this point in her life. In accepting the key, she turned on the charm, revealing that her mother had lived in San Francisco for years and formed many friendships here. "Now I have the key to the city and I wish my mother could see that," she said. "Please Mr. Mayor, don't change the locks."

For days afterward newspaper editors across the nation delighted in relating the mayor's gaffe under articles entitled "Oops! That's Audrey Hepburn"; "Audrey, not Katharine"; and especially "Good ol' what's-her-name." No matter—Audrey counted the mayor's mistake an unexpected windfall in publicity because the story reached every corner of the United States and almost always included her message about helping the children.

She and Robbie flew back to stay at Connie's and visit with Sean for six days. While in her bedroom in Beverly Hills, she met on the phone with Jessica Seigel of the *Chicago Tribune* to promote the Chicago stop on the tour, "An Evening with Audrey Hepburn," another black-tie gala at $200 per plate.

Seigel picked up right away on the earnestness of the messenger and message: "Talking with Hepburn for just a few moments, one quickly sees she is no mere figurehead for the agency. With no prompting, statistics about poverty in the developing world roll from her tongue. Did you know that annual expenditures for health care are $3.50 per person in Africa? Did you know that the infant mortality rate in Afghanistan is 300 deaths per 1,000, compared with 8 per 1,000 in Sweden? And on and on."

On Saturday, February 1, Audrey and Robbie attended the Chicago fund-raiser at the Stouffer Riviere, a luxury hotel just two months past grand opening. The sellout crowd there restored Audrey's confidence in the drawing power of her brand and for four hours' effort earned $100,000 for UNICEF by following the customary agenda: exclusive private-suite cocktail reception, video, children's chorus, speeches, dinner, dancing.

Tribune reporter Jacquelyn Heard mingled in Audrey's direction at the cocktail party, not an easy task given the crush of hangers-on. "Asked how she feels to be the object of such affection," wrote Heard, "Hepburn moved in so close to give her answer, one thought she was about to drop a bomb of a secret. She didn't. She touches you when she speaks. 'I feel fine this evening,' she said, fiddling with the baubles on the inquirer's bracelet. 'I'm a bit nervous, but fine.'"

From the grand success on Lake Michigan the retinue flew south to Miami International to begin a series of events that would culminate with "A Tribute to the World's Children" at the Broward Center for the Performing Arts in Fort Lauderdale.

On Wednesday, February 5, 1992, she raised awareness for the Friday event by touring Broward General Medical Center. She received a bouquet of white tulips, lilies, and roses upon entering, and then proceeded on a tour of the facility. The humanitarian—the press had begun calling her that—shook hands warmly and added hugs as necessary. Anything for the cause. She sat and painted with child patients who had no idea who the nice lady was, but when she headed out of the room to continue the tour one of the kids shouted, "You're special!"

In the neonatal care center she hovered over a newborn of just one pound and three ounces and was told that the fragile little soul would live a normal life. It seemed the longest of long-shots, and Audrey clamped her teeth around the message. This one will live, but 40,000 a day in the Developing World won't, and that's a problem. She said even the United States doesn't do enough for all its children. "This country needs to put children at the top of its priority list," she stated, "in good times and bad times."

Then she threw her hospital public affairs handler a curve ball. She had heard about a clinic called the Children's Diagnostic and Treatment Center just up Andrews Street. The facility cared and advocated for children and adolescents with chronic illnesses and developmental disabilities, including babies born with AIDS and drug addiction. Audrey said she would like to tour it. "Of course,

Miss Hepburn," came the reply.

Reporters and photographers on hand were advised to head to the clinic and that Audrey would soon follow. After the press had departed, Audrey stood deep in thought a moment holding the bouquet she had been given on arrival. Then she asked to be taken back to the hospice care unit she had visited earlier.

There she entered the room of an elderly woman who lay asleep. Gently Audrey placed the bouquet on the tray stand next to the bed and tip-toed out.

On a tour of the children's center moments later, Audrey held on her shoulder a two-month-old African-American baby serendipitously named Tiffany. The warrior said to the gathered media, "This is a very important issue. They are very beautiful babies [here], whether they are cocaine babies or suffer from birth defects." Then she played with children of various ages, and hugged and kissed them, and went on her way.

"So often, with celebrities, there's a public persona and a private persona," Larry Bruce said to reporters afterward. "With Audrey, what you see is what you get—a caring, loving, gentle human being."

They had been on the road three weeks now, and she experienced bone weariness that took her by surprise. She found herself longing for the Jack Russells and La Paisible and primed herself for one more UNICEF benefit.

On Friday, February 7, she appeared with Liza Minnelli at "A Tribute to the World's Children" in Fort Lauderdale. The show was spectacular and Audrey made her usual pitch, but once again attendance fell short of expectations. Compassion fatigue raged in the United States, matched by her own physical weariness.

Two months later she and Robbie returned to the States for black-tie appearances in Indianapolis and Providence, Rhode Island. But through all the stump speeches for UNICEF, the luncheons and galas and accolades, and the commercial flights from city to city, two realities faced her: She must somehow get into Somalia because she envisioned international attention that could address the desperate need of the people. At the same time, she knew she could neither undertake nor complete such a mission for UNICEF. The mathematical equation didn't add up because she possessed so little energy of late. Even working in the garden tired her out. She knew her body as did any trained dancer. She had relied on that body all her life and particularly in these past UNICEF years. She ate healthily, lots of fruits and vegetables, and the energy had always been there. Boundlessly so. But not lately. Lately she felt aches and pains and weakness. So, this is what sixty-three feels like.

Somalia haunted her day and night. A cease-fire had finally been agreed to by Somalia's two most powerful warring clans, and international aid had begun to flow in. But then the NGOs learned what a buzz saw the country was. Soon UNICEF and other agencies evacuated all personnel.

UN Ambassador Mohamed Sahnoun of Algeria sent back reports that grew more dire by the week. "I've never seen a worse situation than in Somalia," he said. "It's appalling." Between the civil war and a crippling drought, 5,000 children under the age of five were dying by the day. By the *day*.

Said a Somali man to an Associated Press reporter from a refugee camp in Kenya, "Before, we never had this violence; rape, looting, disrespect for elders. What have we come to?"

Somalia was the same old story and it made Audrey mad enough to spit. Somalis were accustomed to occasional drought, or to clans fighting each other with spears, but the United States and the Soviet Union had been flooding Somalia with weaponry for years as each side jockeyed for power in the Horn of Africa. Now with the end of the Cold War both superpowers had withdrawn, the government collapsed taking the military and police with it, and rival gangs armed to the teeth destroyed much of the country, including Mogadishu. And both sides had weaponized food, looting water pumps and poisoning wells, driving off farmers so they couldn't plant, and stealing their livestock or leaving it to die. Every Red Cross kitchen in one Somali city had been forced to establish its own graveyard outside for the ones who died waiting in line to be fed. Some had two graveyards. The UN estimated that without immediate aid, a quarter of the population of six million in Somalia would be dead within a couple of months.

The international press reported each new horror, each new atrocity, and finally the reports made U.S. newspapers. But where, Audrey wondered, was the international clamor that should have sounded from all quarters? Why were the mighty Western powers so resoundingly inert—because these were Africans? Black people?

Audrey sat in her home fuming and considered her options. She simply had none until the all-clear was given and it would be safe to enter the country.

Anna Cataldi called La Paisible and said, "Audrey, it's terrible what's happening in Somalia. I want to do something." Cataldi felt she needed to volunteer in the field.

"We're not fit enough to go there and work," said Audrey. "You need young people, strong, perfectly trained. They have no time to train people. The only thing we can do is to use what we have [our names] in order to raise awareness."

But as with Audrey, a fire had been lit under Anna, who heeded her friend's advice about the rigors of volunteering. Instead, she secured an assignment from *Epoca* magazine in Milan to visit Somalia and get the word out about the crisis and international response.

"I was on the phone with Audrey all the time in August. She was very frustrated," said Cataldi. "Very frustrated."

While on standby for Somalia, Audrey flew to Amsterdam for the Danny Kaye International Children's Awards, taped Saturday, August 12, 1992. She knew her UNICEF career must end soon; she had confided as much to Doris. The jet lag, the bad food, and so many inoculations that she referred to herself as a "colander"—all of it added up. And it was time she heeded her own advice to Anna Cataldi; places like Somalia called for young, fit people and not sixty-three year olds who tired more easily by the day.

With her body an engine that was grinding its gears, she recruited another UNICEF ambassador, fifty-six-year-old Dutch entertainer Paul van Vliet, one of the most recognizable names and faces in the Netherlands. The charismatic writer and actor had begun his career as a cabaret host while in college and gone on to found the Cabaret PePijn, which operated for seven years, and then Theater PePijn, which remained vibrant through various incarnations. Audrey had asked van Vliet to sing a duet with her at the first Danny Kaye broadcast in 1988, and now four years later she installed him as a Goodwill Ambassador during the August 12 taping.

Audrey returned to Switzerland for a physical examination and the series of inoculations she would need if and when UNICEF gave the green light for Somalia. She took comfort in the results of blood work and a colonoscopy but knew she didn't feel quite right. For all the talk and endless questions about her thinness, she had been a dancer—an athlete—from age twelve and always felt like one, with a healthy heart despite the cigarettes and a stamina that had allowed for all the international travel and grueling agendas. But now, finally, it seemed that age might be catching up with her. Everything she did, even weeding the garden, seemed to take ever greater effort.

Luca heard of her intention to become boots on the ground in the Horn of Africa. He felt "chills in my back to learn about a Somalia trip." When he visited and took her in his arms that summer, he was immediately concerned. "I almost crushed her. She was very frail; my impression was, 'Mum should take better care of herself.'"

Luca advised as strongly as a twenty-two-year-old son could:

"Don't go, Mummy."

Audrey sighed. "Your brother said the same thing."

Luca said in retrospect, "If you insisted, that's the only time she'd raise her voice. About Somalia, she got very determined." He added, "I wasn't worried at all when she went to the other countries. But this time I had the impression she was burning the candle from both ends. It was too much."

Despite any notion she was tired, Audrey Hepburn would get inside Somalia and bring the press with her. Oh yes, she would. It boiled down to when and how, and for the moment, as August wore on, she could do nothing but sit and stew.

Then, finally, came the green light from UNICEF headquarters. Somalia was a "go."

The Big T

At first glimpse, the 800-foot U.S.S. *Tarawa* amphibious assault ship resembled any typical aircraft carrier in the U.S. fleet, if a little more compact. The *Tarawa* could launch Harrier Jump Jets or Marine helicopters as well as amphibious landing craft, and with her escort ships, the U.S.S. *Cayuga*, a landing ship tank; the *Ogden*, an amphibious landing dock; and the U.S.S. *Fort McHenry*, a landing ship dock, these vessels comprised Amphibious Ready Group 1. The squadron's 2,000 men of the 11th Marine Expeditionary Unit bunked on the various ships and could deploy rapidly and flex U.S. muscle as needed. For all practical purposes, the *Tarawa* and her support ships could put a portable Marine base into any spot in the world.

The *Tarawa*, or "the Big T" as she was nicknamed, had been deployed since May 28, 1992, when she left home port San Diego, and for the Marines and 850 sailors aboard, summer in the Persian Gulf had been brutal. No matter the port of call—Bahrain, Kuwait, Saudi Arabia, or the UAE—temperatures through August had climbed to over 100 by mid-morning. Well over 100. But now it was September 10 and, thank God, finally they were under way for Perth, Australia, which shouldn't be sweltering this time of year, before returning to San Diego. Within the comfort of the Navy's clockwork routine, spirits were high as the ship transited the Strait of Hormuz and pushed into the Gulf of Oman. *Tarawa* commanding officer Capt. Nigel Parkhurst secured from mine watch and prepared for open sea.

That night the ready group received new orders: "Proceed to vicinity of Mogadishu, Somalia." Ah, life in the Navy. Instead of going straight toward off-season Australia, they turned to starboard and headed to another tropical and arid pressure-cooker—Somalia and its civil war.

As he communicated orders to his ships' captains for the turn south toward the Arabian Sea, commander of Amphibious Ready Group 1, Braden Phillips, knew what might lie ahead. Phillips had followed the headlines and understood some basics about Somalia—famine in 1986, civil war in 1990, and overthrow of the military government of Maj. Gen. Mohamed Siad Barre in 1991 by various clans seeking to establish and consolidate political power. A particularly nasty practice of first Barre and then the clans was destroying the water sources of their enemies; by 1992 an estimated quarter-million Somali civilians had died of hunger or thirst. It was, as Phillips understood it, "anarchy."

Around the beginning of September, bowing to international pressure, U.S. President George H.W. Bush had decided to throw a U.S. presence into the Somali maelstrom, where humanitarian efforts by the Red Cross and others were routinely hijacked by warlords from the various clans. At the same time, the U.S. Joint Chiefs pushed back on the president's urge to help in what they considered "a no-win situation."

But Bush kept insisting and Chairman of the Joint Chiefs Gen. Colin Powell reluctantly ordered action. U.S. military C-130s and C-141s began airlifting food into Somalia from neighboring Kenya five days ahead of orders to the *Tarawa* group to redeploy toward Mogadishu.

In Baidoa, a troubled city not far from the border with Kenya, the first airborne food to arrive from the U.S. attracted both armed gangs and starving civilians. Chaos resulted, which proved the instincts of the Joint Chiefs to be correct.

The *Tarawa* carried six Harrier attack jets and four Super Cobra attack helicopters, yet the Joint Chiefs decided the ready group would not display air power or insert its Marines to remedy the chaotic situation on the ground as food began to flow in. Rather, air traffic controllers already aboard the *Tarawa* would be airlifted into the Mogadishu Airport; from there the controllers would guide in a series of C-5A and C-141 transports bearing 500 United Nations peacekeepers from Pakistan. Then it would be the UN's responsibility to protect the food.

Six days after receiving her orders, the *Tarawa* and her escorts had steamed to the Indian Ocean and reached the area of Mogadishu on the eastern coast of Africa. The ships hung ten miles offshore, far enough out that nothing in the Somali arsenal could range it, but within a few minutes' striking distance if need be. Powerful Somali warlord Gen. Mohamed Farrah Aidid seemed to possess an ear well-tuned to saber rattling, because he hurried to Mogadishu when he heard the Marines had come. Aidid had been away for five months, but now his country's affairs became top-of-mind with the *Tarawa* a dot on the horizon.

Upon arrival, task force commander Phillips and Marine Col. Mike Hagee, in command of the Marine Air-Ground Task Force, hopped aboard a long-range CH-53 Sea Stallion helicopter and flew 500 miles to Nairobi to plan for the humanitarian mission ahead. There they huddled up in a strategic session with staff from the recently evacuated U.S. embassy in Mogadishu and with Mohamed Sahnoun, the UN's eyes and ears on the ground in the Horn of Africa. It became an exercise in sandlot football, drawing up plays in the dirt, as the cagey Sahnoun advised what was safe and what wasn't, and what could be done and what couldn't.

In a coordinated effort, Marines and Air Force traffic controllers would establish a beachhead at the Mogadishu Airport under

Colonel Hagee's command and direct the landing of the peace-keepers on U.S. and Canadian cargo planes. The Pakistanis would then proceed to the nearby Port of Mogadishu in force, where they would guard incoming food shipments from looting by the clans and pirates. It was to be the first small step in a long journey of bringing order to a country in shambles.

Audrey Hepburn had gotten her way through elegant diplomacy laid like gold plating over iron-willed persistence. UNICEF had always been eager to send its warrior into the field because of the influx of cash that resulted on each occasion. But even within UNICEF there was hesitation. She kept poking, pestering, until finally Mohamed Sahnoun gave a reluctant okay—international relief efforts had begun, more NGOs were stepping in, and Audrey Hepburn *might* get in and out of Somali alive. Then came a time when the importance of getting the story as seen through her eyes out to the world overruled all sense of caution.

The situation remained dicey. The Bush administration airlift and Red Cross shipments coming into the port of Mogadishu had caused a vicious response from warlord Aidid and rival clans who stole the food as fast as it was unloaded. What supplies made it to the starving masses produced riots.

In short, with hundreds of thousands of armed men roaming the country, in no way would it be safe for Audrey Hepburn. But Audrey was going, and Robbie was going where Audrey went.

On Sunday, September 20, flying east out of Nairobi toward the Somali seaside city of Kismayo aboard UNICEF's twin-engine Beechcraft King Air turboprop, Audrey and Robbie sat together quietly contemplating what lay ahead. Also on the plane were Madeline Eisner, dark-haired information officer from UNICEF headquarters, and young Aussie Ian MacLeod, who had worked with Audrey on the Sydney press tour of 1989 and now served as program officer for Somalia. Kenya-based photographer Betty Press, who had done field work for the UNHCR, was also aboard.

"I was pretty nervous about taking this contract because it was something I hadn't done before," said Press. "I hadn't done anything at that level, working with somebody that famous. But Audrey was very kind to me and told me, 'I'm not going to pose for you. Just take each opportunity and capture what you can.'"

Zooming east, Audrey enjoyed time to call to mind the crash course of information from the UN on Somalia. It was another wretched example of the lasting effects of European colonialism. She had seen it over and over in her travels; she had seen it all her life.

"Are we not reaping the mess we made so many years ago when we enriched ourselves?" said Audrey. "We didn't do a hell of a lot for those people, did we?"

To another reporter she said, "We all have blood on our hands. The Americans with the Indians, the British with the Afghans and the Middle East, the French—you understand what I mean?"

In Somalia, it had been the Italians that colonized northern Somaliland and the British most of the remainder of the country. Since declaring independence from the Europeans, Somalia had been in turmoil. There had been a war with Ethiopia in the late 1970s and a defeat for Somalia that resulted in military buildup—for every dollar spent on education and health, five were spent on the military. While General Barre ruled the country with an iron fist, clans formed to oppose him. Each sought power and prestige; anyone not part of the clan was "other," an outsider, and didn't deserve to live. Civil war broke out and a half-million Somalis were displaced. Many fled to neighboring Ethiopia or Kenya while many more relocated to other areas of Somalia, claiming lands from rightful owners, primarily farmers.

The collapse of the Barre regime in January had released the national military arsenal to the clans, including two factions of the

Hawiye clan that had been fighting for control of Mogadishu for months—one led by General Aidid and the other by Ali Mahdi Muhammad. Audrey learned that among the things Aidid—in fact all the clans—had weaponized was food, and deepening famine had completed Somalia's devastation. Out of a total population of somewhere between 6 and 8 million, approximately 4.5 million Somalis required urgent external assistance. By very conservative estimates, 300,000 Somalis had already died of hunger, and 1.5 million were at immediate risk of starvation, including 1 million children.

On final approach to the Kismayo airport, Audrey marveled at the parched red earth. "Terra-cotta red," she called it. The land-scape looked like a vast dry lake bed, that blood-red dirt puckered and lying in mounds that passed by her gaze at 140 miles per hour in what seemed an unending blur of wave upon wave. She would learn later: These were graves of those already claimed by war and famine. Tens of thousands of graves lying by every roadside.

The plane touched down on the lonely, single airstrip and shot past Kismayo's small terminal. A party of dignitaries awaited with a couple of station wagons flying United Nations pennants and a light truck with a .50 caliber machine gun mounted in its bed, its operator at the ready. As the UNICEF King Air taxied up to the cluster of dignitaries, Audrey knew this was the culmination of all her pleading to get to the children of Somalia. It was finally show time.

Film cameras were ready for the event of Audrey's first steps in Somalia. Ian MacLeod preceded her off the plane. Then a nervous Audrey bumped her head on the bulkhead as she prepared to descend the steps. On the ground she met UNICEF's Representative for Somalia, Mark Stirling, a tall well-built young Aussie with a mop of dark blond hair and a friendly personality. She met many others waiting to see her and introduced them to "my Robert." Everyone smiled pleasantly, but there was no getting around the armed guards—young Somalis who may have been teenagers or a little older, each holding an AK-47 or an Uzi or M-16. And that big gun on the truck—the Somalis referred to a pickup truck mounted with a heavy machine gun as a "technical," and the young, heavily armed males riding in the trucks were "technicals." All the young toughs standing at the edges of the group of officials scanned the terrain as if looking for anything that moved because they wanted to unload a magazine or two at it. Audrey had lived through the big one; she knew an itchy trigger finger when she saw one. And here were many.

"They were our technicals, our security for hire," said Mac-Leod, adopting a when-in-Rome philosophy. "We had to pay for them, and they didn't have much training."

The thin woman who in a few days would capture and hold the attention of the world wore her customary field uniform: cotton Izod shirt, cotton pants, and sneakers, hair pulled back in a ponytail. She had conceded to some lipstick and blush to bring color to unusually pale cheeks at the start—her only allowance for UN cameras that would do important work documenting the trip.

For now, however, only this small reception committee knew of Audrey Hepburn's whereabouts. "There was always a risk," said MacLeod. "We didn't publicize Audrey coming in advance or there could have been a security risk. This was before the kidnappings that happened later in Somalia. In terms of Audrey coming in, that information was on a need-to-know basis."

The group piled into their station wagons and the guards loaded onto the technical, which pulled out first. The three-vehicle motorcade drove from the desolate airport a mile to the edge of Kismayo, Somalia's second-largest city. The young gun-toters chattered away gleefully in the open bed of the truck. Some of them were already chomping on khat, a plant native to the area that had been used for centuries as a stimulant and source of a high. UNICEF had been warned about the practice of khat chewing because just about all the males chewed it and they all carried automatic weapons. Important UNICEF tasks would need to be tackled in the first half of the day, before the technicals were high on khat and more apt to be trigger-happy.

As Audrey described it, "You enter Somalia, number one, without a visa, because there is no government, so you just land, and there are no roads to speak of. There's no government, no electricity, no postal service, no telephones. It's like the moon from that point of view." If this was the moon and a wasteland, it was, to be sure, one heavily armed wasteland.

A week later she would describe the tense situation she had walked into: "There's a truce in Mogadishu shared by the two principal warlords. The rest of the country is really a mayhem of marauding bandits who are likely to hold up a convoy or loot a storehouse. We certainly never went anywhere without guards with machine guns."

First on the schedule, up a dusty road, was a UNICEF feeding center in operation just two weeks, so at the vanguard of the relief effort. A young volunteer explained the center to Audrey and, at first, conditions didn't seem so bad here. The worker said, "It's going really well," and yes, the children were "severely malnourished," but able to sit and eat rations and drink milk, and take a second ration home with them. Audrey was led past hundreds of children three to six years of age, sitting quietly as if shell-shocked. They wore the traditional cotton macawiis, most of them reduced to rags. Their mothers, when mothers sat with children, wore the guntiino draped over one shoulder and tied at the waist, with a head covering. Flies buzzed all about.

Photographer Betty Press began to understand the challenge facing her for the next three days: "It was very difficult lighting. Difficult conditions just getting around—the heat, the flies."

Audrey asked questions to keep her mind engaged. She had come as an advocate for the children. She asked where the food at this center had come from, and how many meals a day the children got, and where they went between meals. That was important: What did they do with themselves the rest of the day?

Moving along through the tour, Audrey saw a forlorn little stick figure of a girl staring vacantly and barely able to sit. Maybe three years old; maybe four. Behind her, another child lay prone, like a rag tossed by the road, maybe alive, maybe dead. And then more such little figures sat or laid about; too many more. Their arms and legs were twigs. Their eyes were saucers of gray with nothing to reveal—the life had gone out of them. And the smell—the volunteers kept cleaning but couldn't quite overcome the stench of unwashed humans and diarrhea and death. The UN worker kept talking about conditions here at the center and how they had improved. Improved? What had it been like here a week ago? Audrey kept moving and talking to keep herself sharp, but the energy she had managed to muster on exiting the plane dropped. And this was just the first visit of the first day.

Next the motorcade knifed into the despair of Kismayo, through dust and impoverished shacks and the rubble of bombs, past Muslim women with their bodies completely covered and pairs, groups, and clusters of men with weapons, to Al Huaraz Camp No. 1, a gathering place for Somalis displaced by war. Someone had managed to find a poster-sized sheet of paper and some magic markers. Written neatly on the paper and hung on a wall of the feeding center was the word WELCOME in brown marker and AUDREY HEPBURN in green marker. Next to it another sign, smaller, an afterthought: Robert Wolders and Betty Press were also welcomed in green marker. Although Press had been misspelled to Price—a clue to the fact it was Australians behind the gesture.

Audrey watched as Unimix composed of enriched maize and bean flour was combined with hot water, stirred, and dispensed to families a container at a time. Oh, the unpleasant smell of it. There seemed to be no logic to how much food was doled out—however big the container, that's how much Unimix was ladled into it. She asked more questions about the equity of the distribution; it seemed there wasn't any. But there was only so much the UNICEF people could control, and the need was so great. The dedication and hustle of the care workers, both from outside and among the Somalis, impressed Betty Press. "They did an amazing job. They just needed the help and the resources to do it."

Audrey's party toured a makeshift city of traditional Somali huts called tukels that looked like igloos and had been thrown up one next to another. They were five feet tall and stitched together of sticks, plastic, cardboard, mud—anything that would provide shelter from the elements. The refugees comprised a vast sea, 10,000 of them, and so many children of three or five or eight who were fascinated by the tall white lady and reached out to touch her as if she'd been heaven sent.

But something struck Audrey as odd. "Starting with the first camps we went to in Kismayo, that's where I noticed after wandering around for some twenty minutes this very strange absence of small children. And I asked about it. I thought perhaps they were in a different—in a hospital or something. No, they're gone." Not, gone as in removed to safety. Gone as in starved and dead and buried. She had to block out the shock of the information and keep her legs moving forward.

The older children that now buzzed about her served as instant proof of what a few days' food could accomplish. The excitement caused by so many foreign visitors ignited further survival instincts. The children wore all manner of rags, most traditional, but here and there appeared a tattered polo shirt or pullover. The healthier ones expended precious nervous energy around her now, but she heard their rattling coughs on the air and when she bent down to peer into a tukel, she'd see the unhealthy ones lying there, little bags of bones, some already dead, others waiting to die. She kept moving and forced smiles, touching the heads or hands of the energetic ones as they quietly, politely mobbed her.

"Funny, funny, funny," she said with a smile. "Funny little girls and boys." But already, the starch had been taken out of her by the sights she had seen, glimpses at every edge of the tableau. "Oh dear, dear," she said, and turned away from the children, so many children, in a vast sea of huts made of nothing.

"What amazed me most of all was how she handled herself in these camps where they were desperate. Desperate," said Betty Press. "The situation at that point was so tragic, and she handled herself with such grace and such dignity. You'd see smiles on people who had nothing to smile about. I realized how sincere she was. How genuine she was. She really cared."

Next the motorcade drove north through parched, rust-red desert to Mokomani village, which was described to her by Ian MacLeod as "an oasis in the desert." The international nonprofit Oxfam, its mission to eradicate poverty, ran Mokomani with support from UNICEF, and seeing patches of green lifted Audrey's spirits and gave her something to focus on. She walked past thriving cornstalks to the edge of the Juba River, seventy yards wide and flowing a muddy brown. Men worked desperately to get an old petrol-driven pump going so Oxfam could demonstrate irrigation in action. They sweated and fumed over the old contraption until it finally turned over and sputtered to life, and Audrey cheered and applauded as a muddy plume of water shot out of a pipe and into irrigation ditches. She watched the flow reach out into the parched earth and touch the growing cornstalks. It was victory, an actual victory here in hell, and she relished the moment.

She toured the village with a UN video camera following. Structures here weren't crude tukels but reeded huts with thatched roofs or sturdy, corrugated metal shacks. One of the village leaders, a tall, thin man of about thirty, spoke English and pleaded with Audrey for diesel fuel and motor oil to run the pump, and for water to drink. These were, he stated, the greatest needs of the village and he expressed them directly to the one in the party with the most perceived power—the thin white woman whom all others catered to.

She was told about the ones, mothers mostly, who couldn't come out to greet her, and she asked to meet one of these people. Inside a hut, she sat down with a frail woman and held her hand and asked the woman through an interpreter for her story—was this her home and where had she come from and did she want to be here? Audrey took on the role of advocate for this woman to make sure she was where she wanted to be. The answer satisfied her—the woman had traveled to Mogadishu in search of food but was now back home in Mokomani.

Said Ian MacLeod, observing her, "No, she doesn't speak the Somali language, but her face and gestures gave such an obvious psychological boost to many of the mothers. They may not have known who Audrey was, but it was clear to them by her aura that she was someone special who was bringing them some hope."

Audrey visited the schoolhouse, a stucco building that showed hasty mortar patches to make it more presentable to the visitors; inside, all the children of the village had gathered to greet her, more than 100 giggling, grinning children showing a spark of life. She tried English on them to no effect, but some knew Italian to Audrey's great surprise—a vestige of the exploitation of colonial times. As she departed, she applauded for the children and they returned the clapping with enthusiasm. It was a beautiful moment in the desert oasis.

"There are some 1,200 people, all of different clans, and they've built their own villages again," she would say of Mokomani to doubters who had written Somalia off. "They've been provided with tools and seeds. They had an old pump for which UNICEF gave the fuel. They're growing maize and tomatoes. They all look well, and they're living together." She believed strongly that this success story proved the naysayers wrong for declaring Somalia a lost cause. She said of the oasis, "They have a common purpose: They're surviving together. Now, is that just a dream? No, it's fact. It's there."

By the time they had arrived back at Kismayo's runway, the desert sun had grown brutal. Here the UNICEF plane awaited to take the party on to Mogadishu. Mohamed Sahnoun, who had given the okay for Audrey's visit and met secretly with the Americans in Nairobi, now arrived to escort Audrey up to the destroyed and dangerous Somali capital. The Algerian Sahnoun was a small man with dark curly hair and a bit of a stoop. He had a kind face, a gentle nature, and protective instincts about Audrey—very much like Robbie's. As she prepared to board the King Air with Robbie hovering nearby, Madeline Eisner asked Audrey to do a quick stand-up with two reporters on why she had come to Somalia. It was the common question, the go-to question, often posed by reporters trained to be cynical or grown cynical in the course of their work. They were used to headline-grabbers and clearly in their eyes, here was another one.

Audrey said she'd wanted to come for a year and a half. She praised these reporters and their media coverage of the Somalia crisis and said, "There's still room for somebody like me to raise funds, which we need desperately."

She was asked for her impressions of Kismayo. Her face hardened under sunglasses. She considered the question, then a long sigh escaped her lungs. "On one hand, I was happy to see as many children already better nourished than I might have a couple of months ago. On the other hand, I saw babies, children, that I don't think will be here tomorrow. I'm very churned up about it. I saw beautiful countryside, with enormous herds of cattle that I was surprised to see, and I'm—" She paused, redirecting herself with the poise and adroitness of a statesman. She smiled and said, "I'm very grateful to be here," and she thanked Ambassador Sahnoun for making it possible.

Upon arrival at Mogadishu, Audrey and Robbie retired with Sahnoun to his UN residence by the airport, a house MacLeod described as containing "this garish Middle-Eastern furniture." There they huddled up with UNICEF people, a military coordinator, and aid workers until Robbie broke up the meeting and ushered Audrey to bed.

The major city around them was a wreck. She later said in a UN statement that she had lived through World War II and seen the destruction of parts of Arnhem and London, "But I've never seen a whole city where there isn't a building that doesn't have holes in it or a roof on it. That city was a total battleground."

It had been a long day with many stops, many faces, and many transactions with desperate Somalis, each needing some of her energy, whatever she had to spare. And she had doled it out, drop by precious and dwindling drop. Watching her, Robbie knew there was only so much to go around, and he worried because he could see her already overdoing it. She had promised to rest to keep up her strength, but how could she rest on this kind of schedule in this barren environment? And a full day in battle-scarred Mogadishu lay ahead.

At 0-dark-thirty on Monday, September 21, the *Tarawa's* flight deck opened and a CH-46 Marine Sea Knight helicopter rose up from the hangar deck, its markings painted over from Iraq military ops so that barely the shadow of the word MARINES remained visible. Alongside were two Super Cobra attack helicopters. Col. Mike Hagee and two members of his staff stepped into the 46 dressed as American civilians about to sightsee in the most lethal place on earth—each carrying an MP6 machine gun in a gym bag if needed because they were about to meet with the top clan leader, Aidid, to discuss a cease-fire allowing for President Bush's U.S. humanitarian presence and also the safe arrival of UN peacekeepers.

At 0600 the three birds went airborne, heading west toward Mogadishu Airport located near water's edge just south of a ravaged city. Four other helos were brought up to the flight deck behind the three that had departed. One would ferry in an Air Force security team and traffic controllers. The other three held Marines ready for combat in case Hagee got into trouble on landing.

As the Sea Knight and its escorts neared the shoreline, the Cobras peeled away and stayed over water while Hagee and his aides landed at Mogadishu Airport, its terminal building pockmarked from small arms fire and explosives. All was quiet and the colonel transmitted an all-clear message back to the *Tarawa*. The platoon of Marines remained on standby in case they would be needed—anything could happen in this first contact between the U. S. military and Mogadishu's top warlord.

Mohamed Farrah Aidid and his interpreter awaited the U.S. representative outside the battered airport terminal building. The clan boss, a bald, well-built black man in his fifties, wore a button-down shirt and khakis and carried a silver-tipped walking stick. He maintained a grim expression and viewed Hagee and his aides through cold eyes that projected confidence—he did, after all, command an army of well-armed and battle-hardened clan warriors spread out through sections of the city and beyond. He expressed to Colonel Hagee a quick disinclination to allow UN peacekeepers on Somali soil because, really, what was in it for him to have foreigners meddling in his country's affairs?

Hagee pulled out a map given to him by Task Force Captain Phillips. He pointed. "Here's your city, and here's the U.S.S. *Tarawa* and 2,000 Marines, right off your coast. You can permit the Pakistani peacekeepers to come in and guard the port, or my Marines will fly in, secure the airport, and see to the port themselves. The choice is yours."

Aidid pulled reading glasses out of his pocket, slowly slipped them on, and gave Hagee's map a glance.

Hagee would later say it took Aidid "a couple of milliseconds" to agree to Pakistani peacekeepers.

When Hagee radioed the okay, the helo lifted off from the *Tarawa* carrying Air Force personnel. It came in for a landing and Aidid observed the security men in black—fully dressed for combat and meaning business—establish a perimeter while the half-dozen traffic-control personnel lugged equipment toward the airport tower to set up operations. Hagee watched Aidid shuffle back a step on sight of his would-be adversaries.

In a while the first U.S. C-141 Starlifter cargo plane appeared in the sky and landed. The first twenty-three peacekeepers of the Pakistani battalion stepped off wearing blue helmets with UN stenciled in white. Hagee recognized Brig. Gen. Imtiaz Shaheen and his officers among this first group. The Pakistani foot soldiers stepped onto the tarmac unenthusiastically, carrying only M16s and not looking to Hagee, or to Aidid standing beside him, like the answer to anyone's security problem.

The moments ticked by for Hagee and his aides, with thousands of well-armed Somali gunmen making no move against the airport. So far, so good. No one had shot anyone, Air Force traffic control had established operations in the tower, and the couple dozen Pakistanis were on the ground and standing by to head to the Port of Mogadishu, located just east of the airport. Hagee felt pretty damn satisfied—and unaware amidst the grime and tension of Mogadishu that a warrior was coming from the general direction of Hollywood.

Held Together by Willpower

Audrey began her Monday, September 21, at Lafoole, a refugee camp and feeding center outside Mogadishu that now housed about 3,600 Somalis. Tukels marked the landscape around some shacks, and she saw hundreds of Somalis of all ages sitting in a group awaiting breakfast. She also came upon a sight that enraged her: Two teenage girls had been tied to a tree by their father. Audrey demanded to know the situation. An interpreter translated their father's explanation: The teenagers were shell-shocked.

Audrey said, "They were so traumatized by shells hitting their house in Mogadishu that their father ties them up for love—otherwise they will wander off and may never return."

Ian MacLeod noted of feeding centers like this one linked to refugee camps, "There [are] a lot of women, a lot of kids, but very few infants because they didn't survive, and very few men because they were off fighting."

A representative, a tall, nervous young black man who seemingly had been appointed to speak on behalf of refugees of the camp, addressed her as soon as she moved within earshot and appealed for more oils and proteins. As with all such interactions, Madeline Eisner scribbled hasty notes to capture what was said in the exchange. Audrey was led to a health clinic and moved from bed to bed. She stopped at the bedside of a tiny bag of bones—a little girl sucking her thumb. Carefully she reached out two fingers and took the child's hand.

"I want to take her home," Audrey said quietly. "I want to pick her up, but I'm afraid she'll break."

Audrey and her group continued through the camp toward the metal-corrugated schoolhouse. On the way she stopped to touch hands with young mothers and children and delight that many had begun to bounce back—she never knew what manner of sights awaited around the next corner.

Betty Press said of Audrey, "She was talking to children, holding them, talking to all the health care workers, and we walked with her as she was taking these tours. It was a very difficult, dangerous situation in terms of disease as well. And she'd be picking up these children and holding them. And I took a picture of her sitting there with all the children around her. She would do things like that. She was just amazingly at-home being there, in a way. Comfortable being there, and people felt that. Somalis can turn on you very, very quickly if they don't see that you're genuine."

The tour passed the pots of Unimix and as usual Audrey recoiled—she couldn't stomach the smell of it, but then none of the UNICEF people could. The group reached the schoolhouse, with rows of neatly arranged children aged five to ten sitting on the floor reciting the alphabet in a room with inadequate ventilation. Audrey smiled widely and invitingly to the children and greeted them all. On the blackboard, under the letters A, B, C, D, and E, Audrey wrote carefully with chalk, "AND LOVE," and drew a heart. Under it she drew four Xs—"These are kisses," she said, "and that's a heart." She scanned the room and all the small faces; some seemed healthier than others and on the air were the always-present, wracking coughs.

Back outside she spied a tiny boy in rags that had once been a macawii. In his hand he carried a red plastic bucket, presumably for food. His arms and legs were like straw and he stood there wide-eyed and dazed. He may have been five, he may have been seven—who knew with growth stunted from malnutrition—but he was clearly disoriented as much by the strangers and the commotion as by hunger. His big eyes showed the now-familiar unfocused stare around a sunken face. These were the ones she always felt most protective of, the ones so easy to overlook, so easy to push aside.

She knelt by the boy and her guide said the boy's mother was sick. Audrey became instantly, fiercely protective of the boy and asked if he had eaten and where he was going. She held his tiny hand and said to the interpreter, "Tell him I'll take him to go and sit down." She said to the boy, "Can I carry you? Can we go get our dinner?" She pointed. "We go there and get our dinner?" She put her face next to his, lovingly, then picked him up the way she picked any of them up—so very carefully, because he might break.

"Oh God, he weighs nothing," she lamented, and posed with the boy as Betty and another photographer snapped pictures. Audrey tried to get a response out of the child in her arms. "Where do you want to sit?" she asked him. No answer. Betty tried to joke with Audrey, but her heart was too busy breaking.

Next Audrey sat with mothers and children and watched them eat until it was time for the UNICEF team to move on. The caravan drove to what was called Medina Hospital, a facility operated by Médecins Sans Frontières. It was a clinic like so many she had seen on her missions, a one-story, green pre-fab building with a red metal roof. In Hollywood it would have been the size of a ranch house owned by a TV star pinching pennies. As she and Robbie unloaded from their vehicle to walk inside, gunshots sounded, sharp reports from not too far off, and then the rattle of machine guns in several bursts. Such were the times that locals didn't bother to turn their heads to see.

Anna Cataldi, also now in Somalia, had just filed a story about the situation here in Mogadishu with her newspaper in Milan:

"The volunteer workers with Médecins Sans Frontières look at us with dazed expressions. Clearly, they are in a bad way. Malaria, amoebas, and now that they've had so much contact with blood, they are testing them for AIDS as well. These brave people stayed in Somalia even during the bombardments, when everyone else had left."

Audrey walked into Medina Hospital knowing what these volunteers faced; it wouldn't be an easy visit. As usual all eyes at the facility fell to the pale, thin, dressed-down movie star as doctors and volunteers gathered round. A doctor led the tour and appealed for more intravenous fluids and more antibiotics. He described the staff passionately in English, his Middle Eastern accent thick. "No salary. They are doing their best for no salary because they are good people."

"Fantastic, isn't it?" said Audrey. The room was small and crowded with their entire party and some doctors; she felt herself swoon a little from lack of oxygen. She mustered the Hepburn discipline and forced a smile that was big and heartfelt. A box office smile.

The doctor worked his weary facial muscles into the closest thing to a smile he could muster. "Thank you very much for coming," he told her, and meant it. A movie star and camera crew were not usual for the clinic.

"Wherever I go in the world," she told the staff gathered around her, "I work for UNICEF, but I always talk about you, because I'm full of admiration, and your courage has been incredible. I think the whole world knows it; you don't need to hear it from me. But I like to be able to tell you, too. Thank you so much."

The caravan pressed on to another refugee camp, this one nearby in Mogadishu. It was as ramshackle as the others, with the tukels composed of just anything, even shards of corrugated steel. But here so close to the port, Audrey could take some comfort that the children seemed a bit better. When she stopped to pose for a picture with a group of them, she studied their faces. "I can tell they've had their lunch," she said to Betty Press with relief. "They look okay."

As she walked through the camp, once again she became the Pied Piper, with a small child gleefully holding each of her hands as she walked, and a mob of them circling around, chattering away at the white lady who seemed to cast a spell on them so easily and for a short time their cares were gone.

Next came UNICEF Feeding Center #1, a white concrete building with bars on the windows. On its roof flew the flag with the red crescent. Here 100 children greeted her and sat and clapped and chanted and she delighted in their enthusiasm. It gave her hope.

The caravan stopped for a quick and austere lunch, and then drove to Mogadishu Port, where UNICEF and CARE officials provided a tour of the offloading of supplies from cargo ships and then the transfer to trucks for shipment inland. But, oh, the trucks, "held together by willpower," she joked, forty- and fifty-year-old cab-over-engine relics that were falling apart, their demolition-derby fenders dented and tires dry-rotted and in shreds.

She stood in the midst of thousands of fifty-pound bags of sorghum stamped USA. She climbed atop the bags piled fifteen feet high and posed for pictures with a CARE representative and with Robbie and looked across the vast warehouse at what seemed enough food for all of Africa. If only there weren't war, or clans— she heard that just that morning in Belet Huen north of Mogadishu, armed gunmen had raided a food depot operated by the International Red Cross. Workers from Save the Children were holed up for fear of their lives, and Audrey knew all this American sorghum could do no good if the people didn't receive it. All of which made the mission of General Shaheen and his Pakistani peacekeepers so vital to the fates of all the Somalis Audrey was meeting in Kismayo and Mogadishu, adults and children.

Up on top of the sacks of sorghum she greeted with hand-shakes the warehouse staff working so hard to load bags into trucks. "Ciao!" she called to them, having learned she had the best chance of communicating in Italian. She climbed down to ground level and watched the ancient diesel truck with the shredded tires lumber out of the warehouse burdened by perhaps eight or ten tons of sorghum and then others pulled out to form a convoy. She could only hope they reached the people and not the bandits.

By now on this second day, Betty began to understand Audrey's physical situation. "I knew she wasn't real strong. It was a big effort for her and that was another thing Robert was very concerned about. I could tell it was hard for her even to get down to the children's level. She would do that, but it was hard."

The agenda moved forward under a punishing Somali sun. Next, Audrey and Robbie were driven a short distance west toward the airport to meet with representatives of CARE and the Red Cross. They were introduced to General Shaheen, an impressive-looking man of fifty wearing a tan Pakistani uniform with a blue beret cocked to one side. He was stocky like a veteran soldier and wore a mustache and sunglasses. The general explained to Audrey that he and his men had just landed and were confined to the airport area because there weren't yet enough of them to proceed to the port in safety. It was a sign of the times in Mogadishu— peacekeeping soldiers were sheltering in place against the violence of the city.

Shaheen led Audrey and Robert to the senior Pakistani officers. "Awfully glad you're here," she said to a major. "We've been waiting for you!" She said it excitedly, then caught herself, and added shyly, "The whole world's been waiting for you, for that matter. Not just me."

Then she asked if she could say hello to all the Pakistani soldiers, and all twenty formed up with fixed bayonets, a long line of men about her height in tan uniforms and blue helmets. She went down the line and shook each hand. "Hello," she said with a smile, and "Thank you for being here." And more hellos. It was, all over again, the moment in *Roman Holiday* when Princess Ann moves along the line of reporters and greets each one with a handshake and a warm word. No Gregory Peck waiting at the end of the line, but to Audrey, at this moment, they all were, in their way, Gregory Peck.

Shaheen would tell a reporter that evening, "This is the first time the blue helmets have been welcomed this way. This is breaking traditions. Breaking new ground, as we say."

Shaheen talked to Audrey about the U.S. Air Force personnel at the airport guiding in more Pakistanis aboard transport aircraft. Col. Mike Hagee of the U.S. Marines was over there with a couple of aides. There were American Navy ships just off the coast, said Shaheen, ready to help guard the food at a moment's notice if need be. But the American leaders, Hagee and Navy Capt. Braden Phillips, had agreed with Shaheen that the best way to proceed was to try to get along with the warlord Aidid rather than antagonize him.

Audrey's mind had latched onto these Pakistani peacekeepers who might just be the salvation of a million Somali children, and that led her to think about the American Marines and Navy boys out there on the ocean, sent here on a mission of goodness and hope. She felt pure joy at the nobility of this mission and it occurred to her that she must find a way to thank the Americans for being here, as she had just thanked the Pakistanis. She knew George and Barbara Bush—this time, the president had done the right thing.

The idea formed quickly and she blurted out to General Shaheen, "Do you suppose I could go out to see the American boys on the ship?"

Warrior Queen

The decrepit little parade of UNICEF vehicles drove toward Mogadishu Airport, which, Ian MacLeod reported, "was almost totally destroyed and still effectively under control of Mohamed Farrah Aidid, the Somali warlord."

Audrey and company exited their cars in the shadow of the control tower, and a red-headed man of medium height in loud civilian attire moved toward them.

"Col. Mike Hagee, United States Marine Corps," said the redhead. "It is a pleasure to meet you, Miss Hepburn," and he shook her hand as if he meant it. Hagee may have been dressed oddly for a Marine in his plaid cotton shirt and civilian slacks, but if ever she saw a man who bore himself like a Marine, in or out of uniform, it was this American with the friendly face who now held her hand. She didn't need to flash the famous Golightly smile; she had him in her power and she knew it. She flashed the smile anyway.

Audrey introduced Robbie, Mark Stirling, and Ian MacLeod. She described their day so far and the visit to the port with its staggering amount of newly arrived food for distribution to a starving country. She mentioned General Shaheen and meeting the peacekeepers who would be charged with the task of guarding the shipments as they were unloaded, and then, hopefully, see the food safely in the hands of children and families who needed it so desperately—she had already seen many children hanging onto life by a thread, which made the Pakistanis and Americans so vitally important.

"I was impressed," said Hagee. "She was very down-to-earth and it obviously wasn't about her, you could tell that. It was about the children. That was her focus and what she was doing. This wasn't about her safety—she was on a mission, which I really admired."

Stirling and MacLeod addressed the question Audrey had posed earlier to Shaheen: Could the UNICEF group, including the film crew, visit one of the warships off the coast to thank all those soldiers and sailors for helping UNICEF? Robbie watched and listened intently, as he always did. Somebody had to look out for Audrey's safety because she wasn't about to do it herself. Now she was all set to hop on a helicopter and fly out over the ocean to expend more precious energy when he knew full well how weary she must already be.

Hagee told the group about the question of legality—how low-key should the mission remain—but said he had spoken with Captain Phillips commanding Amphibious Ready Group 1 and they had agreed it would be a good thing for the men to see Audrey Hepburn aboard the U.S.S. *Tarawa*, which was the base of operations for the U.S. part of the humanitarian mission. In fact, there had been a CH-46 Marine helicopter dispatched for the purpose of transporting the UNICEF team; it should be here any minute.

Sure enough, the heavy-lift, twin-rotor Sea Knight came into view and landed. As crates of supplies were off-loaded out the back of the aircraft, Audrey and party climbed aboard through the door behind the cockpit. Each in the UNICEF party was outfitted with a headset, goggles, and flak vest, then checked out on the military safety harness. Through the headset, Audrey was able to hear communications over what was otherwise a constant roar of engines.

As always, the safety gear sobered Robbie up to the latest escapade this woman had undertaken. Hagee had expressed confidence that there were no safety issues in flying out to the *Tarawa* and back, as in fear of gun or rocket fire, and if the commander on the ground felt that way, why should Robert feel otherwise?

In a moment the bird was airborne and swooping east over water. In a day of adventures, the latest proceeded at 110 miles per hour.

Aboard the *Tarawa*, it might as well have been the president who they tracked inbound aboard the Marine helo. Mike Hagee's radio call had resulted in a hasty meeting on the bridge that included Phillips, *Tarawa* Captain Nigel Parkhurst, Executive Officer Charles Carey, and other officers plus Command Master Chief Earl Brandon. Dignitaries coming aboard for a tour was nothing new. Academy Award-winning actress Audrey Hepburn coming aboard, well, that was another matter.

Audrey was UNICEF—everyone knew that much. Shaheen had told Hagee and Hagee had told Phillips: She's all about business and the business is children. So what would Audrey Hepburn want to see aboard the Big T? How should she spend her time and where should she be taken? Of course, the idea of Hollywood stars and glamour meant more to the officers on the bridge than to the kids below decks, kids who grew up after the 1960s. For these guys an "old movie" was *Jaws*. The guys on the bridge were the ones who had seen *The Nun's Story* and *Breakfast at Tiffany's* when they were young, and *Two for the Road* and *Wait Until Dark* while at the Naval Academy. How would the officers age forty or fifty involve these young pups, the Marines and sailors who had never heard of the long-retired Audrey Hepburn? Sure, they'd be happy to have a woman aboard, and a movie star, whether they knew her or not. But how do you make them care; how do you make them a part of the afternoon?

The idea of a donation to UNICEF came up—pass-the-hat

stuff that would make the ship's company feel like they had skin in today's game. The men checked their watches. Maybe they had an hour if that. *Tarawa* XO Carey gave the job of organizing a donation on the Big T to Command Master Chief Brandon, who hurried off to make it happen.

Phillips and Parkhurst agreed they'd take Audrey and the others up to the flag mess for lunch and a briefing; the visitors could freshen up in the admiral's stateroom now used by Phillips. Then the captains would provide the standard tour of the bridge, airport, hangar deck with the Harriers and Cobras, then maybe the well deck with the landing craft, if there was time. Miss Hepburn would probably appreciate the fact that this ship could do anything needed to guard shipments of food, from putting Marines in trucks ashore to dropping them into critical spots. Whatever was needed, the *Tarawa* could do.

The meeting broke up and word spread through the massive war machine—news that made no sense to anyone: On a too-warm Monday on a too-long deployment, a Hollywood legend was about to pay a call on a U.S. warship off the coast of war-torn Somalia, halfway around the world.

In the bright afternoon sun Audrey Hepburn stepped off the Sea Knight helicopter onto the flight deck of the *Tarawa* looking every inch the warrior queen, striding across the flight deck and trailing a string of servants behind her. All in her party wore aviator headsets and flak vests and she walked like an athlete, the smooth, graceful stride of a cat, a big smile on her face, not knowing quite what to do or where to go. Cameras pointed at her from all around, men on the *Tarawa* taking pictures, and the UN photographers taking pictures and shooting film. She walked and waved and a man called the "air boss" pointed her in the direction she should go.

She walked toward a group of men in khaki uniforms and blue

U.S.S. *Tarawa* ball caps. Two stepped forward with the command look about them. The heavyset one, a man with a gray mustache and fatherly face, offered his hand. "Nigel Parkhurst, Miss Hepburn," he said, "I'm captain of the *Tarawa*."

Parkhurst introduced Audrey to a bright-eyed, fit and trim, clean-shaven officer, another redhead, Capt. Braden Phillips, commander of Amphibious Ready Group 1. Parkhurst explained that Phillips was the officer who had given the okay for the visit. Audrey thanked both captains for receiving her party.

"It was the traditional 'Welcome Aboard,' greeting them, getting them off the flight deck," said Phillips.

Audrey and party—Robbie, Stirling, MacLeod, and Eisner—removed headgear and flak vests and handed them off. The visitors were escorted up steep metal steps to the flag area, space for the staff of the ready group commanded by Phillips and the Marine Expeditionary Unit staff of Hagee. Audrey, Robbie, and the others entered the officers' ward room, also known as the flag mess—the place where the staff officers ate. Suddenly all was quiet for the UNICEF visitors and the two senior officers of the ship. Audrey and her people were offered coffee and lunch in what all the Navy men would remember as a "cordial atmosphere."

In fact, more was offered. "They had a bar," said Ian MacLeod. "We actually got a drink." And after the day they'd had, they needed one.

Captain Phillips laid out the mission of the *Tarawa* as directed by the Joint Chiefs acting on the orders of President Bush. He talked about working closely with Colonel Hagee who was commanding on the ground at the airport. Hagee had met with Aidid and Ali Mahdi and gotten their agreement to let the peacekeepers land. So far, the operation was proceeding without incident, although at last word the Pakistanis remained at the airport even though a second planeload of peacekeepers had landed. The situation was just too volatile to try to truck men armed only with

M-16s to the port when they could at any moment be outgunned 10 or 100 to 1 and facing .50 caliber machine guns or RPGs if the clans attempted to hijack truckloads of food.

Audrey drew on every scrap of information she had studied during her prep work to describe the mission of her party in Somalia. She talked about what she had seen in Kismayo, which she knew was just the barest hint of the suffering of millions. She talked about her day in Mogadishu and said that tomorrow she was off to Baidoa and then to Bardera, places where the situation was said to be very bad. She now clung to hope that the food that had already arrived at the port, the mountain of it she had climbed to the top, and the supplies the Americans airlifted in, could reach those in need.

It was such a pleasant break from the pressure of the mission. "I think they appreciated getting out of Mogadishu for a day," Phillips said with a chuckle. Soon enough he would go ashore and see for himself "what was left after the pillaging by the locals."

Phillips turned his stateroom adjacent to the ward room over to Audrey and Madeline so they could spend some time freshening up and "wash the dust off." The groups reconvened on the bridge, where suddenly Audrey enjoyed an eagle's nest view of the bow and the ocean beyond. She was led next door to what they called the "primary" behind the bridge, the control tower for air operations. Helicopters were coming and going in an impressive, even overwhelming, show of military might.

As she scanned the various radar scopes, and the men in blue diligently went about their work, she noticed Captains Phillips and Parkhurst conferring with other officers. Phillips removed his cap, showing his red hair. He gathered the visitors around him in what Audrey recognized as a photo op. The UN film crew knew to roll camera as Phillips held a piece of paper in hand and explained that when the crew heard Audrey was coming on behalf of UNICEF, they did a quick collection among the men of the *Tarawa*. The paper in his hand was a check and he held it up so she could see. "Between 12:30 and now we got $4,000." He told her it was "from the Marines and sailors of the combined group."

Audrey swooned on her feet as the words sunk in. "You are terrific!" she said, looking about her at all the sailors on the bridge. The gesture had blindsided her. She murmured, "Thank you," and she could barely take hold of the check because her eyes had grown weepy. She was so tired that she could muster no defense against tears now, tears of gratitude and of exhaustion. Phillips deferred to Parkhurst, the ship's captain, and Audrey reached up and kissed him on the cheek. Here's something she could hold onto, something she would remember, like the Oxfam village at Mokomani they had visited the day before. She would speak of this gesture by the sailors and Marines in days to come and tell the world of it. Her new heroes had come through in a most unexpected way.

Parkhurst handed out blue *Tarawa* caps to Audrey and the others in the party and then led her on a tour of the ship, the medical facilities, mess deck, then down to the hangar deck. It was like walking on Fifth Avenue in New York City at lunch hour, this big island on the water teeming with cheerful men, big smiles on their faces, the picture of health.

Behind her, Robbie fretted. The Americans were super-enthused to have her here, and she was following their lead. He communicated his concern to the Navy officers and it reached XO Charlie Carey, who shared the worry. "She didn't look all that well to me," said Carey, who could see exhaustion in her face, "so we were concerned about that." He appreciated the position Wolders was in trying to look after his single-minded woman. Carey said of Wolders, "He was making sure she was pacing herself. I think she would have done anything she was asked; he was more circumspect about 'let's be reasonable.'"

Back on the bridge they rested a moment. Captain Parkhurst asked Audrey if she had any interest in speaking to Marines and sailors who this moment were gathering on the hangar deck. She said that, yes, of course she would. It's why she had wanted to come out to the ship—to thank them. Led by Parkhurst and Phillips, the group made its way back down to the hangar deck. On their approach to that big space, she could hear a dull roar indicating a great many people were ahead.

She had her arm hooked in Parkhurst's and he leaned down and said in her ear, "You know, it's not the academy awards, but there are a lot of people here who would like to see you." She gave him a nervous smile.

The two captains entered the hangar deck with Audrey on Parkhurst's arm and a great explosion of cheers and applause nearly knocked her over. It was the sum total of men at sea for months, and their testosterone, and genuine respect for this woman and her mission.

The officers boosted Audrey atop a wooden crate four feet high and she looked out at a sea of men crammed into every open spot of a hangar deck already packed with aircraft and equipment. Men were wedged in among the jets and helicopters and crates and forklifts. A thousand men now looked up at her with smiles and adoration.

She was handed a microphone. The emotion churned inside her—being here and feeling this unexpected love. More than that. *Support.* Suddenly she realized she must say something, and she didn't even have notes! All she could do right this instant, standing on a wooden crate, was speak from the heart.

"I came to Somalia determined not to cry," she managed into the microphone, swiping at the tears. The men cheered and applauded. She described for them the term 'compassion fatigue,' then held up the check that had been given her by Captain Phillips, more than $4,000, she said, and declared to the men of the *Tarawa*, "Nobody should ever tell me again about compassion fatigue.... I am so touched by this gesture of compassion for the children of Somalia. You young Americans are giving from your hearts." They roared their approval. She looked out at a thousand smiles. An hour ago all they knew was a movie star would come aboard. Now they realized so much more—this was a fellow war fighter. That slim body was lined with steel.

"Most of the guys had heard what the conditions were on the beach," said Phillips, "and recognized the personal sacrifice she was making to carry out her responsibilities as the UNICEF ambassador."

Parkhurst would sum up how all the men of the *Tarawa* felt about Audrey Hepburn's hours on the ship: "Hey, here's somebody important who's visiting us halfway around the world. For her, all these guys are here trying to help in this war-torn country, as if we had become partners on the same mission. She had an expression of extreme happiness to be welcomed in that way. She charmed everybody on the hangar deck, with her smile, her talk, her appreciation of what we were doing. She made them feel good about why they were out there."

Executive Officer Charles Carey said, "She was really well received. Guys loved her. She was clearly tired but man, she was willing to make the effort. If you're not used to getting around a ship, it's exhausting. She was a trouper and willing and happy to say stuff. Everybody was very positive."

After her speech she posed for pictures with sailors and Marines and signed as many autographs as she could within the crush of men on the hangar deck.

And then it was over. Phillips and Parkhurst knew that as the day wore on, the khat-chewing gunmen of Mogadishu grew more volatile and they had to get the UNICEF people back on dry land and whatever safety they could find.

Audrey put on her headgear and flak vest and was led onto the flight deck, with a Navy man on each arm leading her toward the CH-46, its blades spinning just over her head. She hunched low, climbed the steps, and returned to her seat to be harnessed in and soon the group zoomed over the ocean again, heading back to Mogadishu airport.

"It was such a dangerous place," said Parkhurst. "I wouldn't have gone ashore without a platoon of Marines. I think she was very brave. She put strain on her own life."

Back at the airport, journalists caught up with Audrey after the Marine chopper had departed, and all was now dead quiet as the sun began to set. Crews set up cameras in front of a line of UN armored vehicles offloaded from the cargo planes that had arrived that day. Each sported a mounted machine gun with a Pakistani at attention. Audrey stood with General Shaheen on her left and Ambassador Sahnoun on her right. She was asked how it was going on her trip.

"From now on, a whole lot better," she said with a tired smile, "because as you may have seen earlier, a great many more blue helmets came in." She'd made it back to dry land on adrenalin from the *Tarawa* visit, but now her energy flagged by the second and she struggled to put together coherent words for the journalists.

"The U.S. Navy is lying off the coast. I did visit the carrier today. It was a thrill. And from today on, aid—U.S. aid, humanitarian aid in general—will be far better protected and will get where it's supposed to go. So I'm very happy."

Ambassador Sahnoun struggled in unsure English to convey that Audrey's presence represented global effort to bring aid to Somalia. She jumped in to rescue her friend: "If I may quickly tell a story. When I did visit the U.S. ship a moment ago, they had practically no warning of our coming and in an hour, the sailors, the Marines collected $4,000 for UNICEF Somalia." Her smile grew broad and her eyes sparkled in the golden glow of evening light. "Now if that isn't caring and loving. I'm so touched and grateful. What more could we hope for?"

But she sobered in a moment, because Somalia remained Somalia, and the task was as daunting this evening as it had been at sunup. "The greatest problem is anarchy in this land," she stated. "There is plenty of help arriving. There are countless, marvelous organizations—NGOs—and everybody knows what to do, and they can do it, except they're constantly held up by insecurity, lack of security. Aggression, in fact. It's a big deterrent, believe me."

"Are you optimistic?" she was asked by a British journalist.

She smiled. "Very, by nature, and certainly today." He wanted more, and she said, "Of course we're optimistic because we've seen the enormous improvement already in a few weeks' time. Unhappily, we're too late for some, but we are in time for others. And that's why we're here."

It had been a full day and a satisfying one, but she shook with fatigue. And she felt a pain in her stomach. Hunger maybe. A bug maybe. But something. All she knew was, she hurt.

City of Death

Audrey arose on the morning of Tuesday, September 22, 1992, not realizing how much this day would contribute to an ever-compressing timeline: She had only four months to live. To her dismay, the pain in her abdomen remained as she and Robbie boarded the King Air for a hop 270 kilometers due northwest to Baidoa, a city of perhaps 40,000 that had swollen with another quarter-million refugees to become the main stage for Somali's horror show. It was better known lately as the "city of death," Ian MacLeod warned them. Ian had been there and seen it firsthand.

Phoebe Fraser of CARE Australia had seen it as well. Fraser—daughter of former Australian Prime Minister Malcolm Fraser—had first entered Baidoa a month earlier and said of that experience, "As we drove into town a hush came over the car, even the jovial gunmen on the roof were quiet, confronted by evidence of a living nightmare. Men, women, and children so weak they could barely walk wove their way along the main road in search of food. It made for dangerous driving as the reactions of people so close to death are slow and they did not seem to hear or heed the oncoming vehicles." Fraser suspected these poor souls would welcome a quick death by vehicle.

Now it was initiation time for Audrey and Robbie. On the plane ride in, Mark Stirling advised that the weather had changed and the rains had come—it had rained last night, in fact. While that sounded like welcome news for a country short of water, rain brought germs, and with a population weakened by famine, germs brought death. Those quickest to go were the smallest and most vulnerable. As Stirling would say later that week, "The first indication of the rains was the number of children's bodies piled up in Baidoa."

Ian MacLeod offered his assessment: "Baidoa was the epicenter of the famine. I told them [Audrey and Robbie], 'What you saw in Kismayo was bad, and Mogadishu was bad, but this will be much worse.'" It landed as a punch in the gut for both the visitors in this godforsaken land, visitors who had steeled themselves for any and all sights they could imagine. But no one could imagine what lay ahead.

From the air, Baidoa sprawled across a large expanse of low structures surrounded by desert. The UNICEF plane touched down at an airfield just southwest of the city. The group took a short and eye-opening ride into Baidoa, where the structures that seemed fine from a distance came into ramshackle focus close up. The place was a wreck of closed and long-ago-looted shops and houses. And the people, oh, the people. They moved in long and shuffling lines, thousands of ghosts wandering about. The only inhabitants with any sort of health about them were the boys and men with automatic weapons—here, it seemed, every young man was armed to the teeth and subsisting on food that had been looted before it could reach the children and mothers who needed it most.

The UNICEF team reached a facility run by Concern, a volunteer organization that had been founded twenty-four years earlier in Ireland to address famine in the Nigerian province of Biafra. Since that time the amazing volunteers of Concern had touched lives in other corners of the impoverished world, and now had through sheer guts and determination become the first NGO to establish a toehold in the city of death.

Despite their heroic efforts, a sputtering old truck pulled up to Concern's compound every morning before dawn. In fact, it sat parked there when the UNICEF party arrived.

Exiting their vehicle Audrey said, "I walked into a nightmare"—a sight so horrible that it may have shortened her own life: The volunteers who had expected to make a difference in Somalia were tossing sacks into the back of the truck parked there. The sacks were cloth bags containing bodies, Audrey realized. It bothered her that they looked like shopping bags, and they were so easy to toss about. "Over 100 bodies they had collected that morning," said Audrey, "and most of them were very small bodies."

Ian could see Audrey's hesitation to go even one step farther. In another moment she forced herself away from the car because this was why she had come: to see the worst. Ian realized, "It seemed to give her more strength to see it all and then go away and tell the world."

The UNICEF group wandered inside Concern's building. A nurse named Margaret explained that they distribute 15,000 hot meals a day—Unimix and biscuits. Margaret mentioned a "therapeutic center" for the worst cases. Audrey and the others headed that way, across a small bridge. Audrey's friend Anna Cataldi had made this walk on a different day while covering the crisis for the newspaper that had hired her.

She reported: "In order to reach the therapy center we've got to make our way through a sea of haunted faces, nude infants covered with sores, loose bundles on the ground which either cover sleeping bodies or corpses—it's never clear which."

Betty Press said, "It was—" She paused at the memories. "I could not believe it, to see those children, basically, so emaciated. I don't know. It's beyond words, really, to describe that."

The therapy center was a compound with a courtyard dominated by a single tree, and near the tree, as Audrey described it to the press, lay dozens of bundles of blankets each with "these thin,

thin, thin children, of all ages—small, and a little bit bigger—who to me seemed to have gone already. And their eyes were like enormous pools of—" she paused, searching for the word, "—of questioning. They look at you with such—I don't quite know how to say this—saying: "'Why?'"

"They were being more or less force-fed" by the Concern volunteers, Audrey explained. The bags of bones would be arranged on the ground and carefully given "a spoon of something every few minutes, because they can't drink or eat or don't want to anymore. And what amazes me is the resilience of a human being, that they were alive."

Audrey's eyes settled on the wreck of a young boy of, she thought, about fourteen, who lay there trying his best to breathe. "I watched him and watched him fighting for breath—I had asthma all my childhood and, ahhh, I was longing to help him breathe." As she looked at him, "He finally just curled up and died."

In fact, everywhere her eyes fell, in all directions, another drama involving a tiny human played out. "There was one little girl, standing, leaning against a sort of wooden door, motionless," said Audrey. "There was this little white cotton thing that someone had tied around her. I couldn't stand it. I tried to get a flicker of reaction." The little girl merely stared at nothing.

They were wretches, wrecks, abandoned, orphaned, discarded. Tiny little figures, some with mothers present but most alone, with their stomachs distended and their eyes enormous pools of emptiness. "A child that's so traumatized ... seen its parents killed or tortured or whatever ... you can't give him his parents back," Audrey lamented.

Worst of all was the utter quiet. "They are totally silent. Silent children. The silence is something you never forget." She corrected herself. "Sometimes there is coughing. A lot of coughing, because most of them have either tuberculosis or diarrhea—it just sort of runs out of them—or bronchitis, which they can't deal with."

Ian MacLeod noted, "The absolute look of shock and horror on Audrey's face as she could see the pain of the mothers who, also in a pitiful condition, knew they could do nothing to save their children from death." In the tortured hour Audrey's group spent at the Concern feeding center, MacLeod said ten children died.

One of the young Irish nurses drifted up to Audrey and touched her arm. She whispered that maybe Audrey should go to the staff quarters to get away for a moment. The nurse advised that, here, "It's much worse to watch than to work." Audrey forced a smile and said, no, she was here exactly for this: to see the worst and then talk about it to the press.

"The workers that were working there and running the camp were handling it as best they could," said Betty. "I'm sure they saved a lot of lives."

The film crew's director pointed out one of the infants and asked Audrey to try to feed her. Audrey knew with a glance that this child would not make it. She told him no. She decided not to participate in videotaping at certain key points. She always considered filming a "necessary evil" to raise awareness of the desperate situation—but this was too much, and these people deserved privacy, "human dignity" as she described it, even now. Especially now.

She said, "There's this curious, what can I call it, embarrassment, timidity that comes over one when you walk into a feeding center like that, of, I feel I shouldn't be there. I feel I should leave. It's like walking into somebody's room who is dying and the family should be there, only the nurses, you know what I mean, are sort of intruding in some way."

As Robbie described his companion, "It's a love for people that goes beyond sympathy. It is perhaps more than empathy. An ability to project her imagination so that she could actually feel what others are feeling." And for an empath, this was much too much.

So many here were dying in ways she understood all too well from the Hunger Winter. She said, "I wonder if people think about the pain of starving to death, what happens to your body. And it's a very slow process. And it's not something that, just sort of, you waft through and then die."

Her brain clicked into autopilot. The children who were beginning to bounce back with some food, the ones that showed life—she clung to these souls and sat with them, sharing conversations they couldn't understand, but her smile might cause a smile in return. She'd been doing this with children since Ethiopia and the actress could pull it off. Inside, the woman screamed.

"I have been to hell," she would later tell her sons. Hell was Baidoa, and the end of everything.

"UNICEF killed Audrey," said one of her friends, voice choked with emotion even decades later. What the friend meant was, Baidoa killed Audrey.

Luca believed that from Liberation Day in 1945 on, the war relentlessly pursued his mother, that a bullet kept Audrey Hepburn's name written on it. "She knew from a certain point that life was an equation, and that she had to make sense of it," said Luca. "This is the beautiful thing about my mother; the thing I totally miss and the people around her totally miss. She knows she can close the circle. She can come around and meet this bullet from the war." And to Luca, closing the circle meant going into Somalia when she knew it would kill her. It had. She had doled out the last drops of her life force to the wretches in Baidoa, sparing none for herself.

The empath had grown numb by the time the UNICEF party completed the 100-mile flight and touched down just east of the city of Bardera, once a bustling population center of 100,000 in the southern part of the country. Earlier in the year, Aidid's forces had fought for control of Bardera from clans loyal to deposed President Barre. In June Bardera fell to Aidid and became his southern headquarters. By that time, all but 5,000 had fled into the desert or over the border into Kenya.

Robert Press writing for the *Christian Science Monitor* said of Audrey and her mission, "For three days she has flown all over Central Somalia in a small twin-engine plane, landing in towns jammed with unpredictable, heavily armed rebels and marked by bullet-riddled buildings from a civil war still not over."

For UNICEF and other relief organizations, Bardera presented different challenges than Baidoa. The city had been destroyed in battle and become notorious as a kill zone and then, because Aidid had set up shop there, the UN hesitated to send food because the move might have been seen as pro-Aidid and anti-Ali Mahdi. Finally, UNICEF and some NGOs had ventured in and with their arrival, more than 20,000 Somalis had come for food, hundreds dying in that final passage.

On a tour of quiet streets led by one of Aidid's officers, Audrey saw bones lying in heaps in the deserted marketplace—the officer explained these were camels, cattle, and other animals slaughtered for food months back. Even their hides had been boiled to wring out the last nutrients. All the activity centered around the feeding centers, and Audrey spent her time with children and mothers, most of them beyond help.

Such a soul-crushing day her last in Somalia had been. The next morning the UNICEF party flew from Mogadishu over the border into Kenya to visit refugee camps swelled to 50,000 Somalis who had fled their country.

"The dimension of horror is nowhere more evident than in the displaced camps where tens of thousands of people are struggling each day to survive," said Audrey. Once again she described it as "a slice of hell." But at least here survivors who had been fed could begin to relax knowing they no longer were forced to dodge bullets and experience the physical dangers posed by the clans.

In the Kenyan camps "we actually were walking with people," said Betty. "Audrey was holding hands walking with people. Kids would come up. And they were relatively healthy because they were in a refugee camp and being taken care of. It was a different atmosphere. A little bit freer."

At long last they reached Nairobi and the Tudor-influenced, five-star Norfolk Hotel, which sat on four very green acres in sprawling downtown Nairobi. The suffering thousands Audrey had left behind at the camps were geographically close by the opulent Norfolk, and a world away from it.

Emerging from their car she caught sight of Anna Cataldi smiling and waving from the terrace—Cataldi too had just been to Baidoa to witness the plight of the children. Audrey rushed to Anna and they exchanged European kisses. "Beneath the pink shirt she was painfully thin," said Anna, "and I caught myself thinking sadly that she was beginning to look more and more like those children. Audrey had always been thin, but not fragile."

The star excused herself so she and Robbie could find their hotel room. She would track Anna down after a shower and change of clothes, she said. "But when Audrey reappeared, her skin looked no better," said Anna.

The next morning Audrey sat for individual interviews with hand-chosen members of the media. Robert Press, Betty's husband, said, "She received me as a guest in her home, offering a soft drink on ice. Now, that's only a small gesture, but in my years of interviewing people in many countries, it is one of the few times a non-African had been so courteous and thoughtful to this reporter—Africans in their homes almost always offer refreshments."

Press found her relaxed and refreshed, "smiling but very focused on her just-completed UNICEF journey through parts of Somalia—a country in the midst of a devastating civil war. But rather than recount the danger and unpredictability of Somalia ... she gently said she hoped her visit would draw more attention to the needs of the children she had met."

Audrey delighted in relating to Robert Press her *Tarawa* adventure and the surprise donation by the men, which had proven a rare positive moment in her nightmare. Press had been in and out of Somalia for a couple of years and asked about Baidoa and how she kept from feeling overwhelmed. "I don't. I have a jolly good cry every so often," she admitted, adding, "I've always been fairly sensitive, but I think at this point I have had an overdose of suffering. That's why I do need to go home and do other things."

She also sat with Jean Hélène of the French magazine *Le Monde*, Kathleen Openda of the Kenya Television Network, and Anna Cataldi of *Epoca*.

Cataldi wondered aloud to Audrey if perhaps international military intervention could help Somalia away from the edge. "No, absolutely not!" said Audrey sharply, her thinking colored by the war of her youth. "That would be a very big mistake, like killing a snake in the cellar by bombing the whole building."

Audrey saw in Anna's question the idea of military occupation, and to Audrey, that meant war. Luca had heard the sentiment from his mother more than once. "She knew from direct experience that any kind of a war is failure," said Luca. "You cannot have a 'right' war. If you start a war, by definition, you are hurting more than solving. The ones that suffer more are inevitably the frailest ones—the children."

Sitting on-camera with Kathleen Openda from Kenya Television, Audrey was asked again how she copes. "Perhaps I don't," she said. "I give in sometimes. It is heartbreaking … You never walk away from it, ever again. It's an image you carry with you for the rest of your life."

After another rest she met up with her UNICEF colleagues at the doors to the Norfolk ballroom, where two dozen journalists, including those she had met earlier, gathered for the official post-mission press conference. Members of the media represented the BBC, Inter Press Service, ANSA, Reuters, and Visnews.

"Audrey was very nervous because she really wanted to say

the right thing to the world," said Ian MacLeod. "Her hands were shaking. She was so nervous about getting it right. That always surprised me—shouldn't this come easy to an actor?" Not *this* actor—Audrey considered the Nairobi press conference to be the most important moment of her life.

The battered warrior sat at a table and mustered all her remaining strength. Below, the pain in her abdomen remained. Her first words hinted that this wouldn't be a usual press conference: "I want to be very careful how I say this. I don't want to sound overly dramatic. But you really wonder whether God hasn't forgotten Somalia."

Then the story poured out of her. Holding hastily scribbled notes, she reminded reporters that UNICEF had first issued warnings about disaster in Somalia in February 1991. "It was potentially the greatest catastrophe in living memory, and it happened," she said. "In the last four days, I saw it."

She described what she had witnessed in Kismayo and Mogadishu and then added, "Nothing could have prepared me for Baidoa—no matter how good the TV images." She talked about the truck loaded with dead, about a dry wash turned graveyard, about an overwhelmed Concern feeding center, and about the courtyard of children waiting to receive food. "And the silence—the terrible silence broken only by wracking coughs as children with respiratory infections fight for breath." Tears began to flow at the memories.

Cataldi said, "Listening from close by, I was surprised to hear, beneath the gentleness of the Audrey I had always known, an uncharacteristically hard edge to her voice: 'An entire population is on the verge of extinction. Everyone, in government organizations or any other kind, needs to realize the extreme urgency of the situation. There is an immediate need for food, medicines and funds—right now!'"

Anna added, "On this occasion, the usually clear and gentle

voice was low, almost hoarse, as if her sense of indignation were about to choke her."

A reporter asked Audrey if, given everything she had described, all was lost. "Unfortunately, it's too late for many children and mothers, but for many more there is still time," said Audrey. "With the help of the international community; the dedication of relief workers from the NGOs, the ICRC, and UN agencies; with airlifts into the central regions of Somalia; with the protection of UN security guards—with all of these helping hands and thousands of Somalis who work tirelessly to help their own people, we can stop Somalia from falling off the edge of the earth."

MacLeod said, "She was brilliant. She was speaking from the heart, and as a mother."

In many interactions with the press, she hammered home her feelings about war and the consistent theme of colonial exploitation by Europeans that had set up the disasters she now witnessed. "Civil war and the fighting are what impedes reconstructing," she told a reporter. "You can seed and develop, and it all gets destroyed by war. All people must put their weight behind the idea of stopping warfare. We don't want to just help children survive; we want to give them a future."

She returned again to the idea of white-skinned people taking advantage of those who were dark: "We're very responsible for a lot of the suffering in Africa, because we didn't do very much about these populations when they were colonies. We didn't help where education is concerned, and now we're paying the price. We enriched ourselves on the back of these people. Drought is a tragedy of nature, but famine is not."

That evening, Audrey could finally relax after having run the gauntlet of interviews; she had projected strength, composure, and resilience through each. Now she could lower her guard; she invited Anna to her room for a visit. When Cataldi knocked on the door and Audrey called for her to enter, Anna found her friend lying on the bed in darkness.

"Forgive me," said Audrey, "but I have a stomachache and need to lie down. But don't go away; we can still talk if you feel like it. Sit here beside me." Audrey and Anna went back years; Anna was a friend.

As she lay there, Audrey confessed, "I have nightmares. I can't sleep. I'm crying all the time." Then she forced a tired smile and added, "[But] war didn't kill me, and this won't either."

Anna said, "But I had the feeling that sooner or later, war kills you. She was so skinny, I felt something was really wrong."

Cataldi would say later, "Many times since I have asked myself how it was possible that none of us realized her condition. You only had to look at Audrey to see that she was ill."

They parted the next morning—Anna would head next for Sarajevo and another humanitarian catastrophe in the making. Audrey, Robbie, and the UNICEF team were about to move on to the Continent for more press events. "When I hugged her," said Anna, "I was scared. I had a shiver."

Audrey and Robbie boarded a plane and left blood-red Somalia behind. They reached Paris, where she sat for an in-depth, French-language interview with respected journalist Jean-Pierre Elkabbach on his new current affairs television show *Repères*. Elkabbach had offered Audrey a platform to speak exclusively about her mission without the need to revisit ancient Hollywood history.

"You are back from what is called the hell of Somalia," he said to tee her up. "What did you see? Are the odors of the rank poverty you saw and the memory of all the death and dying that you witnessed still very much with you perhaps?"

She hesitated at the intensity of the question. "I think," she began in French, and then paused. "I think that, basically, I am never going to get over that trip. As you say, when you go into a feeding center for little children you're met with that smell of death, you see little bodies being removed, you look into the eyes of the children in those tiny skeletal bodies, and then the little faces—" She closed her eyes tightly. "It's simply unbearable." She forced out the last word in a whisper.

Elkabbach then led her on a thoughtful odyssey of her UNICEF experience. She discussed her role as one who sees what there is to see and then reports on it. He asked her about her many meetings with heads of state, and then she turned to the topic of man's inhumanity to man—civil wars, the prevalence of guns, the exploitation of vulnerable people.

She railed against colonialism that had exploited countries like Ethiopia and Somalia and then cut them loose—ninety-two percent of Somalis can't read or write, she told Elkabbach. As a child she lived in the wealthy Dutch towns of Oosterbeek, Arnhem, and Velp—all had been built by businessmen who worked in the Dutch East Indies. Back then she accepted the grand villas as just the way it was, and only much later understood that natives in Indonesia had paid the price for each villa—people whose skin was other than white. Understanding the wealth of her Dutch hometowns led to her statement, "We all have blood on our hands."

When he asked about her quote from Nairobi, wondering if God had forgotten Somalia, she said that turning to God was "something I've tended to do at certain times." But she quickly grew uncomfortable and segued from the topic, saying, "But God has a lot to do." She turned her attention to Médecins Sans Frontières and other organizations working courageously in Somalia as people representing goodness and light.

From Paris Audrey and Robbie and some others from UNICEF moved on to London for another UNICEF press conference, this one at stately Carlton House Terrace. Beforehand she stopped by a London TV studio to tape an interview via satellite with Bryant Gumbel of the *Today Show* for delayed broadcast on U.S. network television.

Gumbel asked, "I read you quoted as saying you went there

determined not to cry. Why?"

Her face drawn, she smiled an empty smile. "Because other-wise I thought I might, you know, fall apart?" She paused and add-ed, "But I think you might have heard that in connection with a lovely moment which I had there. And little did I expect in Somalia to have a very happy moment. And that is, when we were invited on board the big U.S.S. *Tarawa* carrier, and visited the ship and 2,400 sailors and Marines, and we were there for less than an hour, when at the end we were handed a check for $4,000 which—the boys had collected." Recounting it her voice caught with emotion and exhausted tears flowed. "You see, there I go again," she said.

She ended her appearance with a plea for support of the hu-manitarian effort, as if with her last breath. Signing off with Bry-ant, she forced one more smile and swiped at her tears.

At the London press conference she relived her four days in hell and, bone weary, broke down weeping yet again. "No media report ... could have prepared me for the unspeakable agony I felt at seeing countless, little, fragile, emaciated children," she said. "I'll never forget their huge eyes in tiny faces and the terrible si-lence. I haven't slept at night since then. I sometimes sleep during the day, but I'm having a hard time at night."

Those who had been in Somalia with her had seen signs of physical deterioration—as when Betty had watched her struggle to kneel with a child and then climb upright. But Press also recog-nized the intense Hepburn focus. "She wanted to do that trip. No matter what."

"Audrey complained of an irritating pain in her stomach in the last days in Somalia and when we were back in Kenya and having the press conference," said MacLeod, "but she and Robert were sure it was just a bug from the food or water. It was the usual kind of symptoms that we all felt quite regularly in Somalia."

Robbie would say in retrospect, "Of all our trips [for UNICEF], it was the one Audrey was most determined to make. The trip was grueling emotionally and physically, but Audrey was as much a trouper as on the other trips—she had great energy and courage." Yes, she had been experiencing stomach pains, and yes, they chalked it up to "an amoeba."

Robbie knew her psyche had been shattered by the trip that she had been most determined to make "no matter what." Coming out the other side, the most resilient woman he had ever met was proclaiming before the world that she would never get over Somalia. Had she now proven that she was single-minded and courageous to a fault? Had her victory in conquering all obstacles and experiencing the worst in Somalia been Pyrrhic?

One reporter covering the London press conference understood the perils she had faced. "She is not recognized in many Third World countries, so goes into volatile areas that other visiting dignitaries cannot enter. She admits she feels nervous, 'but not enough to stop me from going.'"

MacLeod had known as far back as their road trip to Canberra two years earlier what a hardy soul Audrey was, but after Somalia, he saw the full picture.

"She was doing something she didn't have to do," he said when asked about warrior-Audrey. "It was something she wanted to do. I was trying to understand, Why are you doing this? She went to places other Goodwill Ambassadors didn't go to. They'd give a concert or go to a gala. Nobody else went to Somalia. She wanted to make a difference to people in the worst situation in the world. So yes, she *was* a warrior."

Danvers - 978-762-4439
240 Independence Way
Danvers, Massachusetts 01923-3653
01/22/2023 02:24 PM

GROCERY
267000001 FRUIT   NF $1.69
055023790 MM S   NF $1.29
218010305 FD COOKIES   NF $4.99
HEALTH AND BEAUTY
052040271 MASCARA   T $9.99
052076889 Maybelline   T $9.99

                    SUBTOTAL $27.95
T = MA TAX 6.25000 on $19.93 $1.25
                    TOTAL $29.20
        Reusable Bag Discount $0.05
    *4224 MASTERCARD CHARGE $29.15
               AID: A0000000041010
                            MASTERCARD
               AUTH CODE: 97474W

Your Target Circle earnings are in!
Open the Target App or visit
Target.com/circle to see your benefits.

SOME PROMOTIONS MAY REDUCE THE
REFUND VALUE OF ITEMS

REC#2-3022-1187-0163-3170-9 VCD#751-752-240

Help make your Target Run better.
Take a 2 minute survey about today's trip

informtarget.com
User ID: 7697 7881 3983
Password: 668 291

CUENTENOS EN ESPAÑOL

Please take this survey within 7 days

Did you earn a little extra?

circle™

Join free.

.com/circle | app

See Target.com/circle for details. ©2019 Target Brands, Inc. The Bullseye Design and Target are registered trademarks of Target Brands, Inc.

Go to target.com/returns for full refund/exchange policy.

Did you earn a little extra?

circle™

Partners

Autumn had erupted in its full Swiss glory by the time they dragged themselves to Tolochenaz on Wednesday, September 30, to be reunited with their home and family. Giovanna took one look at Audrey and grew terrified but said only that la signora must rest. The apples had come in and Audrey prepared her garden for winter. She and Robbie took walks and shopped at the farmers' market and began to heal from what they had witnessed. But she had been right in her pronouncements; she could not get past Somalia.

Sean said, "We had talked on the phone, as we did at least once a week, upon her return from Somalia, and I felt for the first time in my life a chilling and dark cloud enveloping her voice."

To Luca she intimated that she could no longer fight because "evil won."

Another trip to the States loomed. They would visit Sean and Connie and then Audrey would receive an award. This one would be given in Rochester, New York, and they could visit Robbie's mother and two younger sisters. And Audrey would do another round of television interviews for UNICEF and attend another gala in Manhattan. Afterward, they would fly to Antigua to "recharge her batteries." It would be, for the most part, a genuine vacation beginning in mid-October, and until then she could enjoy two glorious weeks sheltered at La Paisible.

"We used to have dinner at either my house or her house," said Doris. "So she came here and said, 'I've got these terrible stomach cramps.' She wasn't well; she wasn't well at all. And Dr. Me said, 'Well, you don't eat the right food, and we're going to have the right food, and you're going to get better.' And then, it didn't get better."

About a week into her downtime at home, a Rochester newspaper reporter called for an interview. By this time Audrey had moved away from vivid descriptions of the suffering in Somalia and focused on positives instead. "Obviously when you go to these places, you see the work of thousands of dedicated people who are having wonderful results," she told him, "and it makes you feel terribly small and unimportant, and full of admiration."

She added that the only way she could ever take on a UNICEF mission was because of her partner Robbie, from Rochester: "I don't do it alone. I do it with Robert. I couldn't do it alone—we do it together. We enjoy it together, we suffer together, we cry together."

But the point of the interview was her upcoming visit to upstate New York to receive the George Eastman Award for Distinguished Contribution to the Art of Film from the International Museum of Photography. "I know that in receiving this award, I'm in extraordinary company," she said based on familiarity with the roster of past recipients of the annual award first given in 1955. They ranged from Buster Keaton and Louise Brooks to Greta Garbo, Jimmy Stewart, and Lauren Bacall. Five years earlier, Audrey had presented the award to her friend Greg Peck on the eve of her UNICEF career.

Audrey and Robbie boarded a plane for the United States on Sunday, October 18, flying first to L.A. to stay with Connie at 615. There Audrey scheduled a visit with Connie's physician to see about the stomach pain that had endured through weeks of rest. After undergoing tests, she and Robbie flew to New York on

October 24 for the Eastman Award ceremony and a visit with the Wolders family. By the time they reached Rochester, abdominal pain had become her constant companion.

"You could tell they were both wiped out," said Rob's sister Claudia. "Neither one of them looked very well. She did not feel good, but she didn't want to cancel the event. She wasn't one to cancel too many things, and it was sold out. This was one of the biggest events in Rochester."

Audrey proceeded with all planned events on the big evening, including a meeting with reporters, the dinner, award presentation, and black-tie gala and dancing. When she and Robbie vanished before 10 p.m. because of her stomach pain, a few grumbled at "typical Hollywood behavior."

"She got through that night," said Claudia. "I don't know how."

At 6 p.m. the following evening, they attended a sold-out showing of *Breakfast at Tiffany's* at the Dryden Theater of the George Eastman Museum. Tickets went so fast that overflow was planned for the nearby ballroom, with a closed-circuit line feeding the proceedings. Audrey dutifully introduced the film and then took questions afterward. By now Robbie knew she was suffering something more than the suspected amoeba and stayed close by. "Nobody knew how ill she was—how could they? I didn't, either. It was quite heroic what she did that night."

They received word the next morning that the tests in Los Angeles confirmed a parasitic infection and she was prescribed a course of powerful antibiotics. Both were relieved and they hurried on to New York City on Tuesday, October 27, for Audrey to receive the Casita Maria Settlement House Gold Medal of Honor for her humanitarian work. Since 1946, the Casita Maria Settlement House on 107th Street had been an educational and cultural center for Spanish-speaking residents of Harlem. Each year New York society, including Ralph Lauren, embraced a gala fund-raiser. This year, Lauren would present the award to Audrey.

"Casita Maria is a jewel and I wish there were many more of them," said Audrey. "It is also very important that Latins can spread their cultural heritage. The more we learn from each other, the better it will be. There is so much hatred in the world. It's hatred that's killing children, not famine and poverty. Children are born loving, not hating, and we teach them intolerance and prejudice."

In the city she sat for another in-studio television interview, this one with Charlayne Hunter-Gault, a groundbreaking African-American journalist and civil rights activist working for the *MacNeil/Lehrer NewsHour*. The highly respected program required that Audrey relive Somalia for a new audience, and she bore down and did just that. When Hunter-Gault posed Anna Cataldi's question about a military occupation of Somalia to restore order and get aid to the people, Audrey was ready.

"I think only in a supportive sense, not in an aggressive sense. First of all, we can't go into Somalia, invade it and occupy it. That is not our right, nor does the UN have that kind of a mandate. The UN guards are still not functioning properly. They don't—are not able to function properly, those that are there, because their mandate is not to fight it out; it's to guard the provisions that are coming in. But the war won't let them do exactly, you know, what we would like to do, and all of that needs negotiating. So it's all very long." She had been at first frustrated and then incredulous that the peacekeepers she had met almost a month earlier still hadn't moved from their bivouac near the airport because of how outgunned they were by Aidid's army.

Hunter-Gault said, "Miss Hepburn, we're approaching the year 2000. Did you ever think there would be this kind of tragedy repeating itself?"

At first Audrey tried to play the optimist, "Let's look on the bright side, Charlayne...." But soon her emotions spilled out. "We see the children dying right in front of us, for most of us on television. I've seen it happen, and I'm filled with a rage at ourselves.

I don't believe in—in collective guilt, but I do believe in collective responsibility. Somalia is our responsibility. It's certainly the British responsibility, the Italians' responsibility, because they colonized that country. And they should be doing more, I think. They have an obligation to those people from whom they benefited for so many years. But it is the international community, and that is the beauty of humanitarian—of relief workers, of humanitarian aid, that regardless of what's going on, of the danger, of the diseases they're getting themselves, they do it, and they don't give up. And that's why I want to not only speak for children but for these extraordinary people who live among the living dead and sleep among moaning bodies in Baidoa, where there is no light after 6 o'clock, and you can't read or even think because there's so much misery around you, and get up in the morning and wash these people and these children, and try and feed them month after month. They're the ones that have to be supported with more help."

Hours later, in their suite at the Plaza Hotel where the gala would be staged, she stepped into the chosen Givenchy gown, green satin below, black and gold brocade above. She pulled the garment up around her body as she had done her entire gala life. Then came a moment that made no sense. With the bodice around her torso, "she couldn't close it because her stomach had gotten so big," said Christa Roth.

Between them, Audrey and Robbie managed to fasten the gown and she proceeded through the evening events, but their alarm now matched the ongoing pain in her stomach. They looked at each other and knew their long-anticipated Antigua getaway wouldn't take place. The next day they flew back to Los Angeles, where Connie's connections meant the best possible medical care.

Before leaving Manhattan they stopped to visit her friend and colleague Larry Bruce, who had begun in Ethiopia with her and had doubted her stamina, then followed the warrior into battle after battle. Strapping, handsome Larry had been there from the beginning of her UNICEF service, and through all the sessions before the U.S. Congress, and most recently on her tour at the beginning of the year—in San Francisco, Chicago, and Fort Lauderdale. He now lay dying of a rare liver disease at only forty-seven. She couldn't believe how far and fast her handsome and vital friend had gone downhill. Her getaway to the States had become yet another nightmare.

In Los Angeles Audrey entered Cedars-Sinai Medical Center. With tests still inconclusive, she was scheduled to undergo exploratory abdominal surgery at the beginning of November. Luca said, "My mother knew her own body. Connie told me that my mother took her hand and said, 'My dear friend, this is it.'"

Doris Brynner said, "I used to tell her, 'You should stop. You should rest.' She'd say, 'I can't. I can't. I've *got* to do this.' And then one day, she couldn't anymore." It had been all or nothing all along for Audrey and UNICEF, and now there was nothing left to give.

The Last Battle

The surgery performed November 2, 1992, revealed cancer that had spread from the appendix to the intestines. A tumor was removed along with a section of her colon. An official hospital post-surgery statement expressed optimism for a complete recovery. All she had to do now, said an oncologist, was wait and heal. But the statement bore no semblance of reality: The doctors had known from mid-surgery that cancer had already spread to Audrey's stomach.

She began a harsh course of chemotherapy and received pain-killers of increasing potency.

She demanded in mid-November to be released from the hospital to stay with Connie at 615. Luca flew to California to visit her that month, unaware of the real story until he laid eyes on her. "I knew my mother well enough to see a layer of despair. When she looked at me, she looked like a mother who was dying," said Luca. "She would smile, but the smile was a mask."

The White House tracked down Audrey at Connie's by phone—President Bush wanted to personally invite her to accept the Presidential Medal of Freedom he had awarded in recognition of five years of UNICEF work. The ceremony would take place at the White House on December 11. Robbie took the call and tried to shield her from the effort of speaking with Bush, but when

Robbie relayed who was on the phone, she felt obligated to speak with the president after the courage he had displayed by sending the amphibious squadron to Mogadishu. She struggled up and out of bed to take the call. Bush believed, based on news reports, that Audrey was mending and cajoled her to attend the award ceremony—he might even have a surprise for her. The best she could offer the American president was, "I'll be there if I can."

Had she made it to the White House on December 11, she would indeed have heard heartening news. Just after midnight on December 9, U.S. Navy Seals and Marine commandos hit the beach off Mogadishu to begin Operation Restore Hope, a U.S.-led, multinational humanitarian mission to take command of Somali ports, liberate the besieged peacekeepers, and assure the safe delivery of food to the starving masses. Some said that Audrey's high-profile mission had forced a lame-duck Bush Administration's hand—Bush sought and secured the support of President-Elect Bill Clinton on the decision. Another amphibious squadron had replaced the *Tarawa*'s group and thousands of U.S. troops were ready to land.

On that same December 9, pain had already driven Audrey back to Cedars-Sinai for a second exploratory procedure. Oh, if it only were an amoeba. But no. Surgery confirmed the spread of cancer in what Sean called a "thin veil" over her entire digestive system. There was simply nothing to be done.

When Audrey regained consciousness, Sean sat beside her to say the surgeons couldn't get all the cancer. In response, according to Sean, she turned her head to look out the window and said just two words.

"How disappointing."

Sean refused to accept any sort of inevitable outcome and in the following days led the charge to find alternative therapies to save his mother and best friend.

"I would usually visit her in the morning and then go to my office under the pretext of work that needed catching up," he wrote. "There I would spend hours reading, researching, and calling every cancer center for the latest treatment or information available."

Robbie said, "I think she always knew what was going on and, sensing our desperation despite all our attempts to remain positive, she tried to let us know that there was no fear."

The terminal diagnosis led Audrey to discontinue chemo and let what she called the "process" of nature take its course—and she wanted to do it at La Paisible. The holidays, the traditional high point of the year, were close by and she needed her touchstones: the house, the dogs, her garden, and the Orunesus—Giovanna and her parents. When Givenchy heard that Audrey wished to fly back to Geneva, he insisted they use a private jet and he enlisted the aid of a mutual friend, philanthropist Rachel Lambert Mellon, known to all as "Bunny."

On December 21 Audrey and Robbie arrived in Geneva in time to see newspaper headlines stating that a convoy of twenty trucks under the control of U.S. Marines and Belgian commandos was en route to Baidoa from Kismayo carrying 300 tons of food— enough for 750,000 people for one day. No, Audrey didn't favor occupation by foreign powers, but the swiftness of the operation and the might of the Western military finally brought to bear on behalf of the voiceless took her breath away.

An unnamed source said at the time, "She cried tears of joy. The one bright spot in her life is the images of the troops feeding the children she fought so hard to save." And then Audrey knew: She could let go of Somalia, and for that matter, of UNICEF. It was time, in Hollywood terms, to circle the wagons and prepare for the end.

Finally, after more than two months, Audrey and Robbie had made it home to be with her house and its family, the garden, her human children, and the Jack Russells. Discussions began about activities for Christmas Day, including a lunch. Before long Christa called the house. "I had Robert on the phone and I asked about her," said Roth. "'Can I come see her?' I asked. He said, 'Why don't you come and join us for lunch on Christmas Day?' I said, 'Are you sure?' And he said, 'Oh yes, Audrey would like to see you.'"

Audrey remained the captain of her ship, and the weeks that followed the final diagnosis would have played out, said Robbie, as "sheer hell if it hadn't been for Audrey's attitude. There was no resentment, no bitterness.... She even said it might have been the best time of her life because she felt the boys and I closer to her than ever."

On Christmas Day La Paisible pulsed with life. Sean had flown in, and Luca and girlfriend Astrid had arrived from Paris. Doris was there as well. Christa sat down with the family, and then, she said, "Audrey came down with her I.V., which was standing next to her chair. At one point she got up and went around the table and gave each of us a Christmas present. It wasn't wrapped. They were all souvenirs—things she had around the house. She gave me a Hubert de Givenchy scarf. She had something for everybody. Then we had lunch and she went upstairs and back to bed."

On December 30 Larry Bruce, head of UNICEF USA and Audrey's partner on so many missions, press conferences, and appearances before Congress, died of liver disease in New York City. When Robbie got the news, he chose to keep it from Audrey.

Doris had been commuting to and from Gstaad, but at the turn of the year, decided to spend nights with Square. For her part, Audrey turned inward to her animist beliefs and watched hours of nature programming on the National Geographic Channel as the disease progressed toward its conclusion.

She had once said to Luca, "I believe that if you lose the connection to the planet, you're dead," and now she sought to reestablish that connection on a quest for personal peace.

By now Robbie had begun to second-guess the intensity of

their UNICEF field work, cramming several missions into just eighteen months and then daring to visit Vietnam and Somalia. And in between, they had circled the earth over and over for various UNICEF activities. Perhaps, he said to Audrey, they should have just enjoyed retirement at La Paisible.

"Think of all we would have missed," she said to ease his conscience. "Think of what we did together!" But as the days counted down, she engaged in her own bouts of second-guessing. Maybe Doris and Giovanna had been correct all along and she had invested too much in the cause. She had done what she could before the engine quit, as planned, but she hadn't seen this catastrophe coming.

Much like Vero Roberti and his dreamed-of trip to Easter Island, Audrey now expressed regret that she never achieved the long-held desire for a family retreat to Australia. Maybe she should have pulled the plug on UNICEF for three or six months back when it mattered, rounded everyone up, and explored Queensland and the Great Barrier Reef—there was already worry about its fragility. No, she couldn't save this world, as it turned out, but with more foresight she could have shared more of this world with her boys.

Hubert and Philippe visited from Paris, and Givenchy and Audrey took a stroll together in the garden, a few steps at a time between rests. While out there, Hubert noticed the fragrance of apples even though the season had long passed. Giovanni the gardener told him that autumn's apple harvest had been stored in the cellar. They would soon send it, "at Audrey's wish, as in previous years, to the Salvation Army."

"She thought constantly of others," said Hubert, who that day faced the unthinkable prospect of saying goodbye to his friend for the last time.

Audrey concentrated all her remaining energy now on worry about how life would treat her companion and sons when she had gone. She kept probing each to determine if her work was done. Said Robbie, "She showed more concern for us than for herself, never letting the pain diminish her qualities. You really can say that her spirit was stronger than the disease."

Luca sensed his mother's question hanging in the air—Will you be all right? "I had started my first job in Milan and was going back and forth," said Luca. "The situation got to a point where I said to my mother, 'I think I had better stay here.' Despite the fact she was weak, and scared, in terrible pain and on morphine, she pulled herself together like the warrior she was."

"No way!" she told Luca.

"But Mummy, you're—"

"This is your first job," she cut in, "and we both worked too hard to get you there. What you're going to do is go to work. Then on Friday evening you can jump on a train and tell me all about it."

Luca said later, "I wanted to be there with her because in those days, the illness was on a fast track. But no, she wouldn't hear of it. She was determined—I find that very honorable of her. It was a decision she didn't make in that moment; it's one she made many years in advance." Now she and Luca needed only to stay the course.

When it came time for her last walk in the garden a week into the new year, Sean at her side, Giovanni told la signora he looked forward to her return to health by spring when they would prepare the garden together. Giovanni and Audrey had formed a deep spiritual bond over the years living on the same property and working in the garden.

"Don't worry, Giovanni," she said with a smile. "I will help you—but not like before."

By now Audrey wanted to see only those within a circle that included Doris and Christa.

"Toward the end," said Roth, "she had a little button which she pushed on to give her more morphine for the pain. I learned afterwards that affects people quite a lot—their psyche and their memory. One day I came and she said to me, 'Ah, I think it's so wonderful that you are coming from so far just to see me!' I realized that she didn't think I was coming from Geneva. She must have thought I was coming from the U.S. or somewhere very far away. When I told that to Robert he said, 'Yes, that is the influence of the morphine.'"

La Paisible remained a focus of activity around Audrey, but without la signora at the helm, its captain, the household wandered off course. By now, morphine was a constant companion. In accordance with her orders, Luca would spend the work week in Milan and arrive at Tolochenaz for the weekend to join Robbie, Sean, Doris, and Giovanna on vigil. "I would see this theater," Luca said. "They were in the war zone, and the tension was eating them up."

Days dragged by until Wednesday, January 20. Doris maintained a vigil at Square's bedside and left the room for just a moment. When she returned, her friend was gone.

Epilogue

At the funeral service, Givenchy tried to eulogize his friend but dissolved in tears. In his place, Sadruddin Aga Khan delivered a touching impromptu speech that's still mentioned today by those who heard it. Audrey was buried in a simple grave in Tolochenaz.

Robbie packed up and left La Paisible for Rochester, where he bought a home. "He was sadder than sad," said his sister, Claudia Deabreu. "He was really, really hurting. I don't think he ever really felt better—Audrey was still such a big part of his life." Rob would spend time years later with Henry Fonda's widow, Shirlee. He succumbed to cancer in 2018.

Sean and Luca memorialized their mother by creating the Audrey Hepburn Children's Fund, and by writing about her. Sean's book, *Audrey Hepburn: An Elegant Spirit* appeared in 2003; Luca's, *Audrey at Home*, in 2015.

Christa Roth retired from UNICEF in 1998 and continues to reside in the Geneva area. Doris Brynner lives near La Paisible as she did while Audrey was alive and misses her best friend every day.

Connie Wald continued throwing intimate dinner parties for Hollywood's elite until her death in November 2012 at age ninety-six. Her son Andrew quoted her as saying at the end, "No flowers, no services—and don't cancel Thanksgiving."

John Isaac suffered humanitarian burnout similar to Audrey's in

1994 after covering events in Sarajevo, including the ethnic cleansing. "The UN had asked me to go to Rwanda before returning to New York and document the conflict between the tribes Hutus and Tutsis, particularly the plight of children who had lost their parents during the unrest. They were called the 'unaccompanied children.' UNICEF had many centers where these children were given shelter. One of the boys named 'Innocent' was describing how his mother and father were hacked to death in his hut while they were hiding and he had witnessed this and later he escaped from Kigali [Rwanda] to Goma [Congo] with an elderly neighbor and he was in one of these unaccompanied children's shelters. He described his experience and looked at me and said, 'Do you know something? You look so much like my murdered father.' Then he asked me if I could take him back with me to my home. At this point, I broke down and had to give some excuse why I could not do that. But all that didn't make any sense to him. He came up to say goodbye while I was leaving, looked at me and said, 'If you ever come back to Africa, please come and visit me.' Heading back home from that trip, my whole journey was marred with this sadness and guilt that I was not able to help him."

Isaac suffered a nervous breakdown, sought psychiatric care, and at one point contemplated suicide. "I had packed away my camera gear and swore, 'I will not take another photo.' One morning while I was in my backyard, I saw a sunflower, and a butterfly had sat on it. At this point I ran inside my house and grabbed my camera and came out and took a whole roll of photos of this butterfly and sunflower. Next day I went back to work. At this point, I decided to turn my camera towards nature, environment, and wildlife and be a voice for the endangered." He continues in that role today as an active photojournalist, lecturer about his life and career, and advocate for nature, particularly the plight of the endangered tiger.

Prince Sadruddin Aga Khan championed environmental causes in his last years, first through his Geneva think-tank Groupe de Bellerive, then through his Bellerive Foundation initiative, Alp Action. He died of cancer in 2003.

Roger Moore would go on to a twenty-year career as one of UNICEF's most vocal and well-traveled advocates before his death in 2017. Christa believed Audrey had greatly influenced Moore's style in the field. "He admired what she had done, and he tried very hard to follow her footsteps and to fit into the mold that she had created," said Roth.

After twenty-nine years, Paul van Vliet continues his role with UNICEF Netherlands that began with Audrey in 1992.

Anna Cataldi's experiences in the Yugoslav Wars would result in her bestselling 1994 book, *Letters from Sarajevo: Voices of a Besieged City*, a collection of letters written by citizens living in terror. In 1998 she became one of ten original United Nations Messengers of Peace and then a Goodwill Ambassador for the World Health Organization, among many other accomplishments.

Dominick Dunne celebrated the memory of his friend by buying a Jaguar XJS convertible the year after her death and naming it Audrey. He kept a notepad in the car because, he said, "I get great ideas in this car." The respected journalist and author died of bladder cancer in 2009.

The initiatives championed by Audrey Hepburn would go on without her, some more successfully than others. Adherence to the 1989 Convention on the Rights of the Child has been in large part a success. Every member of the United Nations has signed on— but the CRC was never ratified by the United States government due to opposition by conservatives and religious leaders.

Operation Lifeline Sudan, with Audrey in-country for its kickoff, became a success in several ways. Said UNICEF's Detlef Palm, "OLS set many precedents: working with non-state actors [meaning a rebel army] to deliver relief; working across borders; creating corridors of tranquility in a war zone. It pioneered many new ways of working: such as 'ground rules' for working with warring parties on both sides of a conflict; introducing a 'code of conduct' as a basis for a vast network of civil society organizations; a 'brand' under which everyone with good intentions was welcome and where everyone could do what they were best at doing; a high level of coordination including a common logistic, security, funding, and reporting network for more than thirty NGOs and several UN agencies." Lam Akol, whom Audrey met in rebel country, would become a political force in an independent South Sudan. Akol said, "OLS saved lives in southern Sudan. That was its declared mandate. However, it is evident that the initiative created an atmosphere conducive to peace as demonstrated by the accelerated peace efforts during its early period."

Some have said that Audrey's mission to Somalia raised such awareness that the U.S. military's Operation Restore Hope resulted. Within a year, 13,000 UN peacekeepers and 25,000 U.S. personnel would save hundreds of thousands of Somali lives by guarding food shipments to Mogadishu, Baidoa, Kismayo, and other places Audrey visited. But the mission would change five months after her death when Aidid's clan ambushed and killed two dozen UN peacekeepers. Aidid and his henchmen became wanted men, leading to an attempt by U.S. Army Rangers and Special Forces to capture clan leadership in Mogadishu that October. The battle of Mogadishu and Black Hawk Down incident resulted in nineteen U.S. soldiers killed and scores wounded. Public outcry in the United States led to the end of Operation Restore Hope, and Somalia went on to become a haven for Arab extremists.

Some of the countries Audrey visited in the Developing World have come back from the brink, but as she predicted, civil wars continue to rage globally and the work of agencies serving children and their mothers in desperate need is unending. In March 1988 when she made the UNICEF decision, she knew the unique power of her "bloody name" and used that name for all it was worth. In some cases she even managed to hold back the tide of oppression and suffering. All these years after her passing, people will smile at the mere mention of her name and they'll say, "I love Audrey Hepburn." The reaction has become universal, a human instinct even in remote places and in that way, a very lasting way, the warrior won her fight.

Author's Notes

1. Comebacks

Audrey Hepburn remained an alluring celebrity for coverage by the press during her inactive period in the 1970s, which provided plenty of material for a biographer, but information doesn't abound regarding Kurt Frings, and so in part I relied on Luca's recollections along with those of Doris Brynner and Anna Cataldi. The press lovingly covered Audrey's return to the screen in *Robin and Marian*, with U.S. release in spring 1976. At this time a Bantam paperback included the screenplay, with an introduction by its author, James Goldman, that presented his fresh, firsthand account of leaving the script at Audrey's hotel in New York. Little was known about her involvement with the evolving film project *Out of Africa* until Anna mentioned it in conversation and pointed me to her book, *La coda della sirena*, released in Italy by Rizzoli in 2018. Sean Ferrer published the letter from Swifty Lazar in the book *Audrey Hepburn: An Elegant Spirit*. Audrey would speak to the press of the challenges of finding good movie roles as she aged, and the story of *Love Among Thieves* emerged through a deep dive into regional press during the time of its production. Evidence points to her restlessness, including comments made by Robbie and by Audrey, who felt she was still young both physically and spiritually and had something to offer the world.

2. Wings, Prayers, and Fate

Danny Kaye's reminiscence of the fateful plane ride that led him to UNICEF seemed apocryphal at first, but international press covered the harrowing Pan American Airlines flight on July 7, 1949, and Kaye provided details in Judith M. Spiegelman's *We Are the Children*, published in 1986. Danny's daughter Dena spoke of her father and the home in which she was raised in the November 2000 issue of *Architectural Digest* and to the Associated Press about his legacy in March 2013, then appeared on the *Rachael Ray Show* that July.

3. Cinderella

Jack Glattbach's 1994 notes to Hepburn biographer Barry Paris formed the backbone of the account of her first appearance for UNICEF, along with reminiscences by Robert Wolders and local press accounts from Macau. Audrey stated multiple times she was at first reluctant to do more than dip her toe in the water on behalf of UNICEF because she loved the quiet life she was leading.

4. The Square

Doris Brynner provided the story of meeting Audrey at the Curtis/Leigh party and detailed their adventures together after both women had separated from their husbands. Luca had covered the meeting of his mother and father in his book *Audrey at Home*, and both Luca and Anna Cataldi spoke of the lack of acceptance of Audrey in Rome. Luca discussed with me his first trip to Japan with his mother and the enduring Japanese love of Audrey Hepburn, and Christa Roth's profound memories of first working with Audrey in Japan rounded out this chapter.

5. The War Diet

Key to understanding Audrey's passion for the UNICEF mission was her experience in World War II as detailed in *Dutch Girl*.

When Luca and I were in the Netherlands together for the launch of *Het Nederlandse meisje*, he told the story of his mother's violent reaction to certain things German, and he and I also discussed it at length later. Extensive research for *Dutch Girl* revealed Audrey's life under fire—which made her no stranger to the bullets and bombs she encountered in the field for UNICEF—and her experiences with the last winter of the war, known as the Hunger Winter. I spoke with many in the Netherlands who confirmed Audrey's accounts to the press of the famine of 1944–45. As an empath, she knew what starvation felt like and couldn't bear the suffering in what she called the Developing World. Audrey's contemporary, Rosemarie Kamphuisen of Velp, provided terrific details about the touch points between Dutch young people and UNRRA relief services. Administrative details were taken from Spiegelman's *We Are the Children*. Luca described the complicated family situation at La Paisible and Giovanna Orunesu's influence with Audrey—the fact that she bucked Giovanna and other voices of dissent regarding UNICEF was significant and took courage all on its own.

6. The Visionary

Bob Geldof's groundbreaking work for Ethiopian relief proved controversial from the start but exerted great and lasting influence on Audrey Hepburn and her UNICEF career. The history of Geldof's humanitarian effort was taken from the press of the day, with his voice drawn from his December 5, 1985, interview in *Rolling Stone* and 1986 memoir, *Is That It?* Luca recounted the experience of watching Live Aid with his mother at La Paisible, which was a day that deflected the course of her life.

7. You Just Decide

Black lives mattered to Audrey Hepburn long before today's organized movement began, and I found it important to establish the Dutch-aristocratic roots of her belief system, as touched on in

Dutch Girl. I am grateful to Horst Max Cerni for connecting me with so many of his UNICEF colleagues who had worked with Audrey in the field, including Fouad Kronfol, George Kassis, and Shahida Azfar, all of whom provided memories of prepping Audrey for her mission to Ethiopia. Christa Roth's memories were profound because of the media scrutiny of this first mission in particular. John Isaac shared his memories of life on the road with his friend Audrey, and his photographs and UNICEF film footage added layers of subtext. Mary Racelis was another Cerni connection who told of her time in-country with Audrey. John Williams documented the Ethiopia mission in a January 1993 piece for the *International Herald Tribune* that was reprinted in the *New York Times* titled "Elegance with an Elf Inside." It was Williams who put in perspective the dangers of that night in Asmara.

8. The Good Egg

John Isaac told the story of the old woman and her chicken and Audrey's reaction, and of Audrey's joke about his "apparatus." UNICEF film footage showed Audrey in action in Mehal Meda, and multiple news accounts and UNICEF footage allowed access to the post-mission press conference in Addis Ababa. The press followed her through the U.S. tour, and those days were easy to recreate. Her appearances in Washington, D.C., were surprisingly difficult to document because of so many competing news stories and a disdain among both press and politicians for celebrities lobbying Congress for various causes. Post-Ethiopia the Hepburn backlash began, and some in the press wondered about her sincerity on the one hand, and naivete of where the money was going on the other. Her fierce reaction set a precedent for reporters who covered international affairs; they learned she was no pushover. Both Doris and Luca spoke of Audrey's exhaustion upon returning from the first mission and press tour, and Luca confirmed that yes, his mother would have parachuted into Ethiopia if necessary.

9. Two Worlds

Connie Wald was a force of nature whose status as a "Hollywood hostess" rated an obituary in the *New York Times* upon her death in November 2012. Much of the detail around the Hepburn/Wald friendship was found in the transcript of an interview of Connie Wald conducted for the writing of the Barry Paris Hepburn biography. Luca brought Connie to life for me, with additional detail provided in Sean Ferrer's *An Elegant Spirit*. Wolders provided specifics about meeting Audrey in a detailed interview conducted for Barry Paris. Audrey told her side of the story of meeting Wolders in a May 1991 *Vanity Fair* interview with Dominick Dunne. Biographers have portrayed Hepburn and actress Merle Oberon as "friends," but Audrey stated they had only met in person a few times. Robbie's mention of the dangers in Ethiopia appeared as an April 17, 1988, press filler in the *Santa Fe New Mexican*. Christa Roth detailed what became the usual practice of pre-travel briefings with Audrey and Robbie at La Paisible. Press coverage and UNICEF documents provided information about the visit to Turkey. Audrey is portrayed today as a media darling, but through her Hollywood career she was known to be aloof and at times a difficult interview because she could shut down fast if asked the wrong question. Various aspects of her off-limits private life were documented in *Dutch Girl*.

10. Camels with Solar Panels

It seemed ironic that as Cannes 1988 opened on the Riviera, there was Audrey in Helsinki auctioning off her artwork. Luca provided details about his mother and Bécassine, and Christa well remembered the origins of the piece of art that Audrey created after Ethiopia for the benefit of UNICEF. Robbie's quote about the camels was taken from Barry Paris's *Audrey Hepburn*. Rucchita's quote was taken from a 2014 interview with Pierluigi Christophe Orunesu that appeared at medium.com. Details of Audrey's first Danny Kaye Awards appearance in the Netherlands emerged from clippings provided by Hepburn archivist Leendert de Jong. Audrey would speak sparingly of her reunion with her father in Dublin; Robert Wolders provided more details in his in-depth interview for Paris.

11. Eye-Opener

As early as the October 1988 mission to South America, the press had begun to lose interest in Audrey Hepburn and her missions. Bringing water to villages and shedding light on street children just didn't resonate like a famine killing millions. Details emerged from photographer Victoria Brynner and from UNICEF documents, supplemented by some brief articles in the press. Spiegelman's *We Are the Children* looked at UNICEF's involvement with street children, and Robbie's quote about street children was found in the Paris interview; Audrey's quote was taken from her speech at UNICEF House. Unfortunately, the PROANDES Project seems to have been short-lived and is now lost to history.

12. Obliged

The story of Max Court and his ring appeared in a Kent newspaper called the *Courier* in January 1947, shortly after Audrey returned the entrusted article to its owner. The *Courier* article contained as much fiction as fact as told by Audrey's mother, Ella van Heemstra, who was then trying to clear her name from charges of sympathizing with Nazis. But the kernels of truth about Audrey helping a downed flier jibe with all evidence presented in *Dutch Girl*. Contemporary press coverage yielded details of the Givenchy retrospective and Audrey's role in it.

13. Return of the Dutch Girl

Leendert de Jong was happy to recount his meeting with Audrey, their June 1988 adventure in Paris, and her appearance in

The Hague in November 1988, with Leendert's archive including local press about the series of events. His anecdote about the moment Audrey tried to adjust a light to better illuminate one of Givenchy's costumes spoke volumes about the relationship of Audrey and Hubert, and about the over-the-top fussiness she could exhibit on behalf of those she loved.

14. Dangerous Road

Horst Max Cerni provided excellent reminiscences about the Central America trip. Additional details appeared in UNICEF documents and film footage. The meeting with Duarte was covered by the press and also on film, providing necessary elements of the conversation and setting. The trip to troubled countries in Central America demonstrated Audrey's deepening commitment to UNICEF and growing self-assurance that she could advocate effectively on behalf of "voiceless" children and their mothers.

15. Unseen Shield

Cerni's description of Audrey's life on the road in Central America captures perfectly the dangers she experienced at this time and the righteousness she felt for her cause. Details about the Mexico leg of the trip were found in newspaper coverage, and UNICEF papers and film footage, with tapes of the Barbara Walters interview available for review.

16. The Big Gun

Rob Wolders spoke of Audrey and the Dutch Resistance in the Barry Paris interview. The UNICEF team's appearance on Capitol Hill was covered in the press, and their testimony can be found in the Select Committee on Hunger's transcripts, Hundred and First Congress, First Session, April 6, 1989, Serial No. 101-3. Audrey's visits to the White House were covered in the *Detroit Free Press* of April 8 and *Chicago Tribune* April 9. Her speech at the National

Press Club was covered in the club's archives.

17. The Adventurer

Luca Dotti spoke of his step-grandfather Vero Roberti with great affection, and an examination of his career and works revealed a man of warmth and significant talent. Unfortunately, not much scholarship could be found about Roberti outside of Italy. His book *Moscow Under the Skin* was released in a UK edition by Geoffrey Bles in 1969, offering glimpses of this journalist's work to an English-speaking audience. The spiritual connection between Vero and Audrey was significant enough that his obituary, written by a journalist friend, mentioned the many prominent people who visited the hospital: "Among all I cannot fail to remember how much attention and affection was shown by the well-known Audrey Hepburn, who was close to Vero, a great actress and also a woman of sensitive and humane feelings whose firm sweetness shines through her smiling eyes." Luca considers his mother's decision to "use her name" on Vero's behalf to be a turning point and one of her life's "aha moments." Audrey spoke of her Sudan mission to French TV journalist Frédéric Mitterand in a May 6, 1989, on-camera interview that was found for me and translated by Sadruddin Aga Khan biographer Diana Miserez. This interview is one of the most candid of her life. Press coverage, UNICEF archives, and the in-depth Wolders interview provided details of the mission to Sudan up to the point where the government ordered her party to turn back. But what happened next? What did she do in the southern Sudan war zone—a trip alluded to by Wolders and by Audrey herself to Mitterand, but clandestine in nature and therefore not documented. Horst Max Cerni, with the invaluable help of Tom McDermott, was able to contact Detlef Palm, the UNICEF representative whose leg work resulted in the secret visit of Audrey and Robbie into the war zone. Detlef Palm's clear and concise recounting of the situation provides the first and only look at Audrey's courageous actions to reach children and women in peril in Sudan.

18. Chicken or Fish?

Luca offers a good-natured and realistic assessment of his adolescent self and the challenges presented to his mother. His reaction to the story of the night flight and flak vest illustrates how "in the dark" Audrey's family was to the true nature of her work in the field. Her blunt statements about the situation in Sudan were taken from her after-action report to the UNICEF executive board. The story of chicken or fish told by Luca was mirrored by Sean Ferrer in an October 2020 interview for *PEOPLE* magazine, and the Bogdanovich anecdote appeared in Barry Paris's Hepburn biography. A tape review of the April 19, 1989, *Larry King Show* appearance showed Audrey's uncharacteristically combative pushback with the host for not appearing to take her seriously.

19. Intermission

Audrey's first exposure to Steven Spielberg via *E.T.* was recounted by Luca. The account of the infamous sixtieth birthday party was first told in *Audrey at Home*, with details provided by Luca and Doris Brynner, who well recalled the moment Engracia collided with Marina Ferrer, to Giovanna's horror. The mutual love of *A Guy Named Joe* by Spielberg and Dreyfuss was recounted in Roger Ebert's December 22, 1989, review of *Always*, and details of the Montana location shoot were taken from the February 1990 issue of *Air Classics* magazine. The letter from Spielberg to Hepburn was auctioned off by Christie's in 2017 with its contents reprinted in the catalog. Accounts of the *Always* shoot were provided by Luca, the Paris biography, and contemporary press accounts. Shahida Azfar's memories of Luca's Namibia visit were forwarded by Horst Max Cerni. Sean Ferrer alluded to the connection between Audrey and plot elements in *Schindler's List* and Luca confirmed it. The visits by Audrey's friends to La Paisible offer charming insights into the private Audrey Hepburn. Leendert de Jong and John Isaac provided their reminiscences of those visits. John and his wife, Jeannette, made another visit to see Audrey and Robbie and reported the same warm experience.

20. Turning Point

The description of Kissinger in the White House Situation Room was taken from *Forum*, a monthly publication of *The Daily Star*, Volume 3, Issue 3, March 2008. Both Luca and John Isaac confirmed that Audrey found Kissinger's remarks highly offensive—and equally motivational. Ian MacLeod provided details of the Australian visit by Audrey and Robbie, and coverage of that visit in the *Sydney Morning Herald* was extensive. Various documents in the Barry Paris Papers at the University of Pittsburgh recounted the Bangladesh visit, including documents from Robert Wolders and Cole Dodge. By this time Audrey and Isaac had become close friends and his perspective was invaluable. Her November 20 speech was found in UNICEF's archives.

21. Reunion

The spiritual relationship between Audrey Hepburn and Anne Frank was covered in *Dutch Girl* from a World War II perspective, but the 1990 diary readings held importance in the timeline of the UNICEF years as one of Audrey's most significant and ambitious fund-raising endeavors. This was *her* baby in partnership with Michael Tilson Thomas. News coverage in the *Philadelphia Inquirer*, *New York Times*, and other papers added depth and perspective to this successful effort that Audrey and Michael Tilson Thomas intended to repeat in coming years. Sadly, Audrey died before that could happen, and no film or video exists of their performances of the Anne Frank material.

22. The Recruit

That Audrey burned out midway through 1990, two years earlier than events would suggest, proved a turning point in development of the book. Suddenly it made sense why she undertook only one mission in 1990 and none in 1991, and why she suddenly sought out Roger Moore for UNICEF work. Despite all the color and fun of *Gardens of the World*, darkness seemed to begin to descend on Audrey in the spring of 1990. She would speak of it in New York to Bridget Foley of the Fairchild News Service and make veiled references to losing vitality in asides to other reporters. Her method of recharging her batteries left family and friends scratching their heads: The self-professed stay-at-home who disliked travel and its jet lag circled the globe multiple times to shoot the *Gardens of the World* segments. The Alan Riding *New York Times* interview took place in April 1991 at La Paisible and proved to be another candid examination of Audrey's mindset and bewilderment that by this time the UNICEF effort had careened off the rails. Roger Moore spoke of Audrey's appeal to him to work for UNICEF in his 2008 memoir, *My Word Is My Bond*, and the Dutch press provided coverage of the International Danny Kaye Awards events.

23. Conqueror

Vo Nguyen Giap's *The Military Art of People's War* lent his perspective to the conflicts that made him a hero and legend. Just because Audrey claimed to be apolitical didn't mean she was; her volatile political statements about Vietnam ran globally only to be overlooked by biographers who seem to have ignored their importance and confrontational nature. Her pronouncements about fourteen million dying children were made to Joan Lunden on *Good Morning America*, December 19, 1989. Photographer Peter Charlesworth's memories of working with Audrey in Vietnam provided terrific insights into her mindset and work ethic in-country.

UNICEF documents and film footage also detail her movements, and descriptions of the mission were also provided to Barry Paris by Jack Glattbach and found in the Paris papers. Audrey would make a return visit to GMA and describe the Vietnam mission and her desire that the U.S. embargo be ended—by that time, U.S. senators had already drafted their letter to Bush expressing the same sentiment; these facts were covered in the press of the day.

24. This Iron Will

Not much has been written about the friendship between Audrey and Prince Sadruddin Aga Khan. Anna Cataldi mentioned in an interview that it was Sadri who first inspired Audrey's interest in UNICEF, and an interview transcript in the Paris papers bore this out. Luca also verified their friendship and the extreme alignment of their political, environmental, and humanitarian views serves as evidence of a close working relationship. Background on the prince was found in the 2017 biography *Prince Sadruddin Aga Khan: Humanitarian and Visionary* by Diana Miserez, with additional information provided by her in our subsequent correspondence. The 1991 Hepburn tour of the United States was widely covered by the press; the Wolders quote about fears of terrorism was taken from the in-depth interview for Paris. Dominick Dunne's May 1991 *Vanity Fair* exposé revealed Audrey's mindset at this point in her life, prompting book agent and deal maker Irving "Swifty" Lazar to entreaty her to write a memoir: "The nature, intent and content of the article is pretty much what your book would be. I have told you this many times, nobody expects you to write a book which would be different than what appears in that article, it is not intended for you to do kiss and tell." But for reasons stated in the narrative, she declined.

25. She's Real

D.C. press covered Audrey's third visit to Capitol Hill, and a review of the tape of the *Larry King Show* showed Audrey's surprise at hearing the voice of Robert's nephew Oliver—Rob's sister Claudia provided the inside story of Oliver's call, and of the subsequent visit of Audrey and Rob to Rochester, with local press supplementing. The botched September 1991 co-starring appearance of Jimmy Carter and Audrey Hepburn at the UN wasn't revealed in the daily press since the event hadn't been covered, but reporter James Warren happened to mention it in his piece "Covering the World at the UN: American media give United Nations beat a low priority," which ran in the *Chicago Tribune* on October 18, 1991.

26. Good Ol' What's-Her-Name

Mandy Behbehani interviewed Audrey for the *San Francisco Examiner* in January 1992 and drew the irate response, "I'm not playing a role," and the honest assessment of life in jeeps, helicopters, and civil wars. The mayor's gaffe, calling Audrey Katharine, led to an unexpected avalanche of press mentions of Audrey and UNICEF. Her visit to the Broward General Medical Center was covered in a February 6, 1992, feature by Berta Delgado of the *South Florida Sun Sentinel*. Interviews with Anna Cataldi brought to the surface conversations with Audrey in summer 1992 about the situation in Somalia and the desire of both women to get there. In written correspondence, Paul van Vliet offered his reminiscences about Audrey's recruitment of him for UNICEF and their work together for the International Danny Kaye Awards. It was clear to Audrey and those close to her that something was amiss with her health, but no one could say what it was or how serious.

27. The Big T

The Department of the Navy 1992 Command History for the U.S.S. *Tarawa* documented its movements in August and September. Interviews with Braden Phillips, Nigel Parkhurst, and Charlie Carey deepened knowledge of the workings of an amphibious assault ship. "The Effort to Save Somalia August 1992–March 1994," a document produced by the Office of the Chairman of the Joint Chiefs and written by Walter S. Poole, provided a blow-by-blow account of command thinking in the White House and Pentagon concerning U.S. response to the situation in Somalia. Ian Mac-Leod and Betty Press shared their memories of working in Somalia with Audrey. The extensive UNICEF film presence revealed conditions on the ground as crews followed Audrey's movements. She would speak of her experiences in a series of press conferences and also on the *Today Show* and the *McNeil/Lehrer NewsHour*, among other broadcast programming. Her mission this time to the most dangerous spot in the world drew as much press as had her first UNICEF field visit to Ethiopia. Mike Hagee, retired Marine Corps four-star general and U.S. commander on the ground in Mogadishu at the time of Audrey's visit, discussed with me meeting Audrey and assessing her conduct and mission in Somalia.

28. Held Together by Willpower

UNICEF's video crew captured the ongoing drama as Audrey progressed through her day, beginning at the Lafoole camp and continuing through the visit with Médecins Sans Frontières and then the stop at the Port of Mogadishu. Ian MacLeod, Betty Press, and Anna Cataldi provided their insights. The meeting with Shaheen and the Pakistani contingent was captured on video as she went down the line greeting each soldier.

29. Warrior Queen

Audrey's visit to the U.S.S. *Tarawa* became a global news story, but only superficially so. What protocols were followed? Who made the decision to allow UNICEF on the ship? What about safety concerns? These questions were answered by Mike Hagee and Braden Phillips, with Nigel Parkhurst providing the perspective of a ship's captain welcoming Audrey and her party aboard and seeing to their needs. As the XO, it was Charlie Carey's responsibility to make sure everything was shipshape—and it was Carey who noticed Robert Wolders fretting over the fatigue of his warrior queen. The donation was also of interest; Audrey would mention it repeatedly in coming months as the high point of an otherwise devastating mission.

30. City of Death

Phoebe Fraser's book *A Single Seed* proved the starting point for understanding the situation in Baidoa. Fraser was first in to attempt humanitarian relief on behalf of CARE Australia a full month before Audrey's visit. Once again, the memories of Ian MacLeod and Betty Press proved invaluable. Some statements made by Audrey were taken from UNICEF document 401534, an account of the post-mission press conference files by MacLeod. Anna Cataldi's reporting for *Epoca* and her book *With a Heart of Gold* were also consulted. Audrey dictated a 13-page account of Somalia she called "The Silent Children" that yielded many quotes found in this chapter. Others were taken from the *McNeil/Lehrer* appearance. *Christian Science Monitor* journalist Robert Press answered my questions about his post-mission interview with Audrey in Nairobi. And each press conference revealed the effects of Somalia on a fading Audrey Hepburn.

31. Partners

In our conversations, Luca discussed his mother's condition upon returning home, and Doris spoke of the alarm she felt at seeing the physical and emotional decline of her best friend Square; Sean's memories were taken from *An Elegant Spirit* and Robbie's from the in-depth Paris interview. Rob's sister Claudia Deabreu discussed the final visit to Rochester in a telephone interview. A review of the Hunter-Gault tape showed Audrey at her most distraught.

32. The Last Battle

My original intention was to end the book with chapter 31 when Audrey enters the hospital for tests. To me the outcome was known and her death has been well-documented. It seemed at first that the warrior's fight was over. But Luca provided rich evidence that his mother fought on and that in some respects her final fight was the most courageous. Sean's account was taken from *An Elegant Spirit* and Robbie's from handwritten notes in the Paris papers. Christa Roth shared her memories of Christmas at La Paisible and visits to Audrey in her final days. Luca's account confirmed that his mother was still his mother in the final weeks of her life. And Doris spoke of the vigil at her best friend's side and the importance of each of those moments.

Acknowledgments

People who knew Audrey love to talk about her. It's not as if opinions are mixed about this subject, which makes all the energy positive, and off you go. The first thank you goes to my friend Luca Dotti for long conversations exploring his mother as a mother, not as a movie star, and as a powerful woman who committed her life to improving the lives of children by "giving a voice to the voiceless." Along the way, Luca connected me with several people who knew his mother best. I wish I had been able to spend time in person with Doris Brynner, Christa Roth, Anna Cataldi, Leendert de Jong, and John and Jeannette Isaac, but a global pandemic got in the way of trips to Europe for face-to-face visits, and instead our interactions took place on the phone and through email. I'm appreciative of their time and patience through my many questions and follow-up correspondence. Luca also put me in touch with fellow creative Vikash Khana, who was working on a film project about Audrey's UNICEF career in parallel with my book and helped fill in many blanks about her media appearances.

It's frightening to me how close we were to losing the story of Audrey's humanitarian career because so much of it had not been documented. I'm grateful to UNICEF veterans Ian MacLeod and Horst Max Cerni for their help. Ian had worked with Audrey in Australia and throughout the mission to Somalia. Horst had accompanied her to Central America. When Horst put the word out to his connections, several other contributors appeared to tell their stories of working with Audrey. These included Mary Racelis, Detlef Palm, Shahida Azfar, and George Kassis, and also Ingrid Kasper, Robert Cohen, Agop Kayayan, Tom McDermott, Mark Stirling, Tarique Farooqui, and Madeleine Eisner. Thank you all for your time and memories—and indeed for your careers of service to those in need around the world. I am also appreciative of the help of Geneviève Wehry of UNICEF for putting me in touch with Paul van Vliet to learn about his friendship with Audrey and the launching of his long and distinguished UNICEF career.

A very special thank you to the photographers who accompanied Audrey on her missions and agreed to interviews about their experiences. These included John Isaac (Ethiopia and Bangladesh), Victoria Brynner (South and Central America), Peter Charlesworth (Vietnam), and Betty Press (Somalia).

Thank you again to Hepburn biographer Barry Paris for placing your research papers at the University of Pittsburgh, and to William Daw and other staff at the University of Pittsburgh Library System, Archives & Special Collections, Curtis Theatre Collection, Barry Paris Papers. Whenever I ask for help, you are there and very welcoming.

For me, curiosity about Audrey's UNICEF career began at its conclusion, with her mission to Somalia. Researching this period kicked off the project; writing about it gave me a narrative voice for *Warrior*. I am grateful to four key members of the U.S. military mission to Somalia for their time and memories. In chronological order by date of our interviews, they are Nigel Parkhurst, skipper of the U.S.S. *Tarawa* in 1992, XO Charlie Carey, squadron commander Braden Phillips, and Marine commander Mike Hagee. Great guys all.

An untold story of Audrey's later life was her friendship with Prince Sadruddin Aga Khan, who must have been important because he stepped in to give a moving eulogy at her funeral. I walk away from *Warrior* so sad that Sadri has passed on and I couldn't have gotten to know him. Luckily, Barry Paris had interviewed the prince in the 1990s and even more fortunately, a biography, *Prince Sadruddin Aga Khan: Humanitarian and Visionary*, had recently been written by a UNHCR colleague, Diana Miserez. Through Diana and her group that includes Azeem Maherali and Nicole Fury, I feel I got as close as one can get to meeting a great man. Thank you all for making that possible.

Any book about Audrey in the UNICEF years must relate back to her formative years in Arnhem and Velp during the war. With this the case, I owe such a debt to my Dutch friends Rosemarie Kamphuisen, Gety Hengeveld, Annemarth Visser 't Hooft, Clan Visser 't Hooft, Robert Voskuil, Maddie van Leenders, and Johan Vermeulen for their knowledge and memories that formed the foundation of my understanding of Audrey in the war.

Because this book resulted in large part from the September 2019 unveiling of the Audrey statue and historical marker in Velp, I wish to thank the people who made that event possible. They include Gety Hengeveld, Pim van Dorp, Rosemarie Kamphuisen, Annemarth Visser 't Hooft, Dick Mantel, and Ben Denekamp of the organizing committee; speakers Geneviève Wehry of UNICEF, Clan Visser 't Hooft, and Sonia Eijkman, Baroness van Heemstra; ballerina Anna Overbeek; musicians of the Koninklijke Rosendaalsche Kapel; Tomas Kruijer and Christine Visser of Overamstel; journalist and TV presenter Hanneke Groenteman; Ester Weststeijn, mayor of Rozendaal; and Mary and Marnix Heersink, Carol van Eert, Marc and Danielle Budel, Johan Vermeulen, Walter Jansen, Luigi Spinola, Domitilla Dotti, and sculptor Yvon van Wordragen. I also wish to express my appreciation to Margreet Mateboer and Kendal Brenneman while on location in Velp and afterward.

Thank you to those at GoodKnight Books, including Mary

Acknowledgments

Rothhaar, Sharon Berk, and Valerie Sloan, Marina Gray, Sarah Myslis, Amelia Williams, Paul Julian, and Sarah Miniaci. And thank you, Nicole Defazio, for your encouragement at key moments.

A final thank you goes to Audrey Hepburn, whose positive energy remains in the cosmos, undiminished by the passage of time. We never met, but we have met, and I value the relationship we have developed over the years.

Selected Bibliography

Airborne Museum. *Moederliefde: Ella and Audrey*. Program for the exhibit, 2017.

Brynner, Rock. *Yul: The Man Who Would Be King*. New York: Simon & Schuster, 1989.

Cataldi, Anna. *La coda della sirena*. Rome: Rizzoli, 2018.

Cataldi, Anna. *Letters from Sarajevo: Voices of a Besieged City*. Rockport: Element Inc., 1994.

Cerni, Horst Max. *Journeying to Paradise and Finding a New "Heimat."* Amazon.com, 2020.

Dotti, Luca with Luigi Spinola. *Audrey at Home: Memories of My Mother's Kitchen*. New York: Harper Design, 2015.

Erwin, Ellen and Jessica Z. Diamond. *The Audrey Hepburn Treasures*. New York: Atria Books, 2003.

Ferrer, Sean Hepburn. *Audrey Hepburn, An Elegant Spirit*. New York: Atria Books, 2003.

Frank, Anne. *Het Achterhuis/The Diary of a Young Girl*. New York: Doubleday, 1952.

Fraser, Phoebe. *A Single Seed*. Melbourne: William Heinemann Australia, 1996.

Geldof, Bob. *Is That It?* New York: Viking Penguin, 1986.

Goldman, James. *Robin and Marian*. New York: Bantam Books, 1976.

Harris, Ben and Sebastian Raatz, pubs. *Anne Frank: A Light in History's Darkest Hour*. New York: Centennial Media, 2018.

Harris, Warren G. *Audrey Hepburn: A Biography*. New York: Simon &

Schuster, 1994.

Hengeveld-de Jong, Gety. *Verborgen in Velp: Nooit vertelde verhalen over moed, verzet en onderduikers. Stichting Velp voor Oranje.* Zutphen: Koninklijke Wöhrmann, 2013.

Jansen, Steven. *Dagboek: Velp en de oorlog 1940–1945.* Zutphen: Wöhrmann Print Service/Koninklijke Wöhrmann B.V., 2006.

Karney, Robyn. *Audrey Hepburn: A Charmed Life.* New York: Arcade Publishing, 2012.

Kershaw, Robert. *A Street in Arnhem: The Agony of Occupation and Liberation.* Philadelphia: Casemate Publishers, 2014.

Matzen, Robert. *Dutch Girl: Audrey Hepburn and World War II.* Pittsburgh: GoodKnight Books, 2019.

Miller, John. *Peter Ustinov: The Gift of Laughter.* London: Orion Books, 2002.

Miserez, Diana. *Prince Sadruddin Aga Khan: Humanitarian and Visionary.* Leicestershire: The Book Guild, 2017.

Moore, Roger with Gareth Owen. *My Word Is My Bond: A Memoir.* New York: HarperCollins, 2008.

Paris, Barry. *Audrey Hepburn.* New York: G. P. Putnam's Sons, 1996.

Press, Betty. *I Am Because We Are: African Wisdom in Image and Proverb.* St. Paul: Books for Africa, 2011.

Roberti, Vero. *Moscow Under the Skin.* London: Geoffrey Bles, 1969.

Spiegelman, Judith M. and UNICEF. *We Are the Children: A Celebration of UNICEF's First 40 Years.* Boston: The Atlantic Monthly Press, 1986.

Stetler, Russel, Editor. *The Military Art of People's War: Selected Writings of General Vo Nguyen Giap.* New York: Monthly Review Press, 1971.

Ustinov, Peter. *Dear Me.* London: Book Club Associates, 1977.

Walker, Alexander. *Audrey: Her Real Story.* New York: St. Martin's Griffin, 1994.

Wasson, Sam. *Fifth Avenue 5 A.M.: Audrey Hepburn, Breakfast at Tiffany's, and the Dawn of the Modern Woman.* New York: Harper Perennial, 2011.

Woodward, Ian. *Audrey Hepburn.* New York: St. Martin's Press, 1984.

Young, John. *South Sudan's Civil War: Violence, Insurgency and the Failed Peacekeeping.* London: Zed Books, 2019.

Index